Written by Jenny Paxton
Copyright © 2023 All rights reserved.
Published by Wild Lark Books
Cover Designed by Wild Lark Books

Wild Lark Books
513 Broadway Street
Lubbock, Texas 79401

Shop Online: https://wildlarkbooks.com

Follow Along @WildLarkBooks
#supportartreadbooks

Fiction | Fantasy
ISBN 9781957864815
eBook ISBN 9781957864846

AN EPITAPH FOR
DESTINY

WILD LARK BOOKS

Wild Lark Books is an independent publisher and bookstore that supports authors as artists. As with all works of art, online reviews and ratings help build readerships and increase the impact of this book.

If Jenny's story has impacted you as a reader, please help support their artistry by leaving reviews online, sharing about it on social media using #anepitaphfordestiny, or chatting it up to all your friends and family.

Your support means the world to us.

Thank you!

~ Brianne van Reenen, Founder of Wild Lark Books ~
Support Art. Read Books.

Learn more about the author at WildLarkBooks.com

An Epitaph for Destiny

Jenny Paxton

Wild Lark Books

Contents

Part One

"Few supernatural creatures are so much Feared as the *Nephilim*. A Nephil is born from the Unnatural and Abominable Violation of a woman by a Demon, and as if to demonstrate its foul Nature, the first act of a Nephil is the killing of its own Mother, for no woman has ever survived long after giving Birth to a Nephil Child. . .The Nephil, when grown, will have Power and Strength beyond that allotted to Mortal Nature, beside sundry other frightful Gifts, and will cause much harm and Evil under its demon Father's instruction. . .

"A Nephil may be recognized by these Traits: some of the locks of its Hair will be white as Wool, and its Eyes will be Gold as an eagle's. It will have Skin resembling as it were Bronze Metal, and its Stature will be great above that of Mortals, as the Holy Scriptures state: 'There were giants in the earth in those days'. And above all, the Blood of a Nephil will be white as Milk. By these signs you may know them without fail. . .

"Nevertheless it is possible to Break the demon Father's hold upon his Progeny. This may be accomplished by Baptizing the Nephil, and the Nephil may so choose to serve God rather than Satan. Few Nephilim have thus chosen, but those who have are named Light Nephilim, for they have chosen to walk in the Light and forsaken the Dark of their heritage. . ."

Sister Angelina di Genoa, *A Brief Treatise On the Nephilim*, c. 1621.

One

In the small West Texas town of Derrick, at the turning of the
year, there was a birth, and there was a death.

In themselves, neither of these events was remarkable: hospitals
are, after all, the usual places for both birth and death, and though
St. Luke's in Derrick was a small hospital, it was no stranger to
either. Nevertheless, the birth and death on this night were unusual. The death was unusual because neither the doctors nor the
nurses had ever actually seen a woman die in childbirth. They
would have said that it simply was not something that happened,
not in a modern hospital in a developed country, not without some
catastrophic complication. But in this case, there had been no
catastrophic complication; the woman, for no good reason anyone
could see, hemorrhaged, and not all the efforts and training and
technology the doctors had to bring to bear could stop it. In the
face of modern medicine, in the face of its obvious impossibility, she
simply bled until she died. It was impossible, it was inexplicable,
but it happened. That was the first unusual thing.

The second unusual thing was that the baby, after her mother
had died, was left utterly alone. This was rare. St. Luke's was a
hospital, and tragedies had happened within its walls: sometimes
parents died and their children lived. But only very rarely were
there no friends, no family, no aunts or uncles or grandparents or

3

godparents, who could take the child in. But the mother had told the hospital staff that she had no family she was in contact with, and the baby's father had been a rapist, whose name she did not even know and whom the police had been entirely unsuccessful in identifying or tracking down; even had she known who he was, no one would have turned the baby over to him. In the violence of the birth, already well underway when she arrived, desperate, at the hospital's door, she had not even given her own full name, and certainly had not named her child. And so the hospital staff found themselves faced with another rare and unusual thing: an orphaned child with no home or place or kin or name.

The nurse who called Child Services, after the mother had been declared dead and the baby placed into a sad little crib labeled "Jane Doe", was quite glad to be able to make a second call as well: she called the local convent, St. Margaret's, to inform them that an unattached and unclaimed child needed their care. The poor little girl had, against all odds, been born with no connections or support whatsoever; thanks to the sisters at St. Margaret's, to the nurse's relief, this would not continue to be the case. Child Services could be informed that a foster home for the unnamed child had already been found.

*

It happened to be Sister Rebecca who was sent to St. Luke's Hospital that night. Sister Deborah, the commander of the house, woke her from a light sleep in her cell, quickly described the situation, and instructed her to go and fetch the orphaned baby at once. This, also, was somewhat unusual, because to all appearances there would have been no reason not to wait until the next morning, and it was then well after midnight; however, Sister Deborah, who had long learned to trust her instincts, was certain that, on this night, with this child, waiting until morning would be disastrous. She knew this with a perfect, crystalline certainty that went beyond question or reason. So she woke Sister Rebecca, and when the younger woman saw the strain and urgency on her face, she shook off sleep at once.

She threw back her light blanket, and sat on the edge of her narrow bed for a moment in her stocking feet, blinking and stretching and trying to wake herself up. Then, blearily, yawning, she straightened the white cotton pants and shirt that were the prescribed habit of Sisters of the Holy Lance (as instructed in the *Rule of the Holy Lance*, she had slept fully dressed), buttoned up a quilted white coat with a red cross embroidered over the left breast, laced on a pair of worn but clean boots, and softly went out into the corridor.

She went first to the empty, darkened refectory, to fill a thermos with hot coffee, and then out into the garage. There were four cars, all white, all several years old but in good repair, lined up there; the rest were out with sisters currently in the field. She had driven them all at some time, and the equipment in their trunks was standardized as ordered in the *Rule*, so she chose the car nearest the garage door and slid into the driver's seat. Then she drove out of the garage, through the commandery-house's gate, and onto the deserted street that led to St. Luke's Hospital.

There were no other cars on the road, and at the two intersections between St. Margaret's and the hospital, the stoplights were blinking red. It was a frosty night, cloudless, and cold enough that she was glad of her coat until the car's heater warmed up. Stars, dimmed by streetlights, gleamed overhead, and all the businesses and houses she passed were dark. Paused at one of the intersections, she unscrewed the cap of the thermos and sipped coffee, as glad for its warmth as its caffeine.

She parked the car in the visitors' lot at St Luke's and went inside. The hospital was silent, with the strained and somehow artificial midnight silence of a place that never really sleeps, and Sister Rebecca made her way to Maternity without meeting a single other visitor.

"I'm Sister Rebecca, from St. Margaret's," she told the nurse at the desk. "I'm here to pick up the baby they called us about."

The nurse looked up, surprised. "I didn't think you'd be here until tomorrow morning!" She rummaged through a stack of papers on the desk, found a chart, and ran her finger down it. "Right. I've got a note here that Dr. Sanchez wants to have a word with you first, then you can be on your way." She put the chart down again. "Wait here just a minute."

Sister Rebecca found a chair and sat down. A few minutes later, a woman in creased green scrubs, a white coat, and wire-rimmed glasses appeared. Strands of her dark hair, peppered with gray, had pulled loose from her ponytail and trailed unheeded around her face, making her look harried. "Sister Rebecca?"

Sister Rebecca stood up. "Yes."

"I'm Dr. Sanchez. Would you step in here please?" She indicated an unoccupied room, and when both of them were inside, she closed the door. "Have a seat."

Sister Rebecca did. "Is something wrong? Is the baby not healthy?"

Dr. Sanchez seemed to have the habit of fiddling with her glasses, and she did so now. Without looking at Sister Rebecca, she said, "I'll be honest with you. We're not. . .entirely sure." She put her glasses back on and looked up. Her eyes were red and exhausted. "To all appearances, she is a perfectly healthy newborn. But there are certain things that are. . .not alarming, exactly, but certainly extremely odd."

Sister Rebecca leaned forward. "Tell me."

"Well, first of all, there is no good reason why her mother died in the delivery room. Really, no reason at all. We did everything to stop the bleeding, we transfused her twice, we even gave her clotting factors, but it just wouldn't stop. It was as if she was hemophiliac, except that she wasn't; we ran the lab work, and no trace of hemophilia. Or any other disorder that could cause uncontrolled hemorrhage like that. We did *everything* we should have done; I even checked my books, after, to see if I missed something, but nothing. That poor woman *should not have died.*"

Sister Rebecca nodded, and understood that part of the doctor's obvious distress and distraction was clearly due to the fact that she must have been the attending physician when everything happened. Obstetricians surely wouldn't ever expect to lose a patient; their job was life, not death. It must have been horrible to lose one tonight, and in such an inexplicable and frustrating way. "I see. So you think that if there was something undetected wrong with the mother, there might be something wrong with the baby too?"

Dr. Sanchez spread her hands in a gesture of pure frustration. "I have no idea, I still don't really know what we're dealing with! But it's a possibility."

"Okay."

"On top of that," Dr. Sanchez went on, taking off her glasses again and turning them over and over in her fingers, "the baby herself has unusual characteristics."

"What kind of unusual characteristics?" Sister Rebecca found herself instinctively taking on a soft, coaxing tone, and realized that made sense: she might be here to take custody of an orphaned child, but at the moment, the distressed and probably traumatized Dr. Sanchez might be the one most in need of her help.

Dr. Sanchez replaced her glasses and looked up, again. "Her hair and eyes are an unusual color, not like her mother's, which may suggest something genetic. She's unusually large for her gestational age—not drastically, but unusually. And, when we drew blood for her routine newborn screens. . ." She trailed off, and raked her fingers along her temples, unconsciously pulling more strands of hair loose from the ponytail.

"Yes?" Sister Rebecca prompted gently. "Her blood test?"

Dr. Sanchez looked up with a desperate, almost wild look on her face. "When we drew her blood for the routine screens, it was *white*."

*

Sister Rebecca stood over the crib, looking down at the sleeping baby, trying to pull herself together and think rationally about what she was seeing. The last few minutes were a blur; she wasn't even sure what she had said to Dr. Sanchez in that unoccupied room, but it had ended with her standing here, looking down at a baby who simply should not exist, should not be what all the evidence said she was. There hadn't been a nephil in a century; they were vanishingly rare, little was known about them, and according to all the lore and literature the Order had at its disposal (which was extensive and very thorough), no one had seen a nephil as a baby since the 1600s.

But Sister Rebecca had read *A Brief Treatise On the Nephilim*, the work universally regarded by the Order as the best and most authoritative work on the subject, written by a sister who had personally helped to defeat one in Italy in the 1600s, and she knew very well all the signs. This baby had every single one. The infant-fine wisps of her dark hair were shot through with strands of pure white, so white that the fluorescents overhead picked out a tinge of blue in them. Her skin had a strange, hard glow, like brushed bronze, like something that wasn't quite skin at all, and when she opened her eyes, vague and unfocused like all newborn eyes, prismatic facets lit up with hot shades of amber and gold. *Not really like eagle's eyes,* Sister Rebecca thought. *Not really like any mortal creature's eyes.*

Clearly this was a night for impossible things, an impossible death and an impossible birth, and there was no way around it: impossible or not, there was clearly a newborn nephil in Derrick. Sister Rebecca returned to the nurses' station, asked for the use of the telephone there, and called the commandery-house.

The house telephone was located in Sister Deborah's cell, and she answered immediately; Sister Rebecca guessed, and rightly, that the commander had been waiting or praying beside it instead of returning to her bed. "Tell me what's happening, please," she said, her sense of urgency unabated. "Do you have the child?"

Sister Rebecca swallowed. "I, um. . ." She rubbed her temples, and decided to cut straight to the chase. "I think I know why you felt so urgent about this."

There was a pause, and she imagined Sister Deborah leaning forward. "Tell me."

"I think. . .I think the baby is a nephil."

There was silence on the line for several heartbeats. "Does she have the signs?"

"Yes," said Sister Rebecca. "All of them. Her mother died of hemorrhage for no good reason, in spite of the doctors doing everything they knew to do. She has white streaks in her hair, and bronzy skin, and gold eyes just like Angelina di Genoa said, and the doctor told me that when they drew her blood for the routine blood tests, it was pure white."

Sister Deborah whispered something that Rebecca did not hear, but which sounded like a prayer. Then she said aloud, "Rebecca, you need to get her back here to the commandery, *now.* The demon-father won't be far behind you, and she must be on consecrated ground before he can get to her. Bring her *now*; never mind the paperwork, we can take care of that tomorrow morning. I'll call the hospital myself. The important thing is to get the child to safety."

Sister Rebecca felt a chill of fear; she had not been taking the demon-father into her calculations, but now she realized that she had been stupid not to. Of course he would be coming to claim his progeny; it was amazing that he hadn't shown up yet. When she spoke again, she heard her voice quivering a little. "I'll bring her right away."

"I'll wake up the sisters to pray, and Brother David will be in the chapel to baptize the child as soon as she arrives. Don't stop for anything."

"Thank you, sister."

Sister Deborah paused. "Remember that God is greater," she said. Then all the lights in the hospital went out.

*

Sister Rebecca felt a sick, helpless fear settle around her, the kind of fear that makes a person neither fight nor run, but want to curl up and hide. Dread, formless and huge, thickened and clogged in her throat, and nausea clenched in her belly; her heart galloped in her chest, and her blood pounded in her ears. Something in her said that this wasn't real, that it was the demon's doing, trying to paralyze her with panic, and she knew it was true; however, functionally, it didn't matter at all. Whether the abject, sickening fear was real or imposed from outside, it was still there, still choking her, still making her muscles weak and her skin cold, still crowding her mind with the yammering compulsion to hide, to cower, to let the demon have whatever it wanted if only it would leave her alone.

She leaned against the wall, feeling the solidity of it, closed her eyes, and took several deep breaths, until she had the abrupt, bottomless terror under some kind of control. It was still there, clenched inside her, making her limbs tremble and her heart race, but she was riding it now, not being whelmed under by it. "I will not fear the terror of the night, nor the arrow that flies by day, nor the pestilence that stalks in the darkness, nor the destruction that wastes at noonday. . ."

Sister Rebecca ran. She knew that it was at least partially, and maybe wholly, not running but *bolting*; however, it least it was in the right direction. In a moment she was back beside the crib, and she caught up the baby as gently as she could, tucking her inside the quilted coat and buttoning it closed around her. The little girl squirmed, and seemed to be gearing up to cry; then, comforted by the warmth and closeness of Rebecca's body, she relaxed. Holding the baby steady with one arm, Sister Rebecca sprinted out of the nursery again, and down the hall to the staircase, not daring to attempt the elevator. Emergency generators were online, true, but this was not a natural power outage; it was deliberate. She must not be trapped.

As she passed windows, she could hear that the wind had risen violently, and it howled and screamed outside, rattling the glass in its frames, pelting it with sand or gravel, even on the third floor.

Down the stairs she went, and after plunging down two flights at top speed, Sister Rebecca noticed that her sickening, debilitating fear had begun to recede; it was the running, of course. Even under demonic attack, her body could not run and panic at the same time. This cheered her a little.

Out the door to the visitors' parking lot, and Sister Rebecca was stopped short by the smack of the icy gale that forced her eyes closed and left her gasping; the temperature had dropped at least twenty or thirty degrees since she had gone inside an hour ago, and she coughed helplessly, feeling that her lungs had been freeze-dried. She pulled up the hood of her coat, leaned into the gale, and fumbled her keys out of her pocket with fingers already burning from cold; when she reached the car door, her hands were almost too stiff and clumsy to open it. But she did, and slid inside.

She looked up as she turned the key in the ignition, meeting her own scared eyes in the rearview mirror, and then looking beyond to the sky. Under the parking lot's lights, she saw that the freezing wind was carrying in a choking cloud of airborne sand and silt; the cones of illumination under the lights were already thick with it, eddies of it whipped across the parking lot's pavement, and she could see the leading edge of the true dust storm bearing down, silhouetted against the stars, moving so quickly she could actually see it move. She had seen dust storms before, of course; all West Texans had. Usually they were more nuisance than true threat. But she had never seen one as fast as this, or as violent, and she could feel the car shaking with every vicious gust. As she punched the accelerator, the wind snatched up a small rock, and drove it into the rear window with enough force to chip the glass.

Sisters of the Holy Lance learned many things in their training, things no typical nun would ever need to learn. One of those things was a certain amount of stunt driving, in case of emergency, and Rebecca made use of that training now. She slewed the car around, sending up a fan of sand and gravel behind her, and stomped the accelerator, still supporting the baby under her coat with one arm; as she peeled out toward the exit, though, her headlights swept over a dark figure standing in the vacant lot across the street. He stood completely unmoving, untouched by the wrenching gale, just staring at her.

There was nothing overtly inhuman about the figure: no red eyes or horns or black vulture's wings. But the moment his eyes met Sister Rebecca's, all the sickening terror she had felt inside the hospital poured back over her, washing out all thought in a kind of voiceless scream. The baby must have felt something too, because she stirred unhappily, and began to make small noises of distress; not cries, not yet, but their beginning. In that shock of naked panic, Rebecca nearly ran the car off the road, but corrected in the nick of time, fishtailing wildly and sending another rooster tail of gravel flying from the wheels in the direction of the demon, in the unlikely event he could feel it. Then she floored the accelerator and tore down the road, thankful that it was as deserted now as it had been when she drove from the commandery-house before.

"God is our refuge and strength, a very present help in trouble," Sister Rebecca recited aloud, almost shouting to be heard over the gale and the scouring of the sand, unsure whether she was fortifying herself, or praying to God, or defying the demon, or all three. She was in the midst of the full dust storm now, and could see barely twenty-five feet ahead; it took all her strength to keep the car on the road against the buffeting of the wind. "Therefore we will not fear though the earth gives way, though the mountains be moved into the heart of the sea—"

Overhead, the bulb in a streetlight exploded with a violent flash, and sent glass showering down over the car; when she reached them, the next streetlight did the same, and the next, and the next. The first stoplight she came to, its arm swaying wildly in the wind and still blinking red, gave a groan of tortured metal as she drove beneath it, and crashed down like a tree into the street; Sister Rebecca only just managed to scrape the car under it as it fell, but she left the rear bumper wrenched off in the road. "Though its waters roar and foam, though the mountains tremble at its swelling!" she shouted into the storm. "The nations rage, the kingdoms totter; he utters his voice, the earth melts! The Lord of Hosts is with us; the God of Jacob is our fortress!"

Everywhere she looked, Sister Rebecca saw the still, black form of the baby's demon-father: standing in doorways and on patios, along the road in every place just beyond the reach of lights, crowding thick behind her, darting along at the edge of her vision, reflecting in every mirror and every window. She glanced to the left and screamed, for the pale face of a creature that had never, not for one second in eternity, been a man, stared in at her from just outside the glass, only inches away, unhindered by the speed of the car, with not a trace of human expression in the bottomlessness of its eyes. Involuntarily, she jerked the steering wheel, jumped the curb, and nearly crashed the car into a closed hair salon; it escaped with only a broken front window, and the car escaped with only the loss of its right rear-view mirror. "He who is in you is greater than he who is in the world," Sister Rebecca recited desperately, and then repeated it: "He who is in you is greater than he who is in the world. Resist the devil and he will flee from you—" She hardly noticed when she passed under the second stoplight, until it, too, crashed down just behind her.

She could see the commandery-house gates, and felt a jolt of relief. But at that moment, the car's engine began to skip and struggle. The car slowed, and though she had her foot pressed to the floorboards, it continued slowing. Identical pale faces, empty of recognizable expression but brimming with deep malice and deeper greed, closed in from both sides, and pale hands reached out, like the carefully composed hands of laid-out corpses. "Resist the devil and he will flee!" Sister Rebecca cried out, her voice shrill with overpowering panic. "In the name of God, I resist you! You have no right to me and no right to this child! Now flee! *Flee!*"

The dead, grasping hands hesitated, and a sense of bottomless hate and rage and famished hunger (but not hunger for food; no, never that) smashed against her like the storm surge of a hurricane.

She had the strong impression that if she had been standing up, in the open, it would have flung her as easily, and as far, as the furious wind was throwing twigs and scraps of litter. But the car's engine abruptly revved back to life, and she accelerated the remaining distance to the gate and through it, onto the commandery-house's consecrated ground.

A scream, not only heard, but smelled and tasted as a bitterness like burning metal, and felt as a scraping pressure against the skin, and sensed as an icepick pain behind the eyes and across the eardrums, ripped through octaves behind her, and every facing window in every commandery building exploded inward. Sister Rebecca drove the car right up onto the lawn outside the chapel, then, holding the baby (crying now, though Rebecca had no memory of when she had begun) tight under her coat, jumped out of the car, gasping for breath in wind as cold as frozen steel. Leaving the car door hanging open, and slitting her eyes against the driving sand, she bolted for the chapel, where a man in white vestments was holding the door open for her; the moment she was inside, he smacked it closed again behind her, and locked it. Stones and gravel hammered against the outside of it as hard as hail, driven by the furious wind, but the door stood firm.

Sister Rebecca stumbled to the nearest pew and collapsed there, gasping, adrenaline still jagged in her. Her hands shaking almost too hard to manage the buttons, she opened her coat, and passed the nephil baby to Sister Deborah, then she flopped back against the back of the seat, panting. For a moment she just sat there, too shocked to form a coherent thought, too exhausted to move. Then she became aware that all of the sisters, awakened to pray as Sister Deborah had promised, and assembled along every stone wall of the chapel, were speaking softly in unison, reciting Psalms together; she also realized that she was seeing this by the light of an assortment of Coleman camping lanterns rather than the usual overhead lights. The power was out in the commandery, and she supposed that it was probably out in the whole of Derrick by now. She could still hear the wind, howling outside, and in the distance there was a rumble of thunder, but inside the chapel all was calm.

Sister Deborah, holding the nephil baby, and Brother David, the man in the white vestments who had held the door for Rebecca, stood beside the marble font at the front of the chapel, talking together softly. Brother David was a priest-brother: only in that capacity could men join the Order, and he was the only brother at St. Margaret's. He was a stocky, balding man, and had been at the commandery longer than many of the sisters.

Sister Deborah looked up, and beckoned to Rebecca. The younger woman stood and walked toward the font; she could feel her heartbeat slowing back to normal, and found that her legs would carry her again. When she reached the others, Sister Deborah said, "You have already protected this child in the face of great danger, and brought her here safely. Would you be willing to stand as godmother?"

Sister Rebecca was taken aback; she had never expected to stand as godmother for anyone—early versions of the *Rule* had actually forbidden sisters to take on that responsibility—and certainly not for a nephil. But then she remembered the colorless face of the demon just outside the car window, its grasping, greedy hands, what it had done to the baby's innocent mother whose name they did not even know, and felt a surge of fierce defiance. "Of course I will."

Thunder crashed again, much closer this time, and the wind continued to wail outside the solid stone walls and the narrow stained-glass windows of the chapel. A flash of lightning, mixing with the silent blue light of the Coleman lanterns, illuminated the wooden benches with their worn velveteen seats, black in the unnatural light, and outlined the rows of arches on each side of the nave as sharply as a spotlight.

Brother David started the christening liturgy, using the old, traditional words. Sister Rebecca found comfort in the agelessness of them, and the poetry and power they brought. "Dearly beloved," he read, "forasmuch as all men are conceived and born in sin, and that our Savior Christ saith none can enter into the kingdom of God, except he be regenerate and born anew of water and of the Holy Ghost—" There was another crack of thunder, this one near enough to rattle the windows in their frames, and the sound of the wind changed: instead of the scraping of blown sand and dust, it shifted to the hissing of sleet and rain.

"I beseech you to call upon God the Father, through our Lord Jesus Christ, that of his bounteous mercy he will grant to this child that thing which by nature she cannot have: that she may be baptized with water and the Holy Ghost, and received into Christ's holy Church, and be made a living member of the same."

Another flash of lightening lit up the chapel, and the sound of the storm outside grew louder. Brother David raised his voice. "Let us pray! Almighty and immortal God, the aid of all that need, the helper of all that flee to thee for succor, the life of them that believe, and the resurrection of the dead: We call upon thee for this infant, that she, coming to thy holy baptism, may receive remission of her sins by spiritual regeneration. . ." Sister Rebecca imagined that she could feel the immensity of this moment, this act, this wrenching of a soul out of darkness and into light. The power of the elements outside was nothing in comparison.

"Amen," all the assembled sisters responded.

"Beloved," Brother David went on, his voice strong over the storm, "ye hear in the Gospel the words of our Savior Christ, that he commanded the children to be brought unto him; how he blamed those that would have kept them from him; how he exhorteth all people to follow their innocency." At those words, Sister Rebecca thought of the demon, doing all in his power to stop her from arriving here with the baby. She narrowed her eyes.

"Ye perceive how by his outward gesture and deed he declared his good will toward them; for he embraced them in his arms, laid his hands upon them, and blessed them. Doubt ye not therefore, but earnestly believe, that he will likewise favorably receive this present infant; that he will embrace her with the arms of his mercy; that he will give unto her the blessing of eternal life, and make her partaker of his everlasting kingdom."

Sister Rebecca thought that the strength of the wind might be lessening a little, and when the next thunderclap came, it was noticeably farther away. The lighting that flashed in the chapel was little more than a flicker, hardly enough to leave afterimages on anyone's eyes. "Wherefore we, being thus persuaded of the good will of our heavenly Father towards this infant, declared by his Son Jesus Christ; and nothing doubting but that he favorably alloweth this charitable work of ours in bringing this infant to his holy baptism, let us faithfully and devoutly give thanks unto him."

Then Brother David turned to Sister Rebecca, and addressed her directly. "Dearly beloved, ye have brought this child here to be baptized; ye have prayed that our Lord Jesus Christ would vouchsafe to receive her, to release her of her sins, to sanctify her with the Holy Ghost, to give her the kingdom of heaven and everlasting life. Ye have heard also that our Lord Jesus Christ hath promised in his Gospel, to grant all these things that ye have prayed for: which promise he, for his part, will most surely keep and perform. Wherefore, after this promise made by Christ, this infant must also faithfully, for her part, promise by you that are her surety (until she come of age to take it upon herself), that she will renounce the devil and all his works, and constantly believe God's holy Word, and obediently keep his commandments."

Sister Rebecca straightened; her part of the liturgy was next. "I ask you therefore," Brother David recited formally, "dost thou, Rebecca, knight-sister of the Order of the Holy Lance, in the name of this child, renounce the devil and all his works, the vain pomp and glory of the world, with all covetous desires of the same, and the carnal desires of the flesh, so that thou wilt not follow nor be led by them?"

"I renounce them all," said Sister Rebecca, and imagined that her words did harm to the demon.

Then Brother David recited the Apostle's Creed, and Rebecca recited it with him silently; all the sisters knew it by heart. "Dost thou, Rebecca, knight-sister of the Order of the Holy Lance, believe this?"

She raised her chin. "All this I steadfastly believe."

"Wilt thou be baptized in this faith?"

"That is my desire," said Sister Rebecca, on behalf of the child, too young to make the decision for herself. Too young, and in too much danger, and presenting too much danger herself.

"Wilt thou then obediently keep God's holy will and commandments, and walk in the same all the days of thy life?"

"I will."

Then Brother David turned to the assembled sisters, and prayed again: "Oh merciful God, grant that the old nature in this child may be so buried, that the new nature may be raised up in her."

"Amen," chorused the sisters. There was a quiet murmur of thunder, almost too far away to be heard, and the wind had died down to fitful gusts.

"Grant that all carnal affections may die in her, and that all things belonging to the Spirit may live and grow in her."

"Amen," said all the sisters again, more loudly. Sister Rebecca had fought many evil things in her time as a Sister of the Holy Lance, and this felt like a blow struck against an enemy, just as much as any she had dealt with weapons, as if each "amen" was the drawing of a sword.

"Grant that she may have power and strength, to have victory, and to triumph against the devil, the world, and the flesh."

"Amen!"

"Grant that whosoever is here dedicated to thee by our office and ministry may also be endued with heavenly virtues, and everlastingly rewarded, through thy mercy, oh blessed Lord God, who dost live, and govern all things, world without end."

"Amen!"

"Regard, we beseech thee, the supplications of thy congregation; sanctify this water to the mystical washing away of sin; and grant that this child, now to be baptized therein, may receive the fullness of thy grace, and ever remain in the number of thy faithful and elect children; through Jesus Christ our Lord."

"Amen." This time the word was spoken with finality, with a solid determination.

Brother David looked at Deborah. "Have you chosen a name for her?"

"Justina."

Sister Rebecca understood immediately, and thought there could be no better name for the girl than that. Like all the sisters, she knew a great deal about female warrior saints, both historical and apocryphal, both within the Order and outside it: Saint Joan of Arc, and Saint Ursula, and Saint Margaret of Antioch, after whom the commandery had been named and who, like Saint George, had slain a dragon. She also knew of Saint Justina, who was said to have repelled all the efforts of an evil sorcerer to influence her, even repelled the attacks of the devil himself; Saint Justina, patron saint against demons and sorcery. No light-nephil could have a more appropriate namesake.

Sister Deborah handed the infant, squirming and apparently in some agitation, to the priest, who said "Justina, I baptize thee in the name of the Father, and of the Son, and of the Holy Ghost." Then, gently and with great care, he dipped her into the water in the font. "Amen!" shouted the sisters, and it was both celebration and battle-cry, both joy and defiance. A sleety gust of wind dashed against the windows, but there was no strength in it now. If there was still thunder, it was too far away to hear.

"We receive this child into the congregation of Christ's flock," said Brother David, "and do sign her with the sign of the Cross." When he touched her tiny forehead with his finger, making the two strokes of a cross, Justina gave one sharp cry, as if a sudden pain had struck her and then gone; Rebecca imagined the darkness in her, inherited from her demon-father, being finally seared away in that moment, cauterized and cut off and made nothing.

"Hereafter," Brother David concluded, "she shall not be ashamed to confess the faith of Christ crucified, and valiantly to fight under his banner against sin, the world, and the devil, and to continue Christ's faithful soldier and servant unto her life's end." And a final time, all the sisters added their amen.

After the christening was over, as everyone left the chapel, they found that the dust and the sleety rain had both been covered over by a mantle of new snow, and the stars were bright again overhead.

***

Interlude One

Excerpt from the Minutes of the Annual Provincial Chapter of the State of Texas, January 27

Sister Patricia (Commandery of Austin, Province of the State of Texas, Chatelaine of the Province, President of the Chapter): Is there any further business to discuss before we dismiss?

The President recognizes Sister Deborah (Commandery of West Texas, Province of the State of Texas).

Sister Deborah: I need to report to the Chapter that a few weeks ago, St. Margaret's took in an orphaned infant, to be raised in the commandery. Our priest-brother has baptized her.

Sister Patricia: You don't really need to ask for permission for that, sister. Of course you should have taken her in and seen her baptized; caring for orphans has been part of the Order's vocation from the beginning.

(Murmur of agreement from the Chapter.)

Sister Deborah: The situation with this child is different. She is a nephil.

(Silence from the Chapter, then muttering.)

Sister Camila (Commandery of South Texas, Province of the State of Texas): May I ask a question?

The President recognizes Sister Camila.

Sister Camila: I hesitate to ask this, and I certainly would never say anything against your due diligence. But, are you absolutely sure? I mean, no one alive has actually seen a nephil in the flesh.

Sister Deborah: We are absolutely sure, yes. All the physical characteristics described by Sister Angelina di Genoa are present, including the white blood. Also, the sister who brought her back to the commandery from the hospital was strongly attacked by the demon-father on the way, so much so that the entire town of Derrick took collateral damage from the accompanying windstorm and the power was out for nearly two days.

(Whispering from the Chapter; several sisters leaning forward. Evidence of greater attention from the Chapter than for several hours prior. Sister Elaine [Commandery of Dallas-Fort Worth, Province of the State of Texas] rolled up her knitting and put it away.)

Sister Marta (Commandery of San Antonio, Province of the State of Texas): I would like to ask a further question.

The President recognizes Sister Marta.

Sister Marta: You said your priest-brother baptized her?

Sister Deborah: That is correct.

Sister Marta: And, you believe it worked? Her demon-father lost his hold on her?

Sister Deborah: All the evidence is that, yes, it worked. There has been no sign of him since the night of her birth, and no further attacks on the commandery-house.

Sister Marta: But you don't know for sure?

Sister Deborah: I suppose not. As far as I know, there isn't an objective test. We would have to wait for her to grow up enough to make free choices, and judge her by those. But isn't that the case for any child?

Sister Marta: Other children aren't nephilim, and other children don't have the powers that she will have.

(Mutters of agreement from the Chapter.)

Sister Elena (Commandery of El Paso, Province of the State of Texas): Wait, has she shown powers? Already?

Sister Deborah: No, she has not. She appears to be a normal infant.

Sister Marta: I move that precautionary measures be taken against this child, until we can know for certain that she will not present a danger to the Commandery or the Order.

Sister Elena: Second.

Sister Deborah: I see no reason to suppose that any demonic associations she was born with have not been completely broken! All the accounts of light-nephilim are unequivocal: the baptism of the nephil, and their renunciation of the devil, even if by proxy, and their consecration by the mark of the cross, will break any demonic connections or influence they have.

(Somewhat uncomfortable silence from the chapter.)

Sister Deborah: Furthermore, exactly what precautionary measures did you have in mind?

Sister Marta: She should be kept under constant supervision at least, and possibly restrained. Certainly she should not be permitted off consecrated ground.

Sister Deborah: And what then? She will grow up knowing that she is distrusted, that she is considered a danger. She will feel that she is being punished for something that may or may not even be in her, and that she can't help and didn't ask for in any case. She will understand that even though she has been baptized, we still consider her contaminated. Will she be inclined to trust us then? If we obviously don't trust her? Will she be   inclined to take the side of God, if the side of God obviously doesn't really want her? Will she be more noble than we are? Would you be, in her place?

Sister Camila: I agree with Sister Deborah! She should be treated as any other child under the Order's protection, until she gives us cause to think otherwise. If we intend to be role models for her, we had better be good ones!

(Various interjections by the assembled sisters.)

Sister Patricia (standing up and raising her voice): Enough! Order, sisters!

(The sisters fall silent, some clearly reluctantly.)

Sister Patricia: Here is the question before us: whether to treat Justina, the nephil child in the Commandery of West Texas, as an ordinary and innocent child until proven otherwise, or as a potential demonic threat. Now, we will discuss the matter calmly and reasonably, and in *good order*.

(Pause.)

Sister Patricia: Now, Sister Marta. Please make your argument to the Chapter.

Sister Marta: The purpose of the Order of the Holy Lance is to protect people from supernatural or extranatural threats. That is our duty and our vocation. A nephil is potentially a very significant threat, and this child should therefore be kept under careful watch and fully controlled, as a precaution. Her comfort must not take precedence over the safety of all the people she might hurt if she does turn out to be a threat. There will be far less collateral damage, and far less potential loss of life and limb for the Order, if she is controlled now, rather than when she has come into her full powers.

(Murmurs of agreement from the chapter.)

Sister Patricia: Does any sister have anything further to add?

(Pause, and no further comments.)

Sister Patricia: Now, Sister Deborah, you may present your response.

Sister Deborah: First, there is no evidence at all that Justina is still vulnerable to demonic influence or control, and much historical evidence to the contrary. All our sources say that a baptized nephil, a light-nephil, is freed from any connection to her demon-father, and if she does choose to do evil, it will be her own free choice, just as it would be for any of us. Therefore, it seems to me that the risk of her turning out to be demon-influenced is minuscule or, more likely, nil, according to all of our history and lore. On the other hand, the risk of pushing her toward rebellion, and doing evil of her own will, is very much higher. If she is treated like a danger, or like a demon *in potentia*, or like someone who is not to be trusted, when she knows she has done nothing to deserve such treatment, she is very likely to rebel. So treating her like a threat is the best way I can   think of to make sure that she actually becomes one.

(Nods and murmurs of agreement from the Chapter.)

Sister Deborah: Furthermore, should we not strive to treat people as Our Lord did? He never treated anyone with suspicion, or assumed the worst of anyone, even people you might have expected him to, like tax collectors or adulteresses or Roman soldiers or thieves. I believe we should do the same with this child. And who knows? Suppose for a moment that there *is*, contrary to all our knowledge and to all good sense, somehow some impossible bit of demonic influence left in her. There is no reason to think so, and much reason to think not, but just suppose. In that case, it may be that our trust and our love may still win her over.

Sister Patricia: Thank you, Sister Deborah. Does any sister have anything to add to her remarks?

The President recognizes Sister Mariana (Commandery of Houston, Province of the State of Texas).

Sister Mariana: It seems to me that it is our duty to give people the benefit of the doubt, just as a general rule. This child being a nephil doesn't change that.

Sister Patricia: Any further comments from the chapter?

The President recognizes Sister Elena.

Sister Elena: I agree with you, but this isn't just personal. There is also a larger duty in play, just as the command to "turn the other cheek" is not intended to apply to soldiers in a just war. We should certainly give everyone the benefit of the doubt, unless it puts more people at risk.

The President recognizes Sister Camila.

Sister Camila: That's true, but in the present case, there is no evidence of risk. Until there is evidence of risk, the benefit of the doubt should take precedence. We should go on the assumption that our history and literature has been right, and Justina poses no demon-related danger after being baptized. If she ever starts to show signs of demonic influence, we can reassess then, but not before. Not preemptively.

Sister Patricia: Any further comments?

(Several seconds of silence, to give any sister a chance to speak.)

Sister Patricia: Very well, we will have a vote. Will the sister-chaplain lead a prayer for the wisdom and kindness of God?

Sister Kate (Commandery of Lubbock, Province of the State of Texas, sister-chaplain of the Chapter) prays.

All the sisters: Amen.

Sister Patricia: Should the nephil child, Justina, be treated as an ordinary, innocent child until she shows clear evidence to the contrary?

The Chapter votes.

Those in favor: Commanderies of West Texas, South Texas, Dallas-Fort Worth, Houston, Austin, Lubbock, Rio Grande.

Those opposed: Commanderies of San Antonio, El Paso, Corpus Christi, East Texas.

Motion passes.

Sister Patricia: The motion is carried, and the child Justina will be raised by the Order as innocent and free of demonic influence, until there is good cause to believe otherwise. Is there any further business to be discussed by the chapter?

(No further business presented.)

Prayers said for peace, protection, courage, and God's favor.

Recitation of the Lord's Prayer.

Two hymns sung.

Dismissal by the President of the Chapter.

***

Interlude Two

Excerpt from the Record Kept by the Sisters at St. Margaret's, About Justina

Sister Rebecca. February 12.

...The truth is, nobody knows very much at all about nephilim. There have only ever been a few dozen recorded to exist in history, and only a handful of those were light-nephilim. The last one was about four hundred years ago, and the monks who raised him didn't keep very good records: at least, nothing like as detailed as we would like to have now. The honest truth is, the best documentation we have about nephilim is nearly all about how to find, fight, and kill them, and not useful at all for *raising* one. We're just going to have to make our best guesses, and trust to God for the rest. Which is terrifying, to be honest.

And the fact that she's a nephil isn't really even the main problem, at least not right now. The main problem is that she's a *baby*. I mean, look at us! We're all Sisters of the Holy Lance, which is basically a monastic order. We're not like typical nuns in most ways, but we are when it comes to the vow of chastity! So none of us has ever had a child, and not very many have taken care of nieces or nephews or other children as babies. I'll be honest: none of us really knows what we're doing at all. Commanderies do foster children pretty often (Justina is the only one at St. Margaret's now, but pretty often anyway, at least averaged across the Order), but not usually infants. We just hope that between the nine of us and Brother David, and advice from the cook (Mrs. Fowler), and books, she won't grow up to be a total mess.

When I agreed to stand as godmother, I never guessed how much it would consist of just standing there looking at her, and thinking, What kind of small creature is this and how do I take care of it? New moms may feel the same—how would I know!—but at least they've had nine months to get used to the idea. . .

Sister Magdalena. March 3.

Took care of the little today. She's already starting to roll over, which the books seem to think isn't an accomplishment due for a few more weeks yet. But who knows what's normal for a nephil baby? We praise her lavishly whenever she does it anyway. Some of us use baby-talk, which is funny; I don't think Sister Deborah had ever baby-talked to anyone in her whole life, and I would almost have bet money that she was physically unable, but she babbles as stupidly as anybody when Justina is there.

This should be some kind of sit-com or something, it really should: nine warrior nuns and a priest, trying to pool their ignorance and raise a baby together. What is the correct developmental stage for Baby's First Crossbow? When should she start practicing forms and hand-fighting? She should probably start walking first, though. When should we start introducing scary creatures, and how should we do it? Should one of us write a cutesy book about them? "A is for Abomination. B is for Black Unicorn. C is for Cat-Shi. D is for Demon." Who knows. . .

Sister Magdalena. March 7.

I noticed something odd about the little today. I had her in the baby wrap across my chest (Mrs. Fowler swears by them, and I have to admit, wearing the baby is by far the easiest method if you're also supposed to be doing chores or paying attention to the Hours or something while you're watching her), and she started to cry. I think she had a wet diaper. Anyway, as soon as she started really crying, I just sort of. . .stopped. I was just standing there, staring at her, completely absorbed in her crying and not even noticing a single other thing going on. After a second I shook it off and got on with what I was doing, but I kept thinking about it. Is she showing some sort of nephilic power? Does her voice have some kind of fascination or glamour to it? I don't know yet. Maybe I just spaced out. Remains to be seen.

Sister Alana. April 12.

We've all noticed that something happens when Justina cries, or even when she just babbles or giggles. It fascinates: you can't *not* pay attention. We've all gotten to where it doesn't completely in-capacitate us every time she does it, but it's pretty clearly something that she's really doing, not just the result of sisters randomly zoning out. It also has to do with her emotions: when she cries, you feel distress. When she giggles, you feel joy (more than the usual for baby giggles, I mean). When she babbles and recognizes you, you feel alert and almost manic.

We have no idea whether she will be able to control this power she has when she grows up, but we hope so, or she will be really difficult to function normally around. It's like her emotions are contagious, and her voice is the vector. . .

***

Two

Justina grew, and quickly. She said her first word at only eight months old, and clearly, with none of the lisping or fumbling that would usually accompany a baby's first efforts to speak; her first full, intelligible sentence came a scant six months thereafter. She did comparatively little babbling, which was actually a relief, because the strange power or fascination in her voice, whatever it was, not only continued but strengthened. By the time she was four years old, she could understand when someone told her she needed to keep silent, and understand why, and she obeyed.

Justina took her first steps at around the same time she said her first word. And she spent very little time toddling; only a few weeks later she walked confidently, and well before she was two years old she was running, confounding both the books' and Mrs. Fowler's predictions. The sisters, despite some hesitation, decided to let her begin her physical training when she was four, in addition to her schoolwork.

In part, this was due to the fact that she was racing through the usual curriculum, not only with speed but with impatience and even a kind of contempt, and needed something else to occupy her. By the time she was five years old she spoke as fluently as an adult, not only in English but in Spanish and Latin as well. She had no patience with books intended for babies, and insisted upon having "real" books read to her from the beginning; immediately upon learning to read for herself (something she accomplished at less than four years old), she embarked upon *The Chronicles of Narnia*, skipping the usual beginner's books altogether.

She took to combat and weapons training with a facility and intuitive understanding that most of the sisters could only envy. Sister Alana, who was the commandery's armorer and bladesmith, made a half-sized and unsharpened sword for her to practice with when she was six, and after she had mastered that, other weapons quickly followed. By the time she was nine, she could spar with any weapon, or unarmed, with any of the sisters, and give good account of herself. Her godmother, Sister Rebecca, trained her with firearms, and she mastered each almost as soon as she could control its recoil. She proved a deadly shot with arrows, too, shortly after she was strong enough to draw a bow.

When she was five, she began to gain control over her voice's power, just as any other child might gain control over her impulses or her temper. Everyone was relieved; they had been afraid that poor Justina would end up with a permanent vow of silence, lest she involuntarily play havoc with the emotions and perceptions of anyone within earshot of her every time she said a word.

But she never sang; at least, she never sang at matins or vespers, or during the Hours. She had been present at the offices since she was a baby, when the sisters brought her, and began to take part in the liturgy, with evident understanding, by the time she was five. But she made no effort to sing the hymns, though she often hummed or sang under her breath during the day. It may have been that she knew something of her voice's power, or guessed, and suspected that if she sang aloud, something might happen.

At the Christmas Eve mass, the year she was nearly eight years old, something did. Many people from the town of Derrick had come to the commandery-house for the service, and the chapel, draped with garlands of pine and lit with candles, was full; Justina sat toward the back. She sat quietly through "O Come, O Come Emmanuel", and through "Adeste Fideles", and through "Joy to the World", with her hands clasped in her lap, as though in fierce self-control, and quiet rapture on her face. It was the "Hallelujah Chorus" that finally opened the floodgates. Of course it was the "Hallelujah Chorus": a song which had brought the king of England to his feet, which had made him feel that if he did not stand he would be swept away, was the song which on that Christmas Eve made a seven-year-old nephil feel that if she did not sing, she would die.

She joined in quietly at first, cautiously. But when nothing went wrong, she sang with abandon, with all her heart and all her voice, her eyes closed, her head tilted back, and her hands slightly spread to her sides. The congregation became aware of a new voice, singing the soprano line: a strong, ringing voice of such crystal perfection that it almost sounded more like a musical instrument than human vocal cords. And they felt it; they felt it as rapture and exaltation, so intense and overwhelming that it was almost fear.

In the power of it, there were other things happening, things no one really registered until afterwards. The flames of the candles arrayed around the chapel quivered; the stained glass windows shivered in their frames. Anyone standing near a wall could feel it vibrating, and all the electric light bulbs overhead swelled in brightness; in the moment, the brightening lights seemed so appropriate, and even inevitable, that no one thought of it, but within a day or two every one of them burned out from the overload. The small microphone in the pulpit buzzed and hummed with distortion, though no one was near it.

At the end of the chorus, after the last dramatic silence and the final, glorious crescendo of *hallelujah*, several people wobbled and nearly fell; Sister Paloma, who had always had a thin frame and low blood pressure, actually passed out for a moment or two. Then, released from the song's grip, the congregation could look back and see whose voice they had heard. Justina was standing there, her eyes still closed and a fierce glory on her face, her dark hair with its white streaks standing out around her head and snapping with static. The hymnals, missals, and prayer books shelved on the back of the pew in front of her were all shaken out of place, and one had fallen over.

When Justina opened her eyes, everyone hastily looked back toward the front of the chapel, not wanting to stare, but they need not have worried; still utterly lost in the rapture of the song, she didn't notice a thing.

*

Even though it was Christmas Day, the next morning Sisters Rebecca and Deborah met in the latter's office to discuss the incident, feeling that there was some urgency to deal with it without delay.

"I never dreamed that her singing would do that," Rebecca said, pulling her chair up close to the desk. "It hadn't even occurred to me, not really. I never thought through what the implications would be of her voice having the power it has."

"It hadn't occurred to any of us." Sister Deborah tapped a pen against the desk. "Why, though, I wonder? I mean, why *singing* in particular?"

Sister Rebecca thought about it. "There's a passage in the Book of Job," she said slowly, "where God is speaking to Job, and mentions that on the day the world was made, the morning stars sang together, and the sons of God shouted for joy. I wonder. . ." She moved her hands, seeking the right words. "She's a nephil, right? Half demon. But demons are actually fallen angels. And if, at the creation of the world, all the angels sang for joy. . ." She paused. "Maybe what we heard yesterday was just a little bit of that. The part of her that sang with the morning stars."

Sister Deborah said nothing for a moment, stunned by the plausibility of it. The idea that Justina had been singing with some kind of primal, celestial power was both amazing and terrifying, but there was no denying that it made more sense than any other explanation she had thought of.

Sister Rebecca dug her fingers into her hair. "Now, what do we *do?*" she cried. "There's no way that the right thing is to stop her from singing. I can't imagine that being a good idea, or God's will either."

Sister Deborah shook her head. "No, I agree with you completely. Aside from the obvious moral nonsense of trying to stop someone from singing hymns to God, I'm honestly not sure whether we even could if we wanted to. After the Triumphal Entry, when the Pharisees told Jesus to make his followers be quiet, He told them that if the followers were silent—"

"The very stones would cry out," Rebecca finished, and nodded. "I have the idea that the same thing would happen if we tried to keep Justina from singing."

Both women sat in silence for a moment. "Well," Sister Rebecca offered, "after all, not every song is the 'Hallelujah Chorus'. I mean, if there was ever a song that would make the walls shake by its pure power alone, it's that one."

Sister Deborah tapped her pen on the desk again. "That's true."

"And she didn't cause any real damage. I mean, she burned out the light bulbs, but that's about it."

"And," Sister Deborah added, "I don't think it's unreasonable to suppose that she'll gain greater control over this as she matures, just as she did over her voice in general when she was younger."

"So," Sister Rebecca suggested hesitantly, "should we just wait and see? Let her sing, and watch what happens?"

=Deborah smiled suddenly. "Why not? Really, why not? Martin Luther reportedly said that the devil runs from music almost as much as from Scripture." She paused, a fierce gleam in her eyes. "If nephilim are made to be weapons, made to do battle, then let Justina take the field in this way, as well as in all the others in which she has such skill. If her singing is a weapon, then let her destroy the gates of Hell with it."

***

Interlude Three

Excerpt from the Record Kept by the Sisters at St. Margaret's, About Justina

Sister Rebecca. March 19.

Justina is eight years old now. But she's not like any other eight-year-old: she can spar competently with any of us, she's tearing through the high school curriculum, and before long she's going to be as tall as some of the sisters! We don't really know what to *do* with her. Surely she can't go out into the field yet! But, what else is there for her to do?

I can really only think of one logical progression, and I have no idea how it would be able to happen. At this point, in order to keep busy and keep improving, until she's old enough to officially declare as a novice and start training in the field, she needs to *teach*. She needs to teach someone younger than herself. She needs the responsibility and moral growth and compassion of that responsibility. But there isn't another child in the commandery, and would setting a child to learn from a nephil really be wise anyway? We still have no real idea of what Justina will be, or what she will be like, or what powers she will have, or even how the powers we already know about will develop. But still, I'm not sure it's really good for her to continue to be the only student and the only child in the commandery. . .

Three

In St. Luke's hospital in Derrick, on a day near the middle of the summer Justina was eight years old, there was another death, and there was another orphaned child left behind.

Unlike in Justina's case, however, there was nothing particularly atypical about the incident. The mother did indeed bleed to death, as Justina's mother had; but it was not inexplicable at all, as she had been in a car accident that was particularly violent. The trauma team at St. Luke's would have been more surprised if she had lived. Also, the woman's four-year-old daughter was left alone, but she had connections: they simply were not ones that particularly cared to take her in. The hospital staff spent more than an hour on the phone, finding this out. And unlike Justina, she had a name: Imani Douglas.

Imani's mother had been able to give her very little, but what she did give, she clearly gave with love. Imani's clothes were worn, but where there were holes, the holes had been (inexpertly, but carefully) mended with mismatched thread, which seemed to come from the kind of pocket sewing kit one sometimes gets for free in motels. Imani's clothes had a few small stains, too, but the stains were faded with washing, and the fabric was otherwise scrupulously clean. Imani's dark hair had been worked into a meticulous, but simple, style of cornrow braids snug against her head, each one

39

with a plastic pony bead at the end; some of the braids were slightly thicker than others, and some were crooked, suggesting that her mother had made them, not a salon. In her arms, Imani clutched a plush rabbit, limp and floppy with wear, its fur matted down from being held, its color (once apparently some shade of blue) faded and washed out to a vague gray.

Keisha Douglas, Imani's mother, had no permanent address at the time of the accident, and all of her and Imani's belongings were in her car. Nearly everything Imani owned was neatly packed in a small pink suitcase, and when Sister Rebecca (who had volunteered this time) arrived at the hospital to pick her up, she brought the suitcase along.

*

Again, Sisters Rebecca and Deborah met in Sister Deborah's office to discuss the new development. Rebecca puffed out a long breath. "*Well.*"

Sister Deborah smiled a little. "I concur."

"So, the hospital said that they called all of Imani's relatives that they could find, and none of them were interested in taking her. Unless they got *paid.*" She curled her lip, revolted and furious, and when she paused for a moment, Sister Deborah guessed (rightly) that she was reciting Hebrews 10:30 to herself, to try to head off the impulse to hunt down such disgusting excuses for family and teach them a lesson. She, Sister Deborah, certainly was.

"So," Rebecca went on after taking a deep breath, "There's a strong possibility that Imani will be staying here for good, and we already have Kevin Orta working on the legal side, just in case one of those deadbeats changes his mind." Kevin Orta was the commandery's lawyer and legal liaison when it needed one, and also a *confrater*: a "friend" of the Order of the Holy Lance, though not an official member, who could be counted on for certain services and could expect support from the Order in return.

Sister Deborah nodded. "Good. The last thing we want is for the poor kid to get uprooted again in a year or two, to go live with some relative that doesn't really want her."

"*And,*" emphasized Sister Rebecca, "I know you've had concerns about how a younger child would get along with Justina. We all have. And we will certainly have to keep an eye on things." Sister Deborah nodded. "But I really think this has the potential to be the best thing we could do for Justina, and a sister, of sorts, will surely be a good thing for Imani too."

"I know that's true," said Deborah. "But keep in mind: Justina has never encountered an *average* four-year-old before: she was about as far from a typical child herself as anyone could imagine. And you know she has trouble being patient with anyone who isn't up to her level, which if we're being honest, is nearly everyone."

Sister Rebecca assented. Justina's impatience with any form of weakness, ineptitude, or stupidity was one of her more unfortunate traits.

"I've placed Imani in Sister Magdalena's cell for now, until we know how the two girls will interact. I would like them to share a cell at some point, but just now it seems better to let Imani stay with someone a bit. . ." She searched for a kind way to put it. "Someone a bit gentler, or with a bit more tolerance for a grieving four-year-old."

Sister Rebecca sighed. She understood; there was no denying that Justina could be harsh, and might well make things worse rather than better for Imani if she wasn't careful. "I know you're right. But I hope and pray that interacting with Imani will mitigate some of that in Justina. If they can have the kind of relationship I hope for. . . If they can truly be *sisters*, not even Justina's singing may be as beautiful as that.

*

Sister Rebecca found Justina in the refectory, wiping tables after supper. "I need to have a quick word with you," she said. "You can finish afterwards." Justina nodded, pulled out a chair, and sat down.

"You know the house took in a new child today. Imani."

"Yes, I heard about it,"

"You will be expected to do many things with her, and help her and guide her. Do you think you can do that?"

Justina wrinkled her brow, confused. "Of course I can, I know how to do everything. I can tell her whatever she needs to know."

Rebecca shook her head. "That is not what I mean. She hasn't had the training you have, and she is also an ordinary four-year-old. You know that you learned things much more quickly than most children."

"Because I'm a nephil," she said thoughtfully.

"Yes, because you're a nephil. Imani can't read yet, or speak as clearly as you could, or fight at all. And she will not learn to do those things as quickly as you did."

"I'll teach her," Justina pronounced, without any trace of doubt.

"I know you will, you and all the sisters. But you must be very patient with her, Justina. You will be frustrated by how slowly she seems to improve, but you *must* be kind. You must help her only as quickly as she is able, and you must not look down on her. She needs you to protect her and love her, not bully her. Do you understand?"

Justina thought about it, and looked down at the table top, tracing on it with her fingertip. "I think so," she said finally.

"Remember that Jesus was always smarter and stronger and braver and more wise than anyone around him, but he still had patience with the apostles, and with everyone, and loved them, even when they did stupid things. He was never mean to them."

Justina nodded, understanding.

"And," Sister Rebecca went on, "her mother just died. I know your mother died as well, but you don't remember her, so it isn't the same. Imani remembers hers, and she is very, very sad. She's grieving. Think how you would feel if I died, or if Sister Magdalena or Sister Deborah died. Only they were the *only person you had*; none of the other sisters were there for you, and you were all alone." Justina thought about it, and her face filled with imagined distress.

"I would feel horrible," she said, almost wonderingly, as if the idea had never occurred to her. "That would be *horrible*! That shouldn't happen!"

Sister Rebecca smiled, just a little, at this reaction. "No, it never should. But it happened to Imani. So, do you think you can be kind and patient with her? Even though she may annoy you?"

Justina pondered this seriously. "She isn't being weak," Justina concluded finally. "She's being as strong as she can."

"That's right, she is."

Justina looked up. "I will be patient with her, and help her," she said decisively. "It's bad for her to be alone. She needs us."

Rebecca stood up, and hugged Justina tight to her then. "Yes," she said, "she does. She does need us."

*

That night, after Sister Magdalena had put Imani to bed on a spare cot, Justina knocked politely on her door. No one answered;

Magdalena had gone to talk to Sister Deborah for a few minutes. Justina softly opened the door and went inside.

At first she thought Imani was asleep. But then, when she got closer, she realized that she was crying, curled into a ball around her stuffed rabbit. Justina hesitated, uncomfortable; then, unexpectedly, she felt a rush of compassion for the child in front of her, and a desire to protect that surprised her with its fierceness. The weakness of tears no longer mattered. She pulled up a chair beside the bed, and rested her hand on Imani's tiny shoulder.

Imani froze, still crying. Justina had no experience comforting anyone, but she knew she had power; when she sang, things happened. She wanted something to happen now. She knew many hymns, and she tried to think of a comforting one; after a moment, she began to sing the one she had chosen.

Shortly after, Sister Magdalena returned to her cell, and found the door ajar. She heard Justina's golden voice singing:

> "Fear not, I am with thee; oh, be not dismayed,
> For I am thy God, and will still give thee aid.
> I'll strengthen thee, help thee, and cause thee to stand,
> Upheld by My righteous, omnipotent hand."

Sister Magdalena opened the door softly; neither of the two girls seemed to notice as she entered, and stood listening.

> "When through the deep waters I call thee to go,
> "The rivers of sorrow shall not thee o'erflow,
> "For I will be with thee, thy troubles to bless,
> "And sanctify to thee thy deepest distress."

Sister Magdalena stood in silence, caught up in the deep comfort and peace of the song, and of Justina's singing of it. It wasn't the same as when Justina had sung the "Hallelujah Chorus" at the Christmas Eve mass. The power here was different, though equally strong; the emotional impact was not one bit less, though it conferred peace and comfort rather than exaltation, and though

Magdalena could feel the air thrumming with the strength of it, the walls and window of the cell did not shake.

"The soul that on Jesus hath leaned for repose

"I will not, I will not desert to her foes.

"That soul, though all Hell should endeavor to shake,

"I'll never, no never, no never forsake."

And when the song ended, Magdalena saw Justina's hand resting on Imani, like a sister's hand, like a mother's, and Imani looked up to her in peace, her tears drying on her face.

***

Part Two

"Any secular person, or persons, whose life or accustomed home is placed in peril by the actions of dark spirits or creatures, should by all means and with all possible dispatch be removed from the danger; this must be the case whether the victims be beggars or serfs, knights or kings, clerks or bishops, for all are one to God, and he shows no partiality. To this end, all houses or commanderies of the Order of the Holy Lance must have the capacity to lodge such persons in a manner befitting their stations, and to give them protection and succor until such time as the said threat has been destroyed. These *hospites* must be served in the refectory with the Knight-Sisters, or with the servants, according to their status, and their lodgings should be located. . .

"The commandery must also permit full freedom of the house to the *hospites*, with all respect and charity, as though giving hospitality to the Lord; as persons in danger of darkness, however, they must be discouraged from quitting the house's consecrated ground. They are not to be restrained, if they have determined in themselves to leave, but their position must be made entirely clear to them, lest they come to harm and God hold the commandery accountable for their blood, as he gave warning to the prophet Ezekiel. . .

"The occasion will arise in which secular persons, of many qualities, may find themselves imperiled, by reason of dark spirits or creatures. Such spirits or creatures being the rightful prey and quarry of the Sisters of the Holy Lance, the nearest house or commandery should dispatch Sisters, in such numbers as are judged necessary by their Commander, to give them battle without delay. . .

"When Sisters go to face creatures of the darkness in battle, they must be "two or more gathered together", as the

Scriptures state, and each Knight-Sister may also be accompanied by two squire-novices. . . All items needful for giving battle to dark foes must be provided by the Order, and the Sisters must carry a full panoply of the same in all sallies, neglecting nothing, lest like the Foolish Virgins, they be found unprepared to their task. The said panoply must include the below-named items in good repair. . .

The Rule of the Holy Lance, approved 1139. Tr. from Latin c. 1387. Tr. to English 1798. Revised English tr. 1936.

Four

Not all hauntings are violent.

Most are not; in fact, most hauntings are not even noticed. A ghost is a footprint, a photograph, a recording: an impression left behind by something which was once there, but is gone. Powerful events or emotions, or powerful personalities, may leave such impressions, but they are ephemeral, and, like a footprint left on a beach, are soon effaced and smoothed over by subsequent events. Most hauntings are worn to nothing before anyone even notices they exist at all.

But some events, especially particularly violent events or ones which continue for a long period of time, may leave impressions deep enough to be noticed. And when they are, the fear or anger or distress they cause does not scour away the impression, but carves it deeper, leading to a more powerful haunting and, in turn, more distress. Therefore, once this situation exists, it will continue to worsen until it is stopped. These types of hauntings are those most people have heard of: the stuff of banging doors and whispers, of disembodied footsteps and shadowy apparitions. Such ghosts have no awareness or volition, but continue to strengthen as frightened witnesses continue, unwittingly, to deepen the original impression.

Most violent hauntings, the kind which cause houses to go through a rapid succession of owners or stand vacant, are, in a sense, accidents: imprints which, by their nature, cause themselves to be reinforced. They are also random, and may be the remnants of any number of events or emotions.

But, very rarely, a haunting may be created deliberately. A few particularly malicious and determined humans have managed it, by repeatedly causing others to experience intense fear or pain over a long period. But other, inhuman forces may also create and shape a violent haunting, and do so very quickly. If a haunting is like an inscription in stone, a human's attempts might be compared to a gradual deepening of the letters by laborious scratching with a small instrument; a demon's efforts, by contrast, would be a sudden, deep gouging. It might happen in a day.

In a house in the town of Barton Draw, two hours' drive from Derrick, it did happen in a day.

Most of the time, when a demon twisted an all-but-unnoticeable ghost into a vicious, terrifying haunting, its purpose was the same as that of most demon actions: to cause suffering, to deceive, to destroy faith. And in this case those were certainly secondary goals, as this demon was never one to settle for one victory when two were possible. But the primary purpose of the haunting was different. This ghost was not a weapon, but bait. Its function was that of any fat, tempting decoy: to draw an elusive quarry out of its covert into view and, if possible, into the line of fire.

The raw material for the operation was not difficult to find. The faint, latent impression of an abusive family, too weak even to have been noticed by the family who currently lived in the house, provided the initial haunting, and the demon, like any practiced craftsman, selected the most useful portions of it to deepen and modify. He discarded the children's fear. He pruned away the wife's silent, simmering, repressed hatred. The husband's potent mixture of pride, scorn, shame, perfectionism, callousness, rage, and need for control were the portions of the latent imprint that would grow best into the kind of haunting the demon wanted, and it was those portions he shaped and built, sharpening them like blades, growing and intertwining them like thorn hedges.

When he was through, the thing in the house was more malicious, more cruel, and more savage than the original abusive father had ever been. If it had a voice, it was a shout, a sneer, a command. If it acted, it bullied and terrorized. If it had any semblances of emotions, they were suffocating arrogance and instantaneous rage. Of the currently-resident family, it would hate the mother with a simple, complete, vicious hatred. It would almost ignore the young daughter, dismissing her with a cold contempt in which there was nothing human. It might attack the father, despising his humanity, though it would not do so right away. And it would be drawn to the son obsessively, seeking to own him, to control him, to remake him; if the ghost had had real thoughts of its own, and could have put the thoughts into words, it would have expressed it thus: "I'll make a man out of you, goddammit."

Satisfied, having fashioned the ghost to his requirements and his liking, the demon set it loose, then watched, savoring the complex, delectable mixture of anger, fear, despair, spite, discord, terror, resentment, disbelief, suspicion. . . It was a delicious banquet the ghost served up to him, and that not even the real goal of the exercise.

The real goal was Justina, his dear, dear daughter. The rest of it was just fun.

*

It started with Tyler. At first, he woke up from strange dreams, disoriented, scared, talking about a mean man he had seen. No one paid much attention; dreams were only dreams, and the stranger they were, the more dreamlike. But then his behavior began to change. He tore the head off his eight-year-old sister Emily's most beloved stuffed animal, then jeered at her when she cried, though he loved his sister. He flew into a temper when the family dog, Mesquite, brushed against him and startled him while he was doing homework, and then he viciously kicked Mesquite, causing the dog to limp for a few days afterwards; but he doted on Mesquite, and had never had such a hot temper before. He made a few attempts to domineer his mother, Sara, as she cooked dinner: attempts which were not made less disturbing by their ineffectiveness. Tyler's teachers sent home concerned notes, reporting that he was becoming a bully, though he had never been a bully before.

"He's twelve years old," Sara's husband, Kyle, said when she told him. "He's just acting out and pushing his boundaries. Middle school is a crazy time for everyone; he'll get over it."

But he didn't. When Sara caught Tyler killing the little lizards in the back yard, flinging them savagely against the sidewalk or against rocks, she insisted on taking him to a child psychologist, and Kyle agreed. "Please," they said to the psychologist, "tell us what's happening with our son. Please help him."

But the psychologist couldn't. After only a few sessions, he was forced to admit bafflement and defeat. He suggested a specialist.

Then, as the demon had known would happen, the thing in the house escalated its attacks. When Sara was in the kitchen, she began to hear whispers; constant, unintelligible whispers, hissing, tittering, scolding. But there was no one there; Kyle was at work and the kids were at school. She told Kyle, but he insisted that it was just the house settling, or the wind outside, or the stereo picking up snatches of stray signal from the ham radio operator next door. All of that seemed plausible, and she tried to believe it.

One day, when she sat down in the living room to watch TV, she had only been relaxing there for a few minutes when she felt a violent *smack* across the back of her head, which threw her off the sofa and sent her sprawling across the coffee table. For a moment she saw stars. Then, when she realized that no one was there (and no one could have done that anyway, not from behind, as the sofa was flush against the wall and there was no room for anyone) and nothing heavy had fallen off the wall to hit her, she bolted blindly from the house, panting.

But, standing out in the yard, in the bright sun and the summer heat, she soon began to feel stupid. What did she think had hit her, exactly? A ghost? She was embarrassed even to think it. Obviously what had really happened was that she had started to drift off to sleep, then jerked awake and toppled over across the coffee table; she only thought someone had hit her from behind, because she was half-asleep. How many times had she jerked awake, believing she was falling? That was all it was. She went back inside.

Then one day, she was in the front yard, deadheading the daisies, trimming back the lantana, and pulling weeds, and had lost track of time. Then she looked at her watch. "Oh!" she cried, and, leaving her clippers and weed-puller on the flowerbed border, she jumped up and dashed to the car to pick up Tyler and Emily. She arrived at the school ten minutes late, with muddy knees and her gardening hat still on her head.

Tyler berated her all the way home, and when they arrived, Sara finally lost her temper. "You will not speak to me that way, young man!" she shouted. "This attitude has gone on long enough! Go upstairs to your room, now, while I think about consequences."

He stood there, looking her straight in the eye, his face full of a terrible, absolute contempt. "Don't you dare tell me what to do, woman."

That was such an odd thing for him to say ("woman"?), that for a moment she was at a complete loss. Then she felt hands close around her throat.

She clawed at them with her fingers, but found nothing there to fight. But she could *feel* the hands, could feel every finger against her windpipe. She struggled, crashing against furniture, but the hands did not move; then she found herself on the ground, dark closing in around the edges of her vision, looking up at Tyler. He was standing over her, staring down, utterly expressionless and remote. Then the hands melted away, and she dragged in a long, sobbing breath.

When she looked in the mirror, she could see the red imprint of large hands on her neck.

She tried to think of a rational explanation; tried with all her might. But she was completely unable to come up with one. So the next morning, in secret, as though doing something deeply shameful, she located a psychic online and called her in.

She showed the woman the bruises on her neck, and told her about the whispers, and the strange new behavior from Tyler, and the blow she had felt that day as she watched TV, which she no longer believed had only been an abrupt waking. The psychic walked through the house, feeling the air with her fingers, sometimes standing with her eyes closed.

"You have a violent, misogynistic spirit in this house," said the psychic.

But Sara had known that already.

The psychic tried to cleanse the house by burning a bundle of sage, but within forty-eight hours the attacks resumed.

She told Kyle everything then, and showed him the bruises. But they had faded enough by then to look like almost anything, not necessarily the imprint of two hands, and he had experienced none of it himself. He refused to believe it. Maybe you dreamed it, he suggested, or maybe you had some sort of accident.

Then, one Saturday, Tyler hit Emily, hit her hard, with his fist, not a childish smack but a punch really intended to do harm. Sarah heard the blow from down the hall, and rushed into the room to her daughter's defense; but as soon as she crossed the threshold, she felt a solid strike herself. It was a hard, furious slap, and it spun her against the wall; if she had been standing in the middle of the room, it would have knocked her down. Tyler looked up, and laughed uproariously, maliciously, in a way he had never laughed before the last few months. Sara looked in the mirror; sure enough, there was a red handprint rising in a welt across the left side of her face.

Kyle was home that day. She went immediately to show him, and this time, he believed her, though with great reluctance. The handprint was obvious and undeniable. He forced himself to ask whether a psychic might be a good idea.

"I already called one," Sara admitted. "She said there was a violent ghost here, and tried to use sage to get rid of it, but it didn't work."

Two days later, Emily had a black eye, given to her by her brother. They were not a churchgoing family, but Kyle hesitantly suggested, "Should we maybe contact a priest?"

Sara agreed. They opened the telephone book and found "Churches" in the yellow pages, then they called them one by one, starting at the top of the list. Eventually they reached a church whose priest agreed to come to the house and see what could be done.

When Father James arrived, he looked nervous, and he was: he had never been called on to deal with a possible haunting before, and had no idea what to expect. But he had done his best to prepare himself, and hoped that if he found himself unable to really do proper battle, he could at least stand firm in the face of whatever was there to be faced, and call in help if it was needed. The husband and wife who had contacted him looked shamefaced, as though embarrassed to call for help from a church they hadn't really believed in, but also haggard and deeply afraid, especially the wife (who, he gathered, had taken the brunt of the violence). He could still see the remains of a bruise across her left cheekbone. He smiled at them both as they ushered him inside, into the living room, trying to put them at ease.

He had decided that his best course of action would be to start with a house blessing, and see what happened. He had chosen an elegant Celtic blessing from the Brigid Liturgy, which he felt was both beautiful and very thorough. "I'm going to start by blessing and consecrating the house," he said. "Is that all right?"

"Do whatever you think you need to do," said the husband, Kyle.

Father James took out a small vial of anointing oil, dabbed some on his fingers, and, turning around, marked the lintel of the front door he had just entered with a cross. "May God give a blessing to this house," he began. "God bless this house from roof to floor, from wall to wall—"

Various objects around the living room began to move, with a faint rattling or clattering. Picture frames bumped against the walls, lamp shades wobbled, decorative objects shivered; the lamps' light bulbs flickered a few times. The air felt heavy, clogged, almost too thick to breathe, and the hissing whispers Sara had been hearing began, thick and fast around them.

"—from end to end, from its foundation and in its covering," Father James continued. "In the strong name of the Triune God, all disturbance cease—"

A cascade of books fell out of the bookcase all at once. All the light bulbs in the room exploded. A vase on the coffee table fell over sideways.

"—all disturbance cease!" Father James tried again. "Captive spirits freed, God's Spirit alone dwell within these walls!"

A small framed picture of the family shot away from its place, sitting on the sideboard, and flew toward Father James. It struck him hard in the mouth, slicing his lip, knocking loose two of his teeth, and flooding his mouth with blood.

He swallowed the blood and shouted the rest of the blessing intended for the front entry, defiantly: "We call upon the Sacred Three to save, shield, and surround this house, this home, this day, this night, and every night!"

"We have to get out of here!" Kyle yelled, grabbing Father James by the arm and bodily dragging him outside. Sara followed, and her face, twisted with fear and fury and despair, was streaked with tears. The door slammed behind them, hard enough to leave a crack in the wooden jamb, though none of them had touched it.

Father James bent over, panting, shocked. He spat another mouthful of blood out into the grass, then he turned to Sara and Kyle. "We need more help to deal with this," he said. "I can't fight it by myself. And you and your kids need a safe place to stay in the meantime."

They both looked at him, nervously, their faces closed; they had told him about the psychic they had already called in, and how she had failed to help. They probably thought he was ready to leave them in the lurch, too.

"I know exactly who to bring in to deal with this sort of thing," he said firmly. "They can be here to pick you up in a couple of hours, to take you to safety. In the meantime, collect anything you safely can, to take with you, and pull your kids out of school; they can keep up with their schoolwork at the safehouse."

Both of them looked relieved to have someone take charge, someone who seemed to have some knowledge of what to do, someone who offered some hope. Father James took out his cell phone and flipped it open. "I'm calling the Sisters of the Holy Lance now," he said, "and I'll stay with you until they arrive."

*

Two hours later, a plain white car, several years old, pulled up and parked along the curb in front of the house. The family, sitting outside with their backpacks and duffles of belongings, Mesquite panting amiably beside them, watched as Father James went around to the driver's side and spoke quietly with someone, then both he and the driver walked around the car and toward them.

The car's driver was a woman in her twenties or early thirties, with chin-length dark-blonde hair. She was dressed all in white: white cotton jeans, a plain short-sleeved white shirt with a small red cross embroidered on it, and sturdy white canvas boots ("waffle-stompers", Kyle had always called boots like that). She looked nothing like a nun, the white clothes and the cross notwithstanding, and not only because she was wearing pants instead of a dress and nothing on her head. (What was that thing called? A wimple? Sara thought it was a wimple. Hadn't there been something about wimples in "The Sound of Music"?) This woman carried herself differently: she moved with a kind of coiled, feline readiness, and her shirt did not entirely hide the hard, athletic muscle through her arms and shoulders. She didn't look like a nun: she looked like a soldier.

She walked over to the family, and shook hands with Sara and Kyle. They noticed the strength of her grip, and the tough callouses on her palm and fingers. "I'm Sister Ella, from the Order of the Holy Lance." Their recitations of "nice to meet you" were dazed and mechanical, but she ignored this. "I'm here to take you to our commandery house, where you'll be safe. Are you ready to go?"

They were, and, after handing Ella the house keys, Father James helped them transfer their belongings to the car, while she approached the front door. He rattled the latch of the car's trunk, but it was locked; she heard him, and called back, "I have equipment in the trunk, so put all the luggage you can in the front, if you wouldn't mind."

Sister Ella approached the door carefully, cautiously. She didn't really expect an attack outside the house's walls, but it wasn't impossible, and she wasn't here today to do battle; her job was to pick up the family, and to verify that there was indeed a haunting present (though from the look of things, it was purely a formality in this case: no one's imagination had created the injuries on Sara or the priest, and the weird aura around the son wasn't imagined either).

She opened the door, slowly, and stepped inside. As soon as her feet crossed the threshold, she knew, as any experienced Sister of the Holy Lance would have known: there was something dark and malicious lurking here, something that wanted to dominate and terrify and cause suffering. She could feel it as a prickling on her skin, a movement of the hair on her scalp, a sense of tightness in the air; she could pick it up as a kind of vibration below the range of hearing. Anyone else might have put these sensations down to imagination, and not irrationally; but Sister Ella had encountered her fair share of hauntings, and knew the difference. It wasn't the very worst she had ever met, but it was certainly bad enough.

She went back outside, and felt a kind of subliminal *snap* of releasing tension as soon as she was back in the open air. Father James met her on the porch and walked with her to the car.

"What do you think?" he asked nervously. Sister Ella wasn't sure whether he wanted her to confirm his response, or tell him he had been overreacting; she wasn't sure whether he knew himself.

"You were absolutely right to call us," she said. "This is a situation we have to deal with, and the family needed to be gotten out immediately, before anyone got hurt worse than they already have."

He didn't look at her. "I never. . . When my predecessor in the parish told me about your Order, and gave me your phone number just in case, I don't think I really believed him. I never thought I'd need to call."

She smiled a little. "No one ever really does, until they're faced with it."

He did look at her then, shamefaced. "I'm sorry."

She stopped walking, and faced him directly. "No, don't be sorry, not for one second. You did everything you could, and everything you should; nothing that has happened here is your fault."

They had reached the car. "God go with you, Sister," said Father James.

*

During the entire drive to St. Margaret's, Tyler sat in the back seat, looking sullenly out the window, silent and motionless. Mesquite nudged his nose under Tyler's hand, whining, but even that elicited no response.

When they arrived, the moment he stepped out of the car and onto the commandery-house's consecrated ground, he collapsed.

***

Five

The family remained in the commandery for three days, as the sisters prepared to remove the ghost from their house. For the first two days and more, Tyler barely moved from his bed in the guest suite, and he was often plainly disoriented and distressed; in fact, at times he acted delirious, as if he had a high fever, though his temperature was normal. A woman with dark, straight hair cut neatly short sat beside his bed, only leaving to attend the Hours, giving him sips of water when he asked, and helping him to eat spoonfuls of hearty oatmeal or porridge when he was awake enough. He learned later that her name was Sister Magdalena. Then, early in the morning of the third day, he woke up properly, weak, but otherwise apparently normal. After matins, he joined everyone for breakfast in the refectory for the first time, accepting Sister Magdalena's supporting arm, but walking under his own power.

He joined his family at a small folding table on one side of the refectory. The square room was plain, and looked more like a school cafeteria than anything else. Folding tables stood in a cross-shaped arrangement in the middle; they were the kind any church or school or club has stacks of, stored away in closets, with fake wood-grain tops, black rubber bumpers all around the edges, and metal legs that could fold up underneath for storage. The refectory floor was made of worn terra-cotta tiles (not linoleum, but real Saltillo tile), and windows high up in every wall would let in a flood of morning sun as soon as the sun rose.

The food was brought in by two girls, the only children they had seen in the commandery: a slightly-built girl who was, Tyler thought, close to his own age, and another girl who seemed a few years older, probably in her mid-teens. He thought the older girl was spectacularly beautiful, in a sharp, almost fierce way, and she was *tall*; so tall, at first he thought there was some sort of optical illusion happening. Maybe the shortness of her companion made her seem taller than she really was. But when she brought bowls of the savory porridgy stuff (it was made with steel-cut oats, which he had never seen used before and didn't recognize, cooked in chicken broth) to his family's table, he knew it wasn't any kind of illusion. She really was six feet tall at least, and that wasn't the only unusual thing about her. Her wavy shoulder-length hair was mostly black, but thick curls of it were pure white, whiter than any hair he had ever seen. Her skin had an odd, almost polished look, as if it was made of metal. And when she looked up he saw that her irises seemed to consist of layers and layers and layers of gold-colored prisms, all flashing and reflecting, bottomless and bewildering. Something in him said, with perfect surety, *this girl isn't human*, and he was shocked to have thought it.

He realized he was staring at her, and that she must have seen him staring. He looked away quickly, flushing. But Justina hadn't noticed. Her attention had been drawn to something else, something she could see on his skin, or inside his skin, that was like nothing she had ever seen before. She ate her breakfast as quickly as she could, and then waited impatiently until the bell dismissed them all; Justina almost never fidgeted, but she fidgeted as she sat through breakfast. Imani noticed, and wanted to ask what had happened, but all meals were eaten in silence. She would have to wait to find out.

*

Justina found Sister Deborah in her office, during the space of time between breakfast before dawn, and prime at sunrise. She tapped on the door politely.

"Come in," called Sister Deborah, and Justina went inside and pulled out a chair to sit down.

A moment later Sister Deborah looked up, smiling. "Justina! How are you this morning?"

"I saw something," she said. "With that boy, Tyler. I hadn't seen him before today; he came to the refectory for breakfast this morning."

Deborah nodded. "What did you see?"

"Maybe everyone else has already seen it, I don't know. But there's something, like a mark, maybe a fingerprint, on his forehead. Here." She pressed her thumb to her own forehead, right between her eyes, to show.

Sister Deborah's face went very serious, and she leaned forward. "No one else has seen that, as far as I know. I certainly haven't. Describe it to me, carefully."

Justina thought about how to frame it. "It looks like something touched him there, and left a kind of smudge, like with ink. Only it didn't seem to be on the surface of his skin, exactly; it was almost as if it was just under a layer of skin, so it still showed through. It wasn't like a tattoo; more like the way you can see veins under the skin on the inside of your elbow. Or like a bruise, only it wasn't a bruise." Sister Alana had several tattoos, from before she joined the Order, so Justina knew what one looked like.

Sister Deborah felt a chill. "And, what do you think it means? The mark?"

Justina had thought through all the things she had learned about that could single out a person that way (though she had never heard of anyone being able to see a physical mark left by them), and come to a conclusion. "I think the ghost in their house did it. I think it's fixated on him, or trying to claim him, or maybe just keeping tabs on him. But I think that mark is where it first touched him."

Dreams, thought Sister Deborah. They said his strange behavior began with dreams. Where the ghost first touched him.

"I think you're probably right, and thank you for telling me," she said aloud.

Justina nodded, and started to get up. "Wait," said Sister Deborah. "What other things have you seen, like this? Things only you can see?"

"Nothing *just* like this," Justina said, "never a ghost's mark or whatever it is." She paused. "But sometimes. . . I can see when people are praying. It's a kind of colored glow around them, different colors for different people. . . I can see song, too. When everyone sings together is the best, it's like. . ." she trailed off, searching for words, finding none. "Does anyone else see those things?"

Sister Deborah shook her head, wordlessly. Then, overcome by curiosity, she blurted out, "What colors?"

"They aren't. . .they aren't like that," Justina said. "Not colors with names."

Just then, the bell rang for prime, and Justina got up, leaving Sister Deborah stunned, and with considerably more to ponder than just a haunted boy.

*

The sisters had researched the history of the house, and carefully collated the stories of all the members of the family (Tyler, surprisingly, could tell them very little: his memory of the last few weeks was vague and hazy, as if he had been half-asleep for most of it). Once they knew Tyler would recover, they were ready to go back and deal with the thing in the house, and on the morning of the fourth day, the weather forecast reported conditions ideal for the operation: hot, sunny, and with high sustained winds.

Rebecca and Magdalena were the ones Sister Deborah assigned to the job. They had both faced hauntings before, and didn't expect anything particularly unusual out of this one; they had hopes of being back to the commandery by vespers that night. And when they left that morning, just after prime, Justina went with them.

"I should go," she had said. "I may be able to see the ghost when no one else can; you need me to help."

"We've both dealt with ghosts before," Sister Magdalena had pointed out. "There doesn't seem to be anything unusual about this one. We can manage it fine."

"And you're fifteen still," Sister Rebecca had added, reflexively protecting her goddaughter. "You can't go out as a squire-novice until next spring."

Justina drew herself up to her considerable height, so that she stood taller than either of them. "You know I can handle it," she said. "I've been training for this since I could walk, and I've been training Imani for years. If I can see a ghost's fingerprint, who knows what else I could see?"

The two sisters looked at each other uncomfortably. They knew she wasn't really wrong about any of those things.

Justina saw them wavering, and pushed her case. "The only reason the *Rule* doesn't allow squire-novices younger than sixteen is to keep the unprepared out of danger. I am not unprepared. I want to help. I want to fight this thing with you."

Rebecca and Magdalena were honest enough to acknowledge that she made good points. They said they would have to put it to Sister Deborah who, as the commander of the house, had the last word.

Sister Deborah did not forbid it.

And so, the summer she was fifteen years old, Justina left the commandery-house for the first time since she was an infant, and though no one knew it, her demon-father watched when she did, his decoy having drawn the quarry into the open just as he hoped.

***

Six

Sister Paloma found Emily, the daughter of the *hospite* family, in the commandery's library after the sisters and Justina had left, curled into one of the big sway-backed velveteen chairs, reading the first volume of *A History of the Order of the Holy Lance.* She looked up when Sister Paloma entered, then went on reading. Paloma smiled a little: a true bookworm, this one. Hiding in a safehouse from a violent ghost, and she just *had* to find something to read.

The commandery library contained a battered, water-spotted sideboard, donated in some long-forgotten decade by a *confrater.* On it sat an electric kettle, a coffee pot, a five-gallon jug of water to fill both, a bag of coffee, and a basket of teabags. Sister Paloma filled the kettle with water, selected teabags, and brewed two mugs of tea.

She took the chair next to Emily, and offered one mug. "Tea?"

Emily looked up, and wordlessly accepted the proffered drink.

Sister Paloma blew gently across the surface of her tea, then sipped. "If you were wondering," she said, "it's really true."

Emily looked up again. "What is?"

"The book." Sister Paloma indicated the one she was holding open on her lap. "The history of the Order. The story's really true."

Emily looked at her suspiciously, trying to decide if Paloma was pulling her leg. "It has *unicorns* in it."

Sister Paloma grinned, liking Emily more and more. "It does indeed, and later on it has other monsters too. But it's true anyway." She pointed at her for emphasis. "You should believe it of all people, you lived in a haunted house!"

Emily furrowed her brow, staring into her steaming mug, seriously considering the weight of this argument. "But unicorns, though," she said.

"Black unicorns," Sister Paloma emphasized, and took another sip of her tea. "Black unicorns aren't anything like most people think of when they think of unicorns. They're huge, and powerful, and they kill people, and only a woman can hurt one. That's why the Order was created in the first place, to fight against black unicorns."

"Why can only a woman hurt one?" Emily asked, curious.

Sister Paloma blew on her tea again, then took a bigger sip. "Nobody really knows," she said. "But it's true. If a man tried to, I don't know—" she wagged her hands vaguely, nearly sloshing hot tea into her lap—"shoot one, the bullet would just bounce off. It wouldn't do anything to it at all, except annoy it. That's just the way it is with black unicorns; it has to be a woman or nobody."

Emily looked down, and turned over a few pages of *A History of the Order of the Holy Lance*. "The book says the Order of the Holy Lance started almost a thousand years ago."

"It did." Paloma took another swallow of tea. "Around that same time, Europe was gearing up for the Crusades, and they created some military monastic orders—basically orders of knights who were also monks. The Knights Templar were the most famous, probably, but there were others too."

Emily sipped her tea, both hands wrapped around the mug, her eyes on Paloma. Paloma went on. "The whole point of those orders was to support the Crusades. They recruited new knights, and raised money, and sent knights to the Holy Lands, and all that sort of thing. They weren't focused on Europe, they were focused on Jerusalem."

"But there were black unicorns," Emily offered.

Paloma smiled. "There were black unicorns. Europe was all about creating military monastic orders then, so they created one for women too, so they could fight bad things like black unicorns in Europe while—"

"While the boys were off defending Jerusalem," Emily finished for her.

Paloma laughed aloud at that. "Yes, exactly! While the boys were defending Jerusalem. But," she added, pausing for another swallow of tea, "there were never very many black unicorns. Enough to create a big problem, but not enough to keep the entire Order of the Holy Lance occupied all by themselves. But there were always other scary things, too."

Emily shivered, and curled herself more tightly around the warmth of her mug of tea.

"So what would you do," Sister Paloma asked rhetorically, "if you were a knight or a peasant or somebody, and you had a ghost or a werewolf or a vampire or something in your village? Who would you call for help?"

"Ghostbusters!" Emily answered gleefully; she had been waiting for days to deliver that piece of cleverness.

Sister Paloma had just drunk another mouthful of tea, and at that she snorted with laughter and nearly choked. When she had recovered herself, she congratulated Emily on a timely joke well delivered; Emily beamed, and seemed to forget her fear for a moment.

"Really, though," Sister Paloma continued, "you would want to call in someone associated with holiness, right? So they could deal with evil things. And you would want to call in someone who could fight. So you'd want a military monastic order. But where were the boys?"

"Jerusalem!" Emily seemed to have nearly forgotten her tea, but if she had also forgotten some of her fear, or at least been distracted from it, it was well worth the waste of a teabag.

"Exactly. So, who was left in Europe to deal with ghosts and vampires and things?"

"The Order of the Holy Lance!"

"The Order of the Holy Lance," Sister Paloma confirmed. "And the more scary things we fought, the more we learned about how to fight them, and the better we got at it. So that even once the Crusades had ended, and the Knights Templar and all the boys were back in Europe, everybody knew: when you had a scary thing, you called the Order of the Holy Lance."

"Not the boys," said Emily.

"No, not the boys," laughed Paloma.

Emily took a long gulp of tea. "So," she said, running her finger around the rim of her mug, "So you know all about getting rid of ghosts. Because you've been doing it hundreds of years."

"Yes, we know about getting rid of ghosts. We even have books about it."

Emily looked up. "You do?"

"Sure, right there." Sister Paloma pointed to a nearby bookshelf, where a row of volumes sat below a curling paper label on which "Ghosts/Hauntings" had been neatly hand-lettered. Emily could read the first few titles from her chair: *On the Cleansing of Dwellings from Unwholesome Presences*; *Ghosts: Footprints That Harm*; *Bump In the Night: A Study of Ghostly Activity and How To End It*; and *The Life and Miracles of Saint Antonia of Aragon*.

Emily sipped tea slowly, regarding the books. "So, what will they do in our house? The sisters who went?"

Sister Paloma swallowed the last of her tea and put the mug down on the tiled floor. "Well," she said, "the first step is to go in and just scope the house out, and see what's going on. Then, once they know what they're dealing with, they can get to work.

*

Rebecca, Magdalena, and Justina pulled up in front of the house in Barton Draw. It looked absolutely ordinary, like any other house on the street: tan brick, sidewalk with the occasional enterprising dandelion squeezing up through the cracks, closed plantation shutters in the windows, trimmed boxwood and yaupon holly, an oak tree in the center of a brick-edged flower bed.

Justina opened the door of the back seat and started to jump out onto the curb. "Wait a minute," said Sister Rebecca. "Sit back down."

For a moment, Justina seemed to consider mutiny. Then she got back into the car and closed her door again.

"Now," said Rebecca, ignoring her goddaughter's impatience, "what is the first thing we're going to do here?"

"I know all this," said Justina.

"I know you do. But tell me anyway."

Justina snorted, but after a moment she said, "The first step is to go into the building and reconnoiter. We'll find out where the activity is the worst, and where the ghost is strongest. We'll also find out how many rooms there are, and what kind, and think about how to cleanse them all." She said this in a rapid, uninflected tone, as if reciting a worn-out lesson she just wanted to get through with.

"Exactly right," said Sister Rebecca. "And what will you take with you?"

"For the walk-through we need shields and vests, in case the ghost throws something at us or tries to hurt us."

"Got it," confirmed Sister Rebecca. "Now, let's get started."

The interior of the house had a slightly stuffy, closed-up smell, as any house would after being vacant and shuttered for four days. But still, they could all feel a sense of coiled watchfulness and hostility there, as if something had been waiting for them. The two sisters, wearing Kevlar vests and light polycarbonate bucklers, positioned themselves so as to cover each other's backs, and Magdalena pulled the similarly-equipped Justina into the formation. "Everyone stay together," she whispered. "No one can go off alone."

"I *know*," Justina hissed back.

"Seriously. Rule One."

"I know!"

They moved through the entire house, including the garage and the attic, carefully noting where the ghost's presence seemed strongest or most aggressive. In the kitchen, they all heard hissing whispers swirling around them, and then abruptly a heavy steel saucepan detached from the overhead pot rack with a loud clatter, and flung toward Sister Rebecca's head as she whipped around to track the noise. Sister Magdalena saw it coming, and smacked it aside with her buckler.

Rebecca looked at the saucepan, then at Magdalena. "Thanks," she said. Magdalena nodded.

Justina crossed the kitchen and bent over to examine the pan, where it had come to rest against the baseboard of the opposite wall. She looked up. "The ghost touched this," she said. "I can see the marks on it."

They went on. In Tyler's bedroom, everyone heard whispering and muttering again, and saw glimpses of a figure out of the corners of their eyes; the stifling sense of being watched, maliciously watched, was stronger than ever. "The ghost's been all over this room," whispered Justina.

"That makes sense," Sister Rebecca whispered back, "since it was so focused on Tyler."

They found a few other, more minor trouble spots in the house, too: the living room sofa where Sara had been attacked as she watched TV, Emily's bedroom where she had been struck by her brother, the place near the front door where Father James had been standing when the framed picture was thrown at him. Justina confirmed that the ghost had left traces in each place.

After finishing the walk-through of the house, they went back outside to the car for supplies. It was time to start driving the ghost out.

*

"Next," Sister Paloma went on, as Emily finished her tea, "they'll need to make the house inhospitable to the ghost, so it isn't comfortable or settled anywhere in it. It's like. . . if you have bugs in your cupboards, you have to shoo them out of the cupboards before you can squish them. So, what the sisters will do is drive the ghost out into the open, and then they can hustle it right out of the house."

Emily blinked at her. "How do you do that, though? How do you make a ghost uncomfortable?"

*

Rebecca and Magdalena did it with sunlight, fire, cedar wood, fragrant herbs, blessed incense, and ceiling fans.

First, they opened every interior door in the house: the door into the garage, the trapdoor into the attic, the pantry door, every closet door, every cupboard, every drawer and cabinet. They turned on every ceiling fan, too, and deployed portable box fans in the garage and attic, to circulate the air. Then they tilted open the louvers of the plantation shutters at every window, and, after unlatching them from the walls, swung the shutter frames themselves wide open. Hot summer sun blazed through the glass and into the rooms, to lie in swathes of gold across the carpeted floors.

"Why are we opening all the doors?" Sister Rebecca dutifully quizzed.

"To make sure the ghost doesn't have any isolated spot to hide," recited Justina, not very interested, "and so the smoke and incense can reach everywhere."

"And," Rebecca went on doggedly, "Why do we open the windows?"

"We let in as much sunlight as we can, because sunlight purifies."

"Exactly."

The ghost had resisted this process, but not strenuously; several shutters had snapped themselves closed again as soon as the sisters and Justina had left the room, and three drawers in the kitchen had slammed closed, open, then closed again. Justina rushed back to reopen them, and this time they stayed open. Whispers hissed around them, and now they had begun to crystallize into nearly-coherent words, slipping over the edge of hearing and then back into silence again.

> get out of here woman
> my house my boy my
> I'll make a man out of
> bitches don't you dare touch
> teach you to ignore me teach you to

They engaged with none of this. It was nothing, just mechanical posturing and bullying. Besides, they knew that the real attacks would come at the next step; everything up until this point had been preliminary, but now it was time for the fight to begin in earnest.

In every room, the women placed a small metal brazier, weighted at the base against spectral attempts to knock it over, and in each one they laid a small fire of blocks of clean cedar wood and dried hyssop and sage. When it was burning, they added the incense, mixed with salt. The smoke drifted up into the room, stirred and dispersed by the fan, and the mingled warm, smoky, spicy scent soaked into carpet, wallpaper, paint, wood, upholstery, and belongings. The ordinary household smells of dust and glass cleaner gave way to the more foreign, more powerful, ageless smell of frankincense and fragrant woodsmoke, a smell redolent of dim naves and voices raised in Latin song, of golden censers and solemn-eyed saints in painted images.

Sister Rebecca arranged and lit each brazier. Justina and Sister Magdalena, meanwhile, stood flanking her, bucklers at the ready, to defend her from attack, and as the ghost found itself torn loose from the walls and floors and ceilings that had been its anchor, the attacks came indeed.

They had lit the braziers in two or three rooms before the ghost apparently became aware of its danger. Then, all at once, all three women felt the air of the room they were in thicken, almost congeal, until it was hard to breathe. A stuffy, musty smell, a smell of damp attics and dark cellars and forgotten corners, fought against the smell of incense wafting in from the braziers already lit, and the temperature in the room dropped abruptly, until they could all see their breaths pluming in clouds from their mouths, in spite of the heat of the day. Sister Rebecca, her hands shaking from the sudden cold, endeavored to light the brazier, but just as the cedar wood caught, the flame leaped up blue and then went out.

"In the name of God, stop this!" sister Rebecca shouted, and this time the fire took hold.

Fragrant smoke and incense drove out the mustiness and stuffiness from the room, and the ghost with them. The sisters and Justina moved to the next room.

The ghost began to slam and lock each door in their faces. They removed the doors from their hinges, and proceeded.

In the living room, things became more dangerous. There were plenty of sharp or heavy objects there for the ghost to fling at them: framed pictures, vases, coffee table books, footstools. And it threw them all at Rebecca, as she worked to light the next brazier. Justina and Sister Magdalena stopped or deflected each item, and soon the smoke of cedar and incense drove the fight on to the next room.

In the kitchen, the ghost began to attack directly. It tried to choke them, as it had done to Sara; because of the salt-coated gorgets they wore along with their Kevlar vests, it failed. Then Sister Magdalena felt a burning, sudden pain down her arm, and saw three vicious scratches appear in her skin, from just below her elbow almost to her wrist, as if a bird of prey had gouged her there with its talons. "Stop, in the name of God!" she shouted.

There was a pause. Then everything in the kitchen—heavy cookware, knives in their knife block, plates and dishes that could shatter into ceramic blades, solid wooden cutting boards—began to shake and vibrate. Magdalena and Justina braced themselves, bucklers ready, to ward off anything that might be thrown.

But nothing was thrown, not then. Instead, abruptly, the sink faucet twisted on full, and what poured out was not water but thick blood. Justina could smell the coppery stink of it in the air. Then she looked around, and saw blood everywhere: oozing out between the tiles on the countertop, dripping from every drawer and cupboard, running in a stream from the vent in the ceiling, squeezing up through the joints in the hardwood floor. The smell of iron and copper became suffocating, sickening.

Something changed. The ghost's voice, previously a half-articulate, half-coherent bullying whisper, became solid and clear, as if a radio had abruptly been tuned to the right frequency. It sounded calm and almost impassive now, in contrast to its earlier fury; it evinced only a kind of cold scorn that had nothing human in it.

"You have no business here, demon child."

Justina looked around for a figure to address, but saw nothing, only walls and floor and countertops curdled with blood. The sudden, perfect stillness in the house made her ears ring. "I'm not a demon. I am Justina, squire-novice of the Order of the Holy Lance, and I am a light-nephil."

The voice laughed, the kind of indulgent, condescending laugh that suggests its owner knows far more than you do. "Oh, demon child. You think a splash of water and some old words can change what you are?"

"Yes!" yelled Justina. "I was baptized on the very night I was born, and again when I was old enough to understand. I was consecrated to God. My demon-father has nothing to do with me any more."

A small paring knife whipped from its block without warning, and flashed toward her. She raised her buckler to block it, but it skimmed neatly around the obstacle and through her skin, leaving a shallow slice across her hand. It was not deep and did no real damage, but it was deep enough to let blood well out. Blood white as milk.

"You can never escape your demon-father," said the voice. "He is in every drop of your blood." The blood on the walls, the floor, the ceiling, began to flow white, overlaying the sticky red.

Justina looked down at her hand, at the cut and the white nephil blood. And she began to see it as something other than white as milk: white as leprosy, white as fungus and mold in damp places that never saw the sun, white as bleached bone and sickness and the film over blind eyes.

"You will never belong to the Order of the Holy Lance. You can't."

"I can and I will!"

The voice laughed again, amused. "How? Tell me that, demon child. How can you possibly, when you can't even destroy a single mindless ghost? This ghost has twisted a child's mind: caused him to do harm his mother and his sister will never be able to fully forget or forgive. This entire family will never be the same. And what can you do?" The voice became viciously mocking. "You can light little nice-smelling fires, and swat at things when the ghost throws them at you. Were you a child it would be cute enough, but as it is, it's only pathetic."

"Of course I can destroy the ghost!"

"Prove it."

Then Justina saw a form at last, a figure, and without sparing a thought for the sisters, she ran after it, drawing a silver-coated knife, dipped in saltwater, from its sheath as she went.

*

Rebecca and Magdalena had seen the sink's faucet begin to pour blood, and they had seen blood streaming and pooling from every surface in the kitchen. But they had not heard the voice. They had only seen Justina freeze, and then stand still, muttering under her breath, oblivious to everything else.

All at once, every knife and blade in the room came whipping through the air toward the two sisters. "Justina!" cried Magdalena, deflecting knives as quickly as she could, while Rebecca worked furiously to light the cedar fire. "Justina, help me!"

Justina gave no sign that she had heard. Magdalena saw a small paring knife flash toward her, saw her try to ward it off and fail; she saw the shallow cut and the trickle of white blood on her hand, and saw Justina staring at it, absorbed, as if nothing else existed in the world. "*Justina!*"

The sage and hyssop caught, but before the cedar could fully light or the smoke could fill the room, a cascade of plates and bowls crashed out of a cupboard to shatter on the floor. The ceramic shards joined the knives whipping through the air, and without Justina's help, Sister Magdalena could not stop them all. Both sisters felt razored shards striking their vests, their shields, their gorgets, and by the time the cedar and incense smoke had spread, they both had several deep cuts in their exposed skin where knives or broken dishes had sliced through. But none of it targeted Justina. Instead, in the middle of the storm of sharp metal and glass, they heard her say "I can destroy the ghost" aloud, and saw her draw her ghost knife from its sheath on her belt. Then, without a glance at the sisters, she bolted from the room, evidently chasing something. "*Justina!* Come back!" Sister Magdalena shouted after her, but she either ignored this, or she never heard it at all.

*

"What happens after they get the ghost out in the open?" Emily asked Sister Paloma.

Sister Paloma was brewing a second round of tea for them both, and opening a package of shortbread cookies (reserved for *hospites*). "Well," she said, "after that it's time to drive the ghost out. They'll open up all the doors and widows, first, to let the wind and fresh air blow through every part of the house."

"Is that why it had to happen today, when it's windy out?"

Sister Paloma poured boiling water into the two mugs. "That's exactly why," she said. "The cedar and herbs and incense scour the ghost loose from the house, and the fresh open air and sunshine drive it away and dissolve it." She handed Emily her mug of tea, and two cookies on a napkin. "It's like. . .if you're trying to get rid of a stain on wood. You sand it off first—that's the incense and stuff—then you wipe away the sawdust and sweep it up and throw it away. That's the fresh air part."

"What about what Father James tried to do?" Emily asked, and blew across the steaming surface of her tea. "The ghost didn't like that."

"No." Sister Paloma sipped her tea slowly, formulating how to describe what the priest had done wrong without making him look bad. "It was the right thing to do, but he did it in the wrong order. The ghost was still so strong when he tried to bless the house, that it would have really hurt him before he could finish. Also, he didn't have anybody else there to watch his back. Sisters of the Holy Lance always go out at least two at a time."

"So they can protect each other if the ghost throws stuff at them."

"Exactly. Poor Father James was by himself, and you never want to try to fight a ghost all alone. That's our first rule: never run off alone."

Emily nibbled her cookie. "So, you're supposed to bless the house at the end? After the ghost is out?"

"Exactly." Sister Paloma dipped her cookie into her tea before taking a bite. "The blessing will make sure that the ghost is totally gone, and make it so that it can't ever come back. It makes it so that God is welcome in the house, not bad things. The sisters will also put salt all around the foundation of your house, and that will help keep bad things from getting in, too."

Emily furrowed her brow over her tea, thinking. "What's so special about salt?" she asked.

"Well," said Sister Paloma, "salt preserves things. Before there were refrigerators, people used to salt things like meat, so they wouldn't go bad. But it works on evil things too, just the same: salt stops things from going bad. It won't drive a ghost out if it's already there, not by itself, but it makes it hard for a new one to get in."

Emily finished her cookies, and took a sip of tea. "And after that, the ghost will be gone? It'll be dead?"

Sister Paloma made a "so-so" gesture with her hand. "Well, yes and no. Yes, the ghost will be destroyed and gone for good. But it won't really be *dead*, because it wasn't ever alive. Ghosts are just. . .recordings, or impressions, remember? So it will be more like. . .recording over a tape, or erasing a file off the computer."

"But it will be gone."

"It'll be gone."

"And we'll get to go home?"

Paloma smiled at her. "If all goes well, you will be on your way home tomorrow."

***

Interlude Four

Excerpt from the Record Kept by the Sisters at Saint Margaret's, About Justina

Sister Rebecca. June 28.

We took Justina out into the field for the first time yesterday. She's only fifteen and a half, which is against the *Rule*, but she made a good point when she insisted we take her: she is far from unprepared, as she has been training practically since she could walk, and her fighting and defensive skills were just as good as you would expect. I quizzed her about what we were doing at every step, and she answered correctly all the way. She knows her stuff, no question about it. Also, she was right: she was able to see where the ghost had been in a way neither I nor Sister M. could.

But still, I'm not as comfortable as I would like to be. Justina thinks she knows everything. I guess it's partly just because she's a teenager: a nephil teenager is still a teenager, it turns out! And the fact that she really *is* extraordinarily gifted and knowledgeable really doesn't help with her humility. But she has no experience, and she does not easily take orders. For instance, she knows very well that the first rule of dealing with a ghost is *don't go off alone*. But she did, repeatedly: to open shutters the ghost had closed, to check out a pan the ghost had thrown, things like that. Then, as we were getting to the end of the scouring part of the process with the braziers, she seems to have had some sort of interaction with the ghost, and apparently it taunted her. She just drew her ghost knife and ran off, even though there were knives and pieces of broken plates flying all around the room, and we needed her help right then more than at any other time. M. and I both got out of it with some bad cuts, and one cut across M.'s jaw needed five stitches. She'll have a scar. I don't think it would have happened if Justina hadn't left her post, and that concerns me. She didn't succeed in engaging the ghost, either; it just led her off and then disappeared. But even with that, all through the rest of the process, she was defensive and not very teachable, and I think she still believes that running off was the right thing to do. Or, at least she's still justifying it to herself. That's dangerous, and I really don't know what to do about it.

It also doesn't help that she really *was* an asset, when she was doing what she needed to do. For example, after we had closed all the doors and windows again and blessed every room in the house, she verified that the marks the ghost had left in different places were gone. We were pretty sure of it, especially since the illusory blood the ghost tried to scare us with had all disappeared, but it was still good to have that proof. None of the rest of us could have done that. She did the same thing after we got back to the commandery, too, and verified that the ghost's mark on Tyler was gone, and that especially was reassuring to him and his family.

All in all, I'm unsettled. I think Justina feels wronged and un-appreciated, because I tried to get her to see the poor decisions she made. But I don't know what I should have done instead! Breaking protocol like that could get someone killed! Probably not with a ghost, but what if it had been something more dangerous? I have the terrible feeling that even though we beat the ghost, we were still beaten somehow ourselves, and I don't know what to do about it.

Or maybe I'm overreacting. She's a teenager, and this was her very first mission. Maybe I shouldn't have expected anything else. M. has called me a worrywart before, and maybe she's right. But I'll be honest: it scares me. Justina will have a lot of power when she grows up; we don't know how much, exactly, but a lot. We just can't afford to make blunders! We can't fail to discipline her, but we don't dare push her to rebelliousness. It's a Catch-22. How do parents *do* this kind of thing?

Sister Magdalena. June 28.

Sister Becca and I took the little on her first mission yesterday. She did well! It's true that she did run off several times, which she knew perfectly well not to do, but honestly, I'm not too surprised. It's only her first time in the field, and it's just a natural impulse to run off to do whatever; why else are ghosts so able to get people alone all the time? It's what they do. It takes discipline to stay with the group, and also experience, which she doesn't have. I expect next time to be better in that respect.

One thing I do find concerning, though; or at least odd. To-wards the end, as we were scouring the kitchen, Justina just zoned out in a weird way, as if she was experiencing something totally different from Becca and me. She told me afterwards that the ghost was talking to her, and called her "demon child", and talked about her demon blood, and rubbed it in how much it had hurt the family. Now, ghosts are just imprints. They can't do much beyond throwing things at you, and insulting you in a really disjointed, generic way. We all heard this ghost do that, and there was nothing out of the ordinary about it. He called us all "bitches": to be expected. But "demon child"? That's weirdly specific and directed. Also, there seems to have been something along the lines of a conversation: ghosts don't have the ability to converse with people that way. They just repeat in a loop.

But this *was* a ghost. Everything about it was textbook ghost, albeit a particularly violent one, and the ghost removal process worked exactly like it was supposed to. There was nothing to suggest anything un-ghostly, except for that one episode with Justina.

Which makes me wonder. For those few seconds, could it be that something else was talking through the ghost, like some sort of ghost puppet? If so, *what*? And why?

Well, what was accomplished? Justina got to stretch her nephilic muscles, and liked doing it. She felt powerful, felt that she was accomplishing powerful things, and in a lot of ways she *was*. But she also broke protocol and put Becca and me in danger, so she had to be corrected, and that got her back up, so she also feels misunderstood and under-appreciated (ah, the joys of teenagers). That's a bit of a worrying combination. And on top of that, something, whether the ghost or something else, made sure her heritage and her half-human-ness were right in the forefront of her mind.

I don't know what it all means. But I can't shake the feeling that we got played somehow.

I'm not as worried about it as Becca, though. Becca is Justina's godmother, and she takes that really, really seriously. That's good, don't get me wrong! But she can fret about Justina sometimes. I say, whatever mistakes she makes, whatever taunts might be leveled about her ancestry, Justina is a light-nephil, dedicated to God both by our choice and by her own. And even if she fails to be faithful all the time, God won't. I don't know what happened yesterday, or even if anything happened of any importance. But I know this: if anything has started putting some sort of nefarious plan into action, it will find that Justina and all the rest of us will put up a good fight. It'll take more than some teenage angst to seduce Justina to the dark side.

***

Seven

After Justina and the two sisters returned to the commandery, late, after dealing with the ghost in Barton Draw, Justina and Imani were in their cell, getting ready for bed after compline.

"What was it like?" Imani asked, a little hesitant. "Were you scared?"

Justina was pulling off her boots and putting them away in her footlocker. "No! Ghosts aren't anything, just hot air." She closed the lid of the footlocker and latched it. "It made me mad, though. The things it said." She clenched and unclenched her hand. "I would rather fight something I can get a sword into."

Imani though about that. "I would've been scared."

Justina peeled off her socks, tossed them into the laundry basket, and pulled on a fresh pair. "Nah. By the time you're fifteen, you won't be scared of anything at all. Evil things will be scared of *us*."

Imani said nothing, and did not look convinced.

Several minutes of silence followed. Both girls brushed their teeth at the cell's small sink, then climbed into their narrow beds; as ordered in the *Rule*, they slept in their clothes, in both symbolic and practical readiness for immediate action.

"I heard you left Sister Justina and Sister Magdalena, when they needed you," Imani said, all in a rush, as if she was ashamed to say it. She didn't look at Justina.

Justina propped herself up on one elbow. "I did not! They didn't need me, they were fine!" She paused. "And the ghost made it personal."

"Personal?"

"It said I shouldn't be there, and that I couldn't really fight evil things because I'm a nephil. Half-demon. It said I couldn't ever really be part of the Order. And it said I could never destroy a ghost, even if it had hurt people and deserved it." Justina paused. Now that she had put it into words, it sounded more petty than it had seemed at the time. "I know must have been lying, but. . ." She couldn't think of anything else to say, and trailed off.

There was silence again, until Justina thought Imani had fallen asleep. Then the younger girl said, in a very small voice, "We'll both be in the field someday. What if you leave me behind?"

Justina heard the edge of fear in Imani's voice. "I would never leave you behind!" she said, honestly shocked, every part of her aghast at the very notion. The idea of chasing a ghost and leaving Imani alone was inconceivable, and it had never crossed her mind.

"But you left them. Sister Magdalena had to have stitches."

Justina said nothing, feeling floored by a sudden visceral realization of what she had done. She understood, now, that she had never taken the danger of the mission seriously, even with knives flying around the room; it had been a game, an exercise, and nothing *really* bad could happen. The possible consequences hadn't been real to her. Imani's voice begged for reassurance, and all at once that made it real. Imani's fear was a consequence she had never considered, and one she simply could not endure.

"I made a mistake this time," she said, an admission she had not made before, even to herself. "But I will never leave you behind. You don't have to be scared, because I'll take care of you."

Justina knew Imani trusted her, and she made a firm determination with herself: she would not leave her comrades in the middle of a fight again, for any reason. And not for the sake of the sisters, or any penance they might impose, but for the sake of her sister's trust.

***

Part Three

Interlude Five

Excerpt from the Mission Reports: Archive at Saint Margaret's

Mission Report.

Date: September 3-4.

Sisters Present: Magdalena, Rebecca. Squire-novice Justina.

Location: south of Plainview, Texas.

Creature/Spirit: vanishing hitchhiker/phantom hitchhiker. (See "phobophage".)

Time and specific location: approx. 3:30am, I-27, just south of Mile Marker 40. The entity seems to have no particular specific date on which it appears, though it has always been reported when the road is entirely deserted apart from the target car (not an unusual circumstance in rural West Texas at 3:30 in the morning). Additionally, the target car must be traveling north, toward Plainview; if traveling southbound, the apparition does not appear.

Actions of concern: the hitchhiker usually appears as a bearded man with a large backpack. He attempts to flag down the passing car, and when it does not stop (because who would, at 3:30 in the morning??), he then appears in the back seat. The driver sees him in the rear-view mirror, glaring murderously. This, not unnaturally, causes the driver to panic, swerve, and often run off the road. Or, alternatively, if there is a passenger in the back seat, the hitchhiker appears right beside them, which naturally causes the passenger to panic, with a similar result. Three fatalities have been reported in the last four years, in single-car accidents, as well as eighteen hospitalizations.

Actions taken: the hitchhiker was successfully drawn out. Justina proved very helpful at this, as she could see the traces where the entity had appeared: not all in exactly the same place, but at many points within a stretch of approximately two miles. She was then able to spot him before either of the others of us. We drove past without slowing, and, just as advertised, he materialized in the back seat with Justina. We then followed the usual procedure with phobophages: we completely ignored him. He shouted and postured and took the form of a decomposing corpse for our benefit, in an effort to elicit the fear reaction he needed, but these efforts were ignored like the rest. After several minutes the entity had used up all its energy stores, and fizzled out.

We drove back south, and put up in the commandery-house in Lubbock for the rest of the night.

The following night we drove to the spot again, just as before. The hitchhiker failed to appear. Justina said the traces were still present, but faded.

Conclusions: It appears that the hitchhiker was drained of energy and driven away.

Recommendations: We should keep an eye on that stretch of I-27 for a while, to make sure the entity is properly gone.

Injuries: none.

Expenses: One full tank of gas, and a further half-tank on return to Derrick. Two meals, in addition to one loaf of bread, some sandwich makings, and one six-pack of Dr Pepper. See attached receipts.

Notes: the steering wheel wobbled a little. The tires on that car may need to be rotated.

Mission Report.
Date: April 28 – May 3.
Sisters Present: Ella, Paloma. Squire-novice Justina.

Location: Dawn, Texas.

Creature/Spirit: tall walker/Walking Sam (See "thanatophage".)

Time and specific location: N/A. Has been appearing all over Dawn for approximately six months.

Actions of concern: Fourteen suicides in the last six months, a very high number in a town of less than 200 people. Many of the victims had reported seeing and being stalked by an elongated shadowy figure with no face, and several had also spoken of uncontrollable, intrusive, out-of-character thoughts of suicide before actually acting on them.

Actions taken: First, we narrowed down the possible causes, and knew that it must be a tall walker. We then tracked down a young man, who was the tall walker's current victim. After we persuaded him to believe that we could help him, he agreed to sit alone in a dimmed room to draw the tall walker out. He was able to sit still while the tall walker slinked closer and closer: you've got to respect his nerve! And when it was close to him and distracted, we killed it with our ghost knives, and waited for every drop of the vapory black stuff they use for blood to drain out. After that it dropped to dust.

Conclusion: we killed the tall walker.

Recommendations: follow up with the last victim (see attached contact information). Under the influence of the tall walker, and in response to the fear it caused, he had begun to drink heavily and also overuse several medications.

Injuries: bruises. No problem.

Expenses: 5 nights in a motel. Three tanks of gas. Meals and groceries. See attached receipts.

Notes: We should have caught this one earlier than we did. Fourteen suicides in six months in a town of that size is way past a statistical anomaly. We should check out what it was in our surveillance protocols that let it go on for so long.

Mission Report.

Date: November 18-21.

Sisters Present: Magdalena, Rebecca. Squire-novice Justina.

Location: San Angelo, Texas.

Creature/Spirit: vampire.

Time and specific location: the vampire had laired in an abandoned house near Lake Nasworthy. Most of the attacks took place in southwest San Angelo.

Actions of concern: several people had been in the hospital with severe anemia, for no apparent reason. Also, there had been several disappearances around the lake. Only one body was found, and despite its considerable deterioration after being in the water, the characteristic punctures over the jugular could be clearly discerned.

Actions taken: We first tracked down the vampire, which took several days. Then we went into the house where she was laired at noon, locked down all the doors and windows with silver, and approached her for parley. She resisted every effort to reason with her, and finally she attacked us, even though it was daytime. Justina was eventually the one who subdued her, and when she refused a last chance to give in, we were forced to stake her and cut off her head.

Conclusion: we killed the vampire.

Recommendations: we should keep an eye on San Angelo for a while. We saw no signs that the vampire had turned any of her victims, but better to be safe.

Injuries: Sister Rebecca was attacked by the vampire first, and thrown against the wall. Extensive bruising, and a dislocated shoulder (reduced on-site). Possible mild concussion. The vampire also threw Sister Magdalena to the ground and went for her throat, though she didn't do much damage before Justina immediately dragged her off. Bruises, defensive cuts on her hands and arms, and two shallow punctures to the throat. Justina received only very minor cuts. The vampire seemed repelled or even frightened by her.

Expenses: 2 nights in a motel. Three tanks of gas. Meals and groceries. See attached receipts. We also replenished the following items in the car's medical kit: sterile dressings, gauze, saline, cold packs, antibiotic ointment, Steri-Strips, Dermabond, and one sling for the arm. See attached receipts.

Notes: I hypothesize that the vampire was repelled by Justina because she smelled her nonhuman blood. It is a point which may need further study later on.

Mission Report.
Date: July 5-8.
Sisters present: Rebecca, Magdalena. Squire-novice Justina.
Location: Abilene, Texas.
Creature/Spirit: Mishipeshu/Underwater Panther.
Time and specific location: usually dusk, on Catclaw Creek.

Actions of concern: there had been four unrelated, unexplained drownings in Catclaw Creek over a period of three months. The creek was not in flood or otherwise hazardous at the time of the drownings, and it isn't a very big creek anyway.

Actions taken: we narrowed down the possible culprits, until we knew a mishipeshu was responsible. We then lured it out of the creek by scattering copper filings along the bank. It was Sister Rebecca who scattered the filings, and just as she was finishing, the mishipeshu attacked her from the water, and grabbed her leg in its teeth. We were able to drive it off her before it could pull her back into the water, and when it attacked a second time, we threw the copper faraday net over it and ran as much current through the net as our portable generator would allow.

Conclusion: the mishipeshu should be banished from the creek for good.

Recommendations: we should follow up with Abilene, to make sure the drownings have stopped.

Injuries: Sister Rebecca's shin, calf, and ankle are mauled, and the tibia is broken. We stabilized the injury and set the break, but she will need continued care at the commandery-house. She will likely need a large number of stitches, as well as a cast, and will be out of action for a while.

Expenses: 3 nights in a motel. 3 tanks of gas. Meals and groceries. See attached receipts. The following items in the car's medical kit need to be replenished: saline, sterile gauze, antibiotic ointment, splints.

Notes: see the ongoing record about Justina.

***

Interlude Six

Excerpt from the Record Kept by the Sisters at Saint Margaret's, About Justina

Sister Magdalena. July 9.

Sister Becca had a close call yesterday. The two of us, with Justina, were looking into several unexplained drownings in one of the small creeks that runs through Abilene, and we figured out that a mishipeshu was responsible, and set about luring it out of the water with copper shavings. It's so ironic, really, that mishipeshu are obsessed with copper and really possessive of it, but they're also incredibly vulnerable to it, because it's such a great conductor of electricity.

You can tell a mishipeshu is coming, because you can hear its voice, but you can't tell where from, because the voice seems to come from every direction at once, including underfoot and up in the sky. So we heard the voice (you can never quite understand the words, but you know you're hearing a mishipeshu), but we didn't know where the creature was until it pounced right out of the water and grabbed Sister Becca. It bit down on her lower leg, held tight, and then just *shook* her back and forth. She was screaming and trying to draw her gun, and I'm pretty sure I was screaming too, and blood was splashing all over the gravel, and I could hear skin tearing, and there was a sort of meaty *crunch* as the bone broke. Then it started dragging her back to the water.

Justina screamed at it to stop. I realize now that I've almost never heard her raise her voice in anger. Did she have some idea of what would happen if she did? Anyway, when she screamed, the scream was a *physical* thing, invisible but completely physical, and it *threw* the mishipeshu back. It wasn't at all like the reaction of an evil thing being confronted with holy objects; those wouldn't work on a mishipeshu anyway. It was more like the thing had been hit by a truck. It crashed back into the water with a huge splash, as if the force that threw it was unbelievably violent, and we just had time to help poor Becca away from the water's edge before the mishipeshu was on us again, madder than ever, all the perch-spines on its back standing straight up and its snake-tail whipping around and tearing up brush by the roots. Justina and I only just managed to throw the faraday net over it and zap it with electricity.

Interesting things, elementals. When the Native Americans said that Underwater Panthers were the opposite and the balance to Thunderbirds, they clearly understood that air or storm energies would counteract and neutralize water energies, and so lightening would neutralize a mishipeshu. Our lightening just came courtesy of a portable generator and a lot of copper mesh. And it worked: when we ran current through the net, there was a hissing sound like water evaporating off a hot griddle, and a smell of steam, and the mishipeshu disappeared.

It wasn't until it was all over that I really thought about what Justina had done. She just *screamed* at a powerful, extranatural creature, and sent it flying back as if it was a bug she'd just hit with a board. Now, we know her voice has a lot of power. We've known that since she was a baby. But we'd never seen it used like this, like a weapon.

We have records of nephilim doing all kinds of violent things to people. But the records never really say *how*; it's always just some version of "they used their powers to do whatever". I'll be completely honest and open with you: in my own personal imagination, I'd always pictured something like the Emperor in Star Wars zapping Luke with his finger-lightening. Don't judge. But now, I think that may have been the wrong image. What if they did it with their voices? With a shout, or a curse, or even with a song?

What will it be like when Justina is grown up, and fully in command of her powers? How powerful will she actually be?

Sister Magdalena. January 10.

Justina is eighteen now. She's pushing seven feet tall, but she hasn't grown as quickly these last couple of years, so we have high hopes ("high" hopes, ha ha. . .) that she may be reaching her full adult height. We all hope so, because if not, we'll soon have to bring in a contractor to raise the lintels of all the doors so she doesn't bash her forehead on them!

On a related note, she recently found an odachi back in the depths of the armory. I don't think anyone has used it in her lifetime, and Sister Alana didn't make it; she says it must have been her predecessor. It doesn't really surprise me, since a greatsword like that isn't exactly convenient for most people to use. Claymores aren't part of our usual equipment either. But Justina definitely has the height and reach for an odachi (or a claymore, for that matter), and she's been practicing with it since. Sister Ella is the best of us with a sword, and she was the one who taught Justina how to use her very first half-sized sword when she was just a little girl; now, she's helping her learn to use the odachi, and says she's astonishingly talented with it. Well, not actually *astonishingly*; we haven't found any weapon yet, or any hand-fighting style, that Justina doesn't take to as if she was made for it.

More and more often these days, she has been suggesting that it's getting close to time to let Imani go out into the field, too. Imani is only fourteen, even younger than Justina was on her first mission, but her birthday is coming up, and the sad fact is that we made an exception to the "all squire-novices must be sixteen" rule for Justina, so obviously she expects us to make one for Imani as well.

I have mixed feelings about it. Would it really be such a bad thing? Honestly, Imani is just as prepared as Justina was. She and Justina are very *different*, in terms of the way they approach things, but equally skilled and well-trained. She will absolutely be capable. But she's just so *young*! It was easier to forget that about Justina, being that she was six feet tall at the time, and capable of bench-pressing any two of the rest of us put together.

Will Imani end up being one of the youngest squire-novices in the history of the Order? It's not my decision, but personally, I expect it. We can only hold off Justina's insistence for so long! We have to be careful, though. Will Imani be fully prepared in terms of knowledge, in terms of physical training? Yes. Will she have the self-confidence to believe that's actually true? Possibly more of a question. But anyway, we'll have to keep a close eye on both girls, to make sure Justina doesn't, without meaning to, bully Imani into doing more than she's ready to do, or comfortable doing.

Or I could be wrong. Imani might be fully aware of how competent she is. I hope so.

***

"Boo-Hag. Also called a mara, ride-by-night, or karabasan, among other names. The root word *mare* or *mara* may be seen in the English word *nightmare*.

"The boo-hag, so named by the negro Gullah culture of the Carolinas, is a most terrible creature, belonging to that *genus* of supernatural creatures which also includes vampires, fear-eaters, and dream thieves: that is, those creatures which have corporeal or semi-corporeal form and which feed upon the life energy, or vital principle, of human prey. This life energy is extracted in varying ways: in the above-mentioned species, it is extracted by means of blood, the eliciting of intense fear in the victim, and dreams, respectively. The boo-hag, in contrast, obtains the human life energy through taking the victim's breath during sleep. It chooses a victim and sits heavily upon his chest (thus giving rise to the name "ride-by-night", and other similar names), then draws his breath, thereby plunging him into a deeply somnolent state which is often plagued by distressing dreams. Upon waking in the morning, he will find himself entirely unrefreshed by the night's sleep, and indeed, if repeatedly fed upon, he will likely perish of pure exhaustion.

"The boo-hag possesses a most remarkable means of defense and concealment, shared by few other supernatural creatures, and none within its own *genus*. In daylight, it is capable of wearing human skin, as a man might wear a suit, and when doing so it is indistinguishable from a true human. This skin is obtained from a victim, usually one who has inconveniently awakened while being "ridden", or fed upon. The boo-hag skins the victim and disposes of the body, which permits it to take the victim's form and identity for a period of time, though only until the skin putrefies. At that point, the boo-hag must find a new skin to wear.

"At night, the boo-hag removes its skin and hides it, much as is also done by selkies, swan-mays, and other similar creatures. In this skinless form, the creature is capable of flight through the air in the form of dust-motes, and may also slip with ease through even the tiniest of openings and cracks, thus permitting it access to its victims. It must, however, return to its skin by dawn, for if daybreak catches it in its unprotected form, it will die. Thus, the simplest method for killing a boo-hag is to prevent it from reaching its skin in time. This may be accomplished by distracting and delaying the boo-hag, burning up its skin (if it can be found), or coating either the skin or the boo-hag itself in salt, which will prevent them from reunifying. Boo-hags may also be killed by fire, though this is much more difficult to accomplish. It will be found ineffective to attempt to kill the boo-hag while it is in its human skin, even should you be able to identify it, for the creature and the skin mutually protect each other while united. . ."

Sister Agatha, Province of Massachusetts, *On the Scientific Classification of Horrors*, 1887.

Eight

The attacks in the town of Mockingbird began in October, the year Justina was nineteen years old, and Imani fifteen. And they began at the worst possible time.

West Texas was a small commandery. But it had never needed to be bigger; it had never needed the numbers of the commanderies of Houston or Austin, because its region was largely rural and sparsely-populated. Less than a dozen knight-sisters had always been able to handle any alarms that came in. But that October, the knight-sisters at Saint Margaret's found themselves well and truly short-handed.

It began when a werejaguar severely mauled Sister Ella, coming close to killing her, and leaving her confined to the commandery-house for weeks. Then, Sister Aisha twisted her left knee while fighting a vampire: not a dangerous injury, or even a particularly serious one, but an injury which left her in a brace and dependent on crutches until it healed. Sister Katie, as the commandery's doctor, could not leave her patients, and Sister Alana, as the armorer and bladesmith, had not gone out on missions in ten years.

Then, within twenty-four hours, the complex algorithms and search protocols embedded in the Order's alert system produced two cases: a haunting in Big Spring, and an unknown predatory creature attacking people in Amarillo. The four remaining knight-sisters set out within an hour of each other.

Then, the very next morning, after terce, before anyone had returned from either mission, the alert system reported the mysterious hospitalizations and equally mysterious deaths in Mockingbird.

Sister Deborah, still the commander but now retired from active duty, called the two teams on their cell phones. Would they be returning to the commandery within the day?

No, said Rebecca and Magdalena. They hadn't even positively identified the creature they were dealing with yet.

No, said Paloma and Katelyn. There were unexpected complications; they had not been able to clear the building. They would not be engaging the ghost until tomorrow.

Sister Deborah was sitting in her cell, her face in her hands, considering the very dangerous possibility of going to Mockingbird herself with Sister Alana, when Justina tapped her knuckles on the open door to signal her presence. "Send Imani and me," she said. "We'll go."

*

It took several hours to drive to Mockingbird from Derrick. Imani didn't say much on the way; she sat silently in the passenger seat, occasionally squirming or fidgeting, trying to read a book but unable to focus on it, watching the flow of prairie shortgrass and spiny amaranth, clusters of yucca and prickly pear, shinneries of mesquite and scrub oak, white cottonfields and ripe, rusty-red sorghum. They passed through towns too small even to have stoplights, dominated by cotton gins or feedlots, and a few tumbleweeds bumped briskly across the highway. The autumn sky stretched blue and bottomless to the horizon.

"Do you want to drive for a while?" Justina asked once.

"Nah, I'm fine," said Imani, not very convincingly. Justina shot her a look, but she was staring out the window.

"What will it be like?" Imani asked finally, as the sun was beginning to decline to the west. "What will we do when we get there?"

Justina thought about it. "Well, first thing, we'll find a motel and check in. It may be getting dark then, and if so we'll have supper and a good night's sleep, then get to work first thing in the morning." She eased the car into the left lane to pass a battered semi-trailer.

"Shouldn't we get right to work?"

Justina shook her head. "No, we don't know what we're dealing with yet. If it's something that operates at night, we would be at a disadvantage. Better to wait for daylight."

"Oh."

Imani sat in silence again, dithering with her book, as miles passed, prairie grass and spears of amaranth rippled in long waves beside the highway, and the sun sank lower. "What if I can't do this?" she burst out suddenly. "What if I freeze, or forget what I'm doing, or miss something obvious—"

Justina was confused. "You won't, why would you?"

"What if I *do*? What if I panic? What if I—"

Justina reached out her right hand gripped Imani's shoulder. "*You won't.* You're fine. The sisters know what they're doing as teachers, and *you* know what you're doing. Sister Deborah wouldn't have let you come if you didn't."

But Imani's fears had been brewing inside her during the hours of the drive, and now there was no stopping them from spilling out. "Of course she would, this time! There wasn't anybody else, she had to send me or send nobody! What if I make a mistake and *someone dies?* I'm not made for this like you are! I'll do the wrong thing at the wrong time or I'll miss all my shots or I'll stab some innocent bystander by accident—"

Justina took her eyes off the road for a moment to give Imani an entirely baffled and slightly exasperated look. "That's silly, of course you won't!"

"*What if I do?*" Imani, to her immense frustration and embarrassment, found herself crying. "I don't have any business being here, *I don't know what I'm doing!*"

"You know what you're doing."

"I *don't*! I'm just faking it."

"Let me tell you something," said Justina, taking a hand off the steering wheel to point at Imani emphatically. "Everyone feels this way on their first mission. Everyone."

"You didn't."

"No," Justina admitted easily, "but I'm not normal. Every one of the sisters I've talked to has said the same thing: on the first mission, everybody feels unprepared and like they're just fakes. But then it turns out fine."

"But what if—"

"What if you do crash and burn?"

Imani nodded.

"I still say that you won't. But even if you somehow do, the Order won't kick you out. God won't kick you out. You'll still be my sister. And you won't make the same mistake twice. You'll learn from it and go on."

Imani thought about that.

Justina spoke strongly, and in her voice there was an underlying bedrock of command. "Don't be afraid."

And whether through the power of Justina's voice or the power of her assurance, Imani was less afraid.

*

Justina and Imani pulled into Mockingbird as dusk was falling. They bought ham sandwiches, packaged in plastic wrap, at a convenience store, then found a motel with its "Vacancy" sign illuminated. After securing the car, they went to their room. It was like a dozen other motel rooms Justina had stayed in while on missions: well-trampled indestructible tan carpet, worn polyester bedspreads in oddly colorless pastel prints, a chipboard desk, patches of enamel worn off all the bathroom fixtures, a clattering air conditioner unit in the window, a vague smell of mustiness and cleaning products.

There was only one chair, and Justina sat there to eat her sandwich. Imani sat on her bed, and though she was hungry, the squashy bread and limp ham and lettuce gagged her, and she could only pick at her supper.

Justina had no such problems. "Okay," she said around a large bite of sandwich, "here's the plan. First thing tomorrow, we'll go to the hospital and talk to the victims. As of a few hours ago, there were five of them, all suffering from acute exhaustion and a depressed immune system." She took a sip of water from the flimsy plastic cup she had filled at the bathroom sink. "Then we'll talk to the medical examiner about the two deaths."

Imani gave up on trying to eat her sandwich, and folded it back up in its plastic wrap. She picked vaguely at the pills on the polyester bedspread.

"Okay?" Justina prompted, as she finished her supper and wadded up the wrapper.

"Sure."

Justina pitched the ball of plastic wrap into the trash can. "We'll figure out what this is," she said. "We'll figure it out, and we's beat it, and then we'll go home. Don't worry, I won't let anything bad happen to you."

Before going to bed, the two girls recited the Lord's Prayer and sang a hymn, as sisters of the Order usually did when away from the commandery and unable to hear the Hours. Justina chose "Soldiers of Christ Arise", as an appropriately bracing hymn for the occasion, and when they had sung it, Imani felt stronger and braver than she had felt all day. She felt, for the first time, quite sure that she and Justina could not only take the field against whatever evil thing was in this town, but defeat it as well.

Of everyone in the motel that night who felt the effects of Justina's power, and there were many, only Imani knew what was actually happening. But it didn't matter. She believed the song, she believed in the power and protection of God, and if her emotions could be braced and clarified and infused with steel by her sister's song, she would gladly accept the gift.

*

"We'd like to talk to the patients who are here for acute exhaustion, please."

The nurse looked up from her paperwork, and saw two young women standing at her station. No, she thought, not two young women; one of them would be a "girl" by anyone's measure. She couldn't be more than fifteen or sixteen years old, and the ledge around the desk hid most of her from view. It was the other who had spoken, and her age was hard to guess, because anyone trying would be completely thrown by her spectacular height. She must be seven feet tall, and she made the girl beside her look even tinier by comparison. They were both dressed in white.

The nurse blinked at them, nonplussed. "I'm sorry?"

"We need to see the patients who are here being treated for exhaustion, and also the doctor treating them. I have a list." She slid it across the Formica, and the nurse took it mechanically, without glancing at it. She realized, flustered, that she had been staring in bewilderment at the prismatic bottomlessness of the young woman's eyes. Some sort of high-tech colored contacts, she guessed. Holographic, or something.

"I'm sorry, but I can't let you in to see the patients. It's against our confidentiality policies. Unless you're with the police, or the CDC?" She made it a question, though she had never seen a pair of human beings who looked less like either police or Center for Disease Control agents.

The tall young woman (*Is she standing on a box? Is there a step there? There's no way she's really that tall*) handed over two glossy identification cards, complete with photographs. "Here's our iden-tification. The Order of the Holy Lance has a longstanding agree-ment with the federal government, and you will find that we are authorized to speak to anyone we need."

Again, the nurse accepted what she was given without looking at it. She felt unaccountably, almost frighteningly, compelled to simply agree to whatever they asked; her usual brisk competence and skepticism had deserted her. With a great effort, she shook off the strange hypnosis, and said, "I'll have to make a call."

The tall woman nodded at her, and smiled. "By all means, call whomever you need. We'll wait."

Shaken, the nurse watched as the two of them (*she really is that tall, what the hell*) moved to the nearby row of molded plastic chairs, and sat down. She quickly found the extension for the Compliance office on her computer, and picked up the phone. As she listened to it ring, her eyes slid back to the impossibly tall young woman with the striped hair and the strange eyes, and without warning the phrase *I wonder what she is* formed itself in her mind. She felt a chill, not because she had wondered, but because having once formed the thought, she couldn't help but keep wondering.

*

"Is she going to let us in?" Imani asked, anxious, watching the nurse talk on the phone to someone.

"It might take a few minutes, but yes," Justina assured her. "Hospitals have to protect patient privacy, but legal or public safety concerns take priority. The Order is authorized, but not as well known as the CDC or something, so they always have to check."

The nurse appeared to be reading information from their ID cards to the person on the line. "What if she doesn't let us through?" asked Imani.

"I guess then we'd have go and talk to a hospital administrator. I've never had that happen, though."

The nurse thanked the person on the phone, picked up the list of patients, then turned to the two girls. "Come with me, please. The first patient is just down here. Dr. Andrews will meet you there."

***

"Evil Kids

"Date: Fri, 16 Jan 1998 19:12:25 -0800 (PST)

"From: "Brian Bethel" (brianbet@camalott.com)

"To: ghost-discuss@lido.com

"Subject: Those Darned Black-Eyed Kids

"I was startled to hear a knock on the driver's-side window of my car. I looked over and saw two children staring at me from the street. I need to describe them, with the one feature (you can guess what it was) that I didn't realize until about half-way through the conversation cleverly omitted. Both appeared to be in that semi-mystical stage of life children get into where you can't exactly tell their age. Both were boys, and my initial impression is that they were somewhere between 10-14. . .

"'Oh great,' I thought. 'They're gonna hit me up for money.' And then the air changed.

"I've explained this before, but for the benefit of any new lurkers out there, right before I experience something strange, there's a change in perception that comes about which I describe in the above manner. It's basically enough time to know it's too late. . .

"'C'mon, mister. Let us in. We can't get in your car until you do, you know,' the spokesman said soothingly. 'Just let us in, and we'll be gone before you know it. We'll go to our mother's house.'

"We locked eyes.

"To my horror, I realized my hand had strayed toward the door lock (which was engaged) and was in the process of opening it. I pulled it away, probably a bit too violently. But it did force me to look away from the children. . .

"I turned back. For the first time, I noticed their eyes.

"They were coal black. No pupil. No iris. Just two staring orbs reflecting the red and white light of the marquee. . .

"I ripped the car into reverse (thank goodness no one was coming up behind me) and tore out of the parking lot. I noticed the boys in my peripheral vision, and I stole a quick glance back.

"They were gone. The sidewalk by the theater was deserted."

Counterpoint One

It was Jamie Marquez's day off, and he was spending a pleasant hour lovingly disassembling, cleaning, reassembling, and polishing his shotgun; dove season had begun, and he and his brothers had plans to bag a good haul of them that weekend. Jamie's wife had a recipe (she passed it off as a family secret, but he, Jamie, happened to know that she'd found it on Pinterest) for grilled dove in prickly pear barbecue sauce, and he would never hear the end of it if she had to get *squab* from the *grocery store* to make it with, when the prickly pears had come from their own back yard. The horror!

The doorbell rang.

Jamie put down his oily cloth on a paper towel, carefully laid aside the partially-assembled shotgun, and went to answer it.

Two boys stood on the porch. Their ages seemed oddly nondescript—they might have been eight or fifteen—but he guessed them to be close to the age of his daughter, who was in seventh grade. Both wore plain hoodies, one brown and the other navy blue, and despite the beautiful weather (the kind of weather that, quite honestly, made Jamie want to go dove-hunting on the spot, instead of waiting for the weekend like a responsible adult), both had their hoods pulled up, shadowing their faces. They didn't shuffle, or sway on their feet. Neither had earbuds in under his hoodie. Both stood still, straight, at ease, and absolutely nothing like any other doorbell-ringing children Jamie had ever seen on his porch, not even well-practiced cookie-selling Girl Scouts (who tended to be the most relaxed and poised of any). These boys were unquestionably on a mission, and one they were entirely comfortable with.

One boy, slightly taller than his companion, took one step forward. "We would like to use your telephone," he said, his voice smooth and almost uninflected. "Let us in please."

This struck Jamie as odd. Using the phone (who ever used the full word "telephone" anyway?) wasn't a big favor, but it was a favor, and even an adult would normally be a little more apologetic about it. But this boy clearly had perfect, unquestioned confidence that Jamie should and would and must comply.

Jamie was not a nervous man. He was not given to much imagination, or to superstition, or to teasing his mind with conspiracy theories or spooky stories. He had read *The Shining*, and enjoyed it, but (contrary to the predictions of the rave reviews printed on the flap) had not felt compelled to sleep with the lights on afterward. But something about these two boys was weird. Unsettling. Something was off. Ordinarily, he would have invited two children into the house to use the phone without a second thought; this time, he hesitated.

This was not according to the script, and both boys seemed very slightly discomforted by it. Both, in perfect, inhuman unison, tilted their heads to the left; the quizzical gesture would have been cute under different circumstances, but here it was unspeakably creepy. Jamie decided that he would just have to be rude. They could use someone else's phone. He started to close the door.

"We need to come in, please," said the boy again. "You need to invite us." He took one more carefully-measured step forward; Jamie had the impression that those steps were carefully rehearsed and possibly scripted, the way telemarketers had to ask a certain number of times whether you were *sure* you didn't want to hear their unprecedented money-saving offer. Somehow, without being aware of it, he had stopped closing the door, and had actually swung it open wider.

"Let us in, mister," said the boy, his voice silky and persuasive and not at all childlike. "We're just kids. We'll be gone before you know it. Just let us in for a quick moment."

Jamie still knew that something was drastically wrong. But the terrible, visceral feeling of *wrongness* was fading. Instead, the thought formed itself across his mind, as if from outside himself: *They're just kids playing around, pretending to be creepy. Nothing to worry about. Why not let them in? No big deal. They'll be gone before I know it.*

He stepped back, clearing the wide-open door. "Come on in," he said.

The two boys moved forward, perfectly in step. As they did, they pulled back their hoods, revealing two pairs of eyes as black and opaque as tar from lid to lid.

And they came in, but not into the house, and not to use the phone. Instead, all at once, Jamie felt an intolerable pressure inside his head, as if his brain had swelled to twice its proper size. As the pressure built, he screamed and clutched at his eyes, sure they would be pushed right out of their sockets from inside; his vision went red, and he didn't realize his legs had given way until the floor crashed against his knees. He screamed again, blindly, desperately, amazed his skull had not burst like a boiling egg with a cracked shell.

Then what had invaded his brain sank in, squeezed tight, and settled. The pain receded. Jamie stood up, slightly confused, seeing the door and wondering who had opened it. He wondered if he had tripped. He shook his head, and returned to cleaning his gun. But things had changed, though he had no consciousness of it. New memories, new ideas, and new motives had seeped into him, and when he admired his newly-cleaned and reassembled shotgun, it was no longer doves he intended shoot with it.

***

Nine

After they had finished at the hospital, Imani and Justina talked to the county medical examiner about the two deaths. They pulled up in front of the County Coroner's Office, and parked their car in the nearly-empty parking lot; Justina chose a parking space shaded by an impressive live oak tree, and the car's tires crunched over the scatter of acorns that littered the pavement beneath it. The building itself was made of taupe brick, and its architects had evidently aimed for an air of impressiveness and authority, but failed to achieve it, as it only looked grim and unfriendly. Inside was not much better; an oversized arrangement of artificial flowers in a faux-Grecian urn, which sat on the receptionist's desk, made the place feel like a funeral home.

"We need to speak to the county medical examiner, please," Justina told the receptionist. She handed their identification across the desk.

Again, the two girls waited patiently as the receptionist made a verifying phone call. Then, after signing in, they were shown to a glass door with the words "Dr. Leonard Smith, M.D., Chief Medical Examiner, Mockingbird County. They went inside, pulled two chairs up to the medical examiner's desk, and waited for him to finish typing something on his computer. If either of them had ever gone to a public school, they might have thought this felt similar to being called in to the principal's office. Imani shifted awkwardly in her chair, and it squeaked against the linoleum tiles of the floor.

"*There*," said Dr. Smith in evident triumph, jabbing a key on his keyboard emphatically and whirling his swivel chair around to face them. Justina guessed that he had just composed and dispatched an important email. She was right. "Now then, what can I do for you two lovely ladies?"

"We need you to tell us about the two people who died under unusual circumstances in the last week. Brian Perry and Debra Price."

"Right." He leaned back in his chair, and it groaned under his not-inconsiderable weight. Even in the air conditioning (which both girls felt to be excessive), his shirt had wet patches of sweat under the arms. "Not too much to tell, to be honest. Now that first one, Brian Perry, had COPD—chronic obstructive pulmonary disease, you know."

"We know," said Imani.

"Right. Well, he had that. Not too bad, though; he wasn't on oxygen or anything. No reason for him not to live for many more years, and die of something completely unrelated. But then one night his lungs just quit working."

Justina leaned forward. "How do you mean, 'quit working'?"

"Well," said Dr. Smith, "he just wasn't getting enough air. Like what you'd see if someone smothered him with a pillow, only no one did. First thing we looked for, signs of smothering. Nothing."

"Was it fluid in his lungs?" offered Imani.

"If it was, I'd've told you straight off." Imani flushed, embarrassed. He went on. "No sign of fluid or any kind of edema. No blood either. It was like something just sucked the air out of the room, so he died. In his sleep, looked like. Never even woke up."

"Thank you," said Justina. "And the woman? Debra Price?"

"Well," said Dr. Smith, "as I recall. . ." He trailed off, swiveled to face his computer again, and clicked his mouse several times. Apparently he found the information he wanted, and swiveled back to face him. When no one is in here, he must amuse himself by just whirling round and round in that chair, thought Imani.

"Yep, I was right. She had arrhythmia. Uneven heart rate. But it was well under control too, just like Brian's COPD. Seems she'd had a pacemaker since she was in high school, and hadn't had any problems since it was put in. But then one night, just a week after Brian, her heart just stopped."

"Her pacemaker gave out?"

Dr. Smith looked at his screen again, but apparently the short glance didn't warrant a full chair-whirl; he settled for just turning his head this time. "Nope, it was working fine. An ambulance chaser was all set to sue the pacemaker manufacturers, the bastard, but even he couldn't make out anything wrong with it. Her heart just up and quit, like maybe from severe nervous strain or stress, or overexertion."

"And neither of the deceased showed any sign of foul play, or anything suspicious?" Justina prompted.

"Of course not, didn't I just say?" Dr. Smith seemed to be getting testy. Maybe he has another important email to compose, Justina thought.

"All right. Well, thank you for your time," said Justina.

Seeing that the interview was at an end, Dr. Smith became expansive again. "Pleasure to meet you," he said, and gave each of them a hearty handshake. His plump hand was sweaty. "Always nice to get a visit from charming young ladies!"

"Thanks again," said Justina.

*

Back in the car, Imani said, "Well that was awkward."

Justina snickered. "We're *charming young ladies,* apparently."

Imani laughed aloud at that. "And the stupid thing with the chair! *Whoosh!*"

Justina pointed the car at the parking lot's exit, then thrust a fist out in front of her, as though leading a cavalry charge. "Whoosh!" She cried. And with that they headed back, bursting with laughter, to the motel.

***

Counterpoint Two

Transcript of Dashboard Camera Footage, Officer Paul Bradley,

Midland, Texas

September 30, 2:17am

Officer Bradley: [singing]

[chip bag crinkling, soft drink pop tab opening, sounds of eating and drinking]

Officer Bradley: (singing) I hate traffic duty, I hate traffic duty, nobody is here, just me and my coke. . .

[static, three seconds]

[sound of tapping]

Officer Bradley: (yelp of surprise) Shit!

Officer Bradley: (muttering) What the hell are kids doing out here this late, come on! I ought to be arresting their parents, not sitting here watching for speeders at two [inaudible].

[sound of car window being rolled down]

Officer Bradley: What can I do for you kids? It's really late, do you need a ride home?

Young female voice (unidentified): Yes, we would like a ride to our mother's house.

Officer Bradley: Sure, where do you live?

[pause, one second]

Young female voice: You have to invite us in, mister. We can't come in unless you do.

Officer Bradley: I have to. . .what?

Young female voice: Invite us in. You have to invite us in now.

[pause, three seconds]

Officer Bradley: I. . I'm not sure I. . .

[pause, five seconds]

Young female voice: Invite us in. Now.

[pause, one second]

Officer Bradley: Sure, hop in.

[pause, seven seconds]

Officer Bradley: What the fuck! What's wrong with your eyes? Wait! I—

[static, one second]

Officer Bradley: [sustained sound of screaming]

[sounds of crashing and clattering inside the car, sound of liquid spilling]

[static, three seconds]

[pause, thirty seconds]

Officer Bradley: What the hell just happened? Shit, my coke! Ow! Well, that'll teach me to nod off.

Officer Bradley: [singing]

***

Ten

"So," said Justina, "What do you think?" They were back in their motel room, after stopping by a grocery store on the way back from the county coroner's office, and Justina was assembling two thick sandwiches.

Imani was stretched out on her stomach on her bed, with a pillow wadded under her arms, flicking through a book on her e-reader. The Order had wasted no time in digitizing their library, once the technology was available, and e-readers loaded with every reference book at the Order's disposal had been added to each car's standard equipment. She looked up. "What?"

Justina opened a package of sliced turkey luncheon meat, and piled it onto bread. "What do you think?" she repeated. "About the creature that we're after?"

Imani twisted around and sat up. "Well," she said, "it attacks people in their sleep, and drains the energy out of them. It can't be a vampire, because there are no puncture wounds."

Justina added thick slices of cheddar cheese to the sandwiches. "Dream thief?" she suggested.

Imani thought about it. "I don't think so," she said seriously. "The victims we talked to all described having bad dreams, so whatever attacked them wasn't siphoning the dreams off. It had to be getting their energy in another way."

Justina layered lettuce onto the sandwiches, then added mustard to her own and pickles to Imani's. "What then?" she prompted, finishing the two sandwiches and handing one to Imani on a paper plate.

"Thanks," said Imani, and took a big bite. Then she put the sandwich down, and began ticking off points on her fingers. "The one victim with COPD seemed like he died of not being able to get enough air, even though there was no mechanical reason for him not to. He wasn't smothered by anything, and he didn't have any fluid in his lungs. Maybe something took some of his breath, and his lungs weren't strong enough to make do on what was left."

"Solid assumption," said Justina, smiling.

"Nobody saw anything," Imani went on, picking up her sandwich and gesturing with it. "So it's something that can move around undetected."

"Looks like it," Justina said.

"So, something that drains people's energy, while they're asleep, but still leaves them dreams. Something that can make a pre-existing problem worse, to the point where the person unexpectedly dies, like the woman with arrhythmia did. Something that can steal people's breath." She looked up, hoping for approval. "Boo hag?"

"Boo hag," Justina concurred, smiling broadly, absurdly proud. "I'm pretty sure you're right, and that's what we've got."

Imani reached for her e-reader, and tapped several times with one hand, her forehead wrinkled with thought. She held her sandwich with the other hand, off to one side to keep from getting crumbs on the screen. "Boo hags, boo hags," she muttered to herself, until she found the page she wanted.

She looked up. "So, what do we do now? How do we hunt it?"

Justina finished her sandwich, and sipped from a bottle of water. "Well, the easiest thing would be to find its skin and burn it. That way we don't have to engage it at all."

"How do we do that, though?" wondered Imani, rolling back onto her stomach. "It could be anywhere. A boo hag has got to be good at hiding its skin."

"Well, it only makes sense that it would attack close to where it's laired, rather than far away. Do you have the list of home addresses of the victims?"

Imani got it out, and they found the locations on a map. Sure enough, all of them were clustered closely, within only a few blocks. "What's there?" Imani asked, leaning close. She popped the last bite of sandwich into her mouth.

There wasn't much of note. It was a residential area, with no conveniently obvious place for a skin-changing monster to spend its free time or hide its stolen human skin.

"We better go look," said Justina. "Maybe there's an abandoned house, or a shed or something." She picked up the keys to the car and got up.

"Seems like it would want to choose a cool, dry place," Imani said, thinking it through as she put on her boots. "So the skin would last longer." She stopped. "Wait, what about the identity it's taken? It would be disguising itself as a person now, wouldn't it?"

Justina hadn't really thought about that side of it. "You're right, it probably would." She twirled the keys thoughtfully.

"Would you *see* it?" Imani wondered. "If we met the boo hag in its human skin? Would you be able to tell?

"I don't know." Justina knew that she often did have the ability to *see* supernatural or extranatural creatures, even when they were able to disguise themselves to everyone else, just as she had seen the ghost's mark on Tyler that day several years ago in the commandery. "It's definitely worth a try." She tossed Imani a water bottle, and Imani caught it neatly.

"Let's see if you can spot a monster," she said.

*

Imani and Justina canvassed the neighborhood together most of the rest of the afternoon. At each house, they asked questions: had anyone noticed anything strange? Any neighbors acting in an unusual way? Any new people in the neighborhood they didn't recognize? (After all, Imani reasoned, the boo hag might still be using a skin from before it arrived here.) They said they were looking into the hospitalizations and deaths, trying to find a pattern.

Several people looked at them askance: two nuns? In pants? One of them remarkably unusual-looking and intimidating, and the other obviously too young even to have a driver's license? Looking into something like this? Weird. No thanks. Others talked to them, but had nothing to report: no one new that they had noticed, no one acting strange that they had noticed, no odd activity. That they had noticed.

"No one notices anything!" Justina complained. "Whatever happened to looking out for your neighbors?"

"What do you have to look into?" one man asked curiously. "The news said that there wasn't foul play or anything suspicious. What are you investigating?"

"It can't be a coincidence," Imani said, "everyone getting sick just within this few square blocks."

"Everyone lived within a few blocks?"

The two girls blinked at him. "Yes," said Imani. "One of the victims lives just three doors down from you."

He looked down the street where she pointed, as if he expected to see a sign in the front yard. "Huh! Well, who knew." He shook his head. "I wish I could help you girls! But I haven't seen anything. Good luck, though."

They thanked him, and went on.

"They don't really take us seriously," said Justina. "You're too cute, that's the problem."

Imani snorted. "I'm the only thing that keeps them from fleeing the scene at the sight of terrifying seven-foot you."

"*You girls*," Justina muttered, still nettled. "He'll be singing a different tune if we save him from a boo hag that's sucking his breath.

It was nearing sunset as they approached a house near the end of a cul-de-sac. It looked like every other house they had seen that day: red brick, two multi-trunk oak trees inside cement-bordered flowerbeds, a plume of pampas grass growing in one corner, the house's address stenciled on the curb along with a Texas Tech University emblem. The woman who opened the door seemed no less ordinary: middle-aged, t-shirt clad, blonde hair so obviously dyed that there was something innocent about it. Imani asked the usual questions, and the woman answered politely, but gave them no useful information.

It wasn't until they turned away from the closed door that Imani realized that something was different. Justina put a hand on her shoulder, pulling her to a halt, and said, "That was it. That was the boo hag."

Imani stared at her, then back at the door, feeling a chill. She had wondered, in spite of everything she knew, whether she herself might pick up on something amiss, something wrong, about the boo hag wearing a suit of human skin; evidently not. She imagined the creature watching them through the window, watching with stolen human eyes, and the skin between her shoulder blades crawled.

"Let's go," said Justina, drawing her down the sidewalk toward their car.

Imani trotted to keep up with Justina's long strides. "What did it look like?" she asked, in a hushed voice, as if the boo hag might be able to hear them.

Justina was silent for several paces. "It looked horrible," she said finally. "I could see right through the skin, and the boo hag inside was. . .just a wet red nightmare, like raw meat.   And it had a huge mouth that could gape like a rattlesnake's mouth." She paused. "No wonder it wants to hide that. Too bad it has to do it by killing and skinning people."

Imani shuddered. She was glad she hadn't been able to see the boo hag, but at the same time, having to leave it to her imagination was somehow worse.

*

They returned to the motel to regroup, and to plan their attack on the boo hag that night. Imani was stretched out on her stomach on her bed, poring over the documents on her e-reader again. "I still don't see how we'll be able to find its skin in time to stop it from attacking anyone," she said. "Even if we know which house it's probably in, a house is still a big place to hide something like that."

Justina looked up from the small plastic vials she was carefully filling with saltwater, but said nothing.

"This book says that boo hags like to hide their skins in the spaces underneath staircases, but the house we saw is only one story."

"Maybe there's a basement," Justina suggested.

Imani flicked through pages, her forehead creased. "I don't know, I don't think we can rely on that."

Justina screwed the caps onto the vials and stowed them one by one in a battered aluminum ammunition box, the kind designed with individual compartments to hold shotgun shells. It had slots in the back, so a belt could be threaded through for convenient carrying, and the crest of the Order painted in red on the lid.

"I guess we'll have to, though," she said. "The boo hag won't hold still and let us douse it in saltwater without a fight. That's got to be our last resort."

"This book says that a boo hag can also be killed by fire," Imani said.

"Sure, but we have to assume it'll be in someone's house, sucking their breath," Justina pointed out, latching the ammunition box and beginning to thread it onto her belt. "We can't exactly go throwing around burning tar or whatnot in someone's bedroom."

Imani went back to the book. It did mention that fire could only be used on the boo hag itself in the form of something that would stick to it, like burning tar; otherwise, the creature would simply revert to its semi-corporeal dust mote state and escape.

There was silence for a few minutes, as Justina began to fill an ammunition box with vials of saltwater for Imani, too. Imani herself stacked her two fists and rested her chin on them, thinking.

"It'll be dusk in half an hour or so," said Justina presently. "We should get over there, so we can start looking for the skin as soon as the boo hag leaves it behind."

Imani said nothing. She had been fine for most of the day, but now that it was actually time to face the monster, she felt anxiety rising up in her again, closing her throat and knotting her stomach. Again, she found herself picking nervously at the mauve pills on her polyester bedspread.

Justina led them in two hymns, and Imani, her voice only slightly shaking, read a passage from the book of Ephesians. Then they recited the Lord's Prayer together and, having completed the accepted substitute for vespers while away from the commandery-house, they set out as dusk began to fall.

*

In the car, Imani said, "I was thinking."

"What about?" asked Justina, without turning from the road.

"I think you'll probably be able to see the boo hag leaving the house when it goes out to hunt, even after it. . .dematerializes, or whatever they do. You'll be able to see where it's going, who it might be attacking."

A stoplight turned red, and after bringing the car to a halt, Justina shrugged in acquiescence. "I don't know, probably. She paused. "I wonder what *that* will look like."

"But if that does happen," said Imani, refusing to be sidetracked, "and you do see it, you ought to follow. I'll stay at the house and look for the skin."

Justina shot her a startled look. "Absolutely not! I told you I would never leave you, and I won't!"

"But what if tonight's victim is like those two people who were killed? Brian Perry and Debra Price? What if we don't find the skin in time and someone dies?"

The light turned green. They drove on, but Justina said nothing.

"Even if there's just a chance you can get enough salt on it to stop it from getting back into its skin, I think you should try."

Still Justina was silent. They had nearly reached the neighborhood, and twilight was falling, before she said, "Is your phone charged up?"

"Of course," said Imani, and held it up.

"We need to text each other every five minutes."

"Are you agreeing with me?" Imani asked. "Just making sure."

"Only if I hear from you *every five minutes*," said Justina, pointing her finger at Imani emphatically with each word.

"Sure, every five minutes."

"I mean it!" Justina felt that Imani was not regarding this stipulation with the appropriate degree of gravity.

"I will text you every five minutes," said Imani solemnly.

"Good then."

They drove in silence for perhaps half a minute, and then Imani burst into giggles. A moment later, Justina started laughing too. "I really do mean it, though!" she said. "Six minutes, and I'll be running to your rescue, don't you doubt it."

"I know," said Imani, serious this time. "I know you will, and the same goes for me. If I don't hear from you, I'll be running to your rescue too. Saltwater and lighter fluid in hand."

"Saltwater and lighter fluid in hand!"

***

Counterpoint Three

Eddie Sosa had been an overnight security guard at Panhandle Shooting Sports for three years. It wasn't a glamorous job, and most nights it was stupefyingly boring, but it paid the bills, and didn't require much of him besides watching monitors, occasionally strolling around the building, and not falling asleep. It could be a lot worse. He had his satellite radio in the control room to pass the time, he always brought a vacuum flask of strong coffee, and there was always the tiny off-chance of getting to be a hero if anything ever happened.

In his years working there, nothing ever had. But then, one night in early October, that changed.

He had just arrived and settled himself in the control room, and the owner, Elmer Preston, was leaving for the evening after locking up the front door. Eddie watched him on the monitor as he left. Elmer Preston was a big man, still sturdy and solid, his belly only just beginning to show signs of an impending paunch, though he was past sixty years old; his round head, however, was perfectly bald and shiny, reflecting back the light of the motion sensor as he walked past. He had owned the firing range for close on thirty years, and Eddie personally fully expected him to go on owning it for thirty more.

Eddie poured some coffee from his thermos into a mug, leaned back in his chair, and watched idly as Mr. Preston headed down the front walk toward the parking lot. Then the picture dissolved into static for a moment: this was not particularly unusual, as the security cameras hadn't been updated in the last decade, and Eddie, as he always did, gave the monitor a brisk smack with his hand. He had never been sure whether this actually did anything, but on the chance it did, he thought best to leave well enough alone, and kept doing it. The static proved more stubborn than usual this time, however, so he smacked the monitor again.

This time it cleared, and he saw that Mr. Preston had stopped. Two kids were standing there, wearing nondescript clothes and hoodies with the hoods up; Eddie couldn't even tell whether they were boys or girls. It was hard to imagine that they could have run quickly enough to simply appear on the camera like that, in only a couple of seconds of static, but they must have. He leaned forward, dropping the front legs of his chair back to the floor, and watched more closely.

They stood as straight and still as soldiers at attention, nothing like children would normally stand. One of them was evidently talking to Mr. Preston, inaudible over the security camera feed; he (or she, he still couldn't tell which) gestured with his hand, but the gesture had something oddly rehearsed about it, as if it had been called for in a script rather than being a spontaneous addition to the conversation.

Mr. Preston seemed uncomfortable; his body language was stiff and guarded, and he was visibly edging—not moving confidently, but unambiguously *edging*—back toward the door. He shook his head; he was saying no to something.

Eddie wondered if he should go to help. He didn't see any danger—it was just two kids!—but clearly there was something off, even if he wasn't sure what it was. He drained his mug in a long gulp, and started to get up.

Mr. Preston stopped edging toward the door, and stood still, his arms limp by his sides, looking around vaguely, as if he didn't know where he was. The child spoke again, and Mr. Preston answered.

Snow and static ran across the monitor screen again. Eddie took the time to administer his usual all-purpose smack to it, and when it cleared this time, there was no sign of the children. They must have run off as quickly as they'd come, though he couldn't imagine how they had managed to time it so perfectly with the glitch of static on the monitor. But he didn't give it too much thought, because he saw immediately that Mr. Preston had fallen to the concrete of the front walk, and he was thrashing back and forth and clutching his head in evident agony.

Eddie sprinted from the control room, through the entrance foyer, and outside. Seizure? he wondered. Or had the children hit him with something? Had he tripped and fallen while the camera was blocked by static? Eddie dropped to his knees beside the crumpled Mr. Preston, trying to remember everything he knew about first aid.

But already the seizure, or whatever it was, seemed to be passing. Mr. Preston wasn't thrashing any more, but just lying on the concrete groaning.

"Mr. Preston?" Eddie said cautiously. "Can you hear me? What happened?"

Mr. Preston squinted up at him, as though the security lights hurt his eyes. He groaned again.

"Mr. Preston? Did you fall? Did those kids do something to you? Do you want me to run and see if I can catch them?"

Elmer Preston began to lever himself painfully into a sitting position, rubbing his head. "Ooh. . .what happened? I think I tripped. I must have tripped. I think—" He sat up, feeling his head gingerly as though checking for cracks. Eddie hovered, ready to catch him if he collapsed, but he stayed upright, only swaying slightly. "I think I'm okay. Just tripped, that's all." He paused, and for the first time seemed to register the rest of what Eddie had said. "Kids? What kids?"

Eddie blinked at him, suddenly concerned; maybe he was more injured than he seemed. "There were two kids, standing right here on the sidewalk. You were talking to them. I saw it on the monitor camera." He paused. "You don't. . .you don't remember?"

Mr. Preston creased his brow, thinking hard. "No," he said finally. "I don't." With a grunt of effort and a hand against his temple, he gingerly got to his feet.

Eddie reached out a hand. "At least let me walk you to your car," he said. "Are you sure you can drive? I can take you to the urgent care clinic, it's just down the street."

Mr. Preston shook off his hand impatiently. "I'm perfectly fine," he said. "I tripped, and got my bell rung, and that is all. Stay here and keep an eye on the firing range like you're supposed to. I'll see you tomorrow."

Eddie watched Mr. Preston cross to his car, get inside, and drive off. When he drove, his car didn't weave or swerve; he really did seem to be okay. Eddie turned and headed back inside. He shook his head. The fact that Mr. Preston didn't remember the kids at all was worrying; very

"*What kids*". Worrying, no doubt about it. And, too, where had they gone? Where had they run off to?

***

Eleven

Imani and Justina stood outside the house where the boo hag had laired, looking up at it in the dusk. It had gotten cool after the sun went down, and both girls had their hands tucked into the pockets of their white jackets; the oak trees whispered and rustled in a fitful, gusty breeze over their heads.

Justina looked down at her sister. Imani's face didn't show much paleness—it never did, under her dark skin tone—but Justina could see the wideness of her eyes, hear her too-quick breaths, see how much her hands were shaking (even through her jacket pockets), read her tight posture. She could smell the sharp sourness of fear pouring off of her.

Justina did not like casually touching people, especially strangers. She would do it, if the mission required it: she had even shaken hands with the annoying Dr. Smith, the county medical examiner. But she did not usually enjoy much close physical contact, or seek it out for its own sake, even within the commandery; for example, unlike Imani, she was not generally fond of spontaneous hugs. When she touched someone, it was with full deliberation. This tendency was partly due to her own natural preference for personal space, but also from an idea that her touch might have some as-yet-undiscovered latent power in it, and for this reason should probably be treated with some caution.

It was, therefore, of some note when Justina caught one arm around Imani's shoulders and pulled her tight into a hug. "You can do this," she said with perfect certainty. "You have been trained by the best, you have all the tools you need, and God is for us." She took a step back, and faced Imani squarely. "Tell me, who are we?"

"We are the Sisters of the Order of the Holy Lance," said Imani. "We are a sword in God's hand against the forces of evil."

"Too right we are."

They turned to face the house again. "Do you have all your gear?" Justina asked. "Saltwater? Lighter fluid? Ghost knife?"

"Yes, yes, and yes," said Imani.

"All right, then, lets get to it," Justina said. As they approached the front door, she added, "Did you know that sisters of the Order are technically permitted to break into houses in exigent circumstances, just like the police?"

"The unexpected perks of the job," said Imani, making a valiant (and not altogether unsuccessful) effort at bravado.

Justina grinned, and pulled a neat set of lockpicks in a leather case out of her pocket. She set to work methodically on the house's front door.

Suddenly she stopped short, and looked up. "Imani," she said softly. "It's happening. Now. The boo hag just left. Can you see it? Just there." She pointed.

Imani squinted, and thought she might have seen something in the cone of illumination under the streetlight; something like a gust of wind-blown sand or snowflakes. It might have been the creature, but she couldn't be sure. "Not really," she admitted.

Justina hesitated, caught between two bad options: leave Imani alone, or allow some innocent person to be attacked, and maybe even killed, if they couldn't find the skin right away. She froze, agonized with indecision, the lockpick motionless in her hand.

"Go after it," Imani told her. "It's okay, I want you to. You may save someone's life, and at the very least you'll save someone a trip to the hospital. It's the right thing to do. Go."

Justina took a few steps down the walk, then turned back, still hesitating. "Go!" hissed Imani, already carrying on with the lock-picking where Justina had left off.

"Every five minutes," Justina reminded her.

"Yes, every five minutes, just *go!*"

Justina turned and ran after the tenebrous form of the incorporeal boo hag, as it glided through the chilly air in search of prey. It drifted, looking to her nephil eyes something like a humanoid-shaped mist of blood droplets suspended in water, but with hungry eyes and gleaming teeth, until it singled out a house, and sifted inside through the minuscule crack around a window.

Justina could not follow that way, and she had left her set of lockpicks with Imani. Never mind. No time to worry about it, and the Order paid for repairs in cases like this. When she reached the front door, she simply snapped the doorknob, wrenched the deadbolt out of the jamb, and went inside.

Meanwhile, Imani was hunting frantically for the skin inside the house that was the creature's lair. Trying to think of any place that would be cool and dark and dry, she slammed cupboards open and closed, crashed through piles of pots and pans in the kitchen, flung clothes and shoes and out-of-season Christmas decorations willy-nilly out of closets, rooted under every bed and every large piece of furniture. She clawed through stacks of sheets and towels in the linen closet, sneezing on the disturbed dust. Nothing. She yanked out every drawer from every dresser: still nothing. She dug through tools and scraps of lumber and rakes and leaf blowers in the garage, pulled the ladder down and checked the attic: more of the same. She began to feel frantic. Where could the skin be hidden?

Somewhere handy, somewhere hidden, somewhere cool and dry and dark. . . She ran back into the house, trying to think of some place she hadn't checked yet.

Justina crept softly into the house the boo hag had targeted. It was an ordinary, rather charming house, decorated with Southwestern art, but Justina had neither time nor inclination to appreciate the pottery or the woven rugs. This house had two stories. She found the downstairs bedroom: empty. She loped up the stairs three at a time, and looked into the first bedroom she came to: empty again, and evidently being used as a painting studio.

It was in the bedroom at the end of the hall, the master bedroom, that she found what she was looking for. A woman lay on her back in the bed, nerveless and deeply asleep, apparently barely breathing, and her right hand drooped over the edge of the bed, limp and somehow pitiful. On her chest crouched the boo hag, fully corporeal and fully unmasked, a flayed-looking thing of stringy sinew, covered with slimy ichor, its jaw gaping open wider than should have been possible in a rational universe. Its raw hands, nothing but skinned bone and tendon, held down its victim's shoulders, its long, almost fleshless fingers curled tight. It was sucking out her life energy with her breath, in the form of a misty vapor traveling from her mouth to the boo hag's gaping gullet.

Justina saw this, and felt a swell of rage almost crystalline in its cold perfection. This thing, this blot on creation, dared, *dared*, to attack one made in the very image of God Almighty? Before she even realized she had moved, she had lunged across the room, grabbed the boo hag in hands that splintered its brittle bones, and flung it off its victim. The creature weighed no more than the flensed corpse it essentially was, and it had barely reached the top of its arc before it smacked into the wall, with a repulsive meaty squelch and crunch.

It fell to the ground, but in a moment it was back up on all fours, righting itself with insectile speed, snarling, all its backward-facing teeth bared and gleaming with thin slime. Then, all at once, its lidless cadaver eyes fixed properly on Justina for the first time. She pounced at it, intending to pin it with her ghost knife and then douse it in saltwater, but with a shriek it bolted for the door like a spider, blurring halfway into dust motes as it did. Of all the possible responses the creature might have had, abject flight was not one Justina had seriously considered, and it took her off guard.

She knew that she had the ability to *see* the reality of supernatural creatures. It had never occurred to her that there was something which they, in turn, might be able to *see* in her. She didn't know that some creatures saw her as something like an avenging angel, descending in terrible power and righteous wrath.

She knew the boo hag was escaping, and could not allow it. It would only attack someone else, and that was unacceptable. Texts from Imani had been coming to her phone regularly, but evidently she had not been able to find the skin. The fight needed to end here.

Without even thinking about what she was doing, Justina shouted "Stop!"

And the boo hag did. It froze in an arachnid crouch, semitransparent and semicorporeal, snarling and clenching its bony fingers, unable to flee any further.

Justina could feel it, what she had done. It was something like a muscle, something she could move and flex at will, something she could stretch out and touch things with. She could actually *feel* the slippery, squirming creature she was holding with it, though she never moved so much as a finger of her physical body.

For a moment she stared at the captured boo hag with a perfect fury, in rage that such a thing could exist and pollute the earth. Then—

"Burn," she said softly, and the frozen steel in her voice was terrifying. "*Burn!*"

The boo hag burst into flames so hot they were white. There was a very brief screech from the creature, then only the overwhelming stink of charring meat and bone. The flames were so hot that the boo hag was reduced to ash in seconds, and the ash dropped in a small heap to the carpeted floor.

Justina turned, and saw that the woman who had been the boo hag's last victim had woken up, and had seen everything. She sat in her bed, eyes and mouth both stretched open, shock written on every inch of her, unable to say a word.

*

The next morning, Justina and Imani had finished checking out of the motel, and were enjoying a complimentary breakfast of muffins and toast in the motel's dining area before heading back to Derrick.

"So you just told it to stop, and it stopped," said Imani, spreading a slice of toast thickly with strawberry jam from a plastic packet. There were only five tables in the tiny dining alcove, and none but theirs were occupied, so she didn't whisper.

Justina nodded. "But it didn't stop just because I said so, like it was following orders or something. I *compelled* it, somehow, or maybe I just immobilized it. I could actually *feel* it. I made something physically happen. Then I just. . .made it burn."

Imani took a bite of toast. "Could you do it again, do you think?"

Justina turned her plastic butter knife over and over between her fingers, and considered it. "I think so," she said finally. "I can't explain how I did it, but it was just like moving any muscle. I mean, you couldn't exactly *explain* to anybody how you move your arms, right? You just do it."

Imani nodded slowly. "I see how that could be."

They sat in silence for a moment, thoughtfully chewing their toast.

"What if it hadn't been a monster?" Imani asked. "Would it have worked on anything? A person, even?"

Justina was silent. Finally she said, "I think so. Maybe not as easily; a person is more complex than a monster that just functions on base needs. Even a vampire or something like that is more complex than a boo hag. It might be harder for me to get a good hold."

Imani sipped from a paper cup of Lipton tea, then put it down and twirled the cardboard sleeve around it. "I wonder what the sisters will think," she mused.

There was a TV mounted to the corner of the ceiling, tuned to a cable news station; the two girls had been ignoring it. But in the silence after these words, they both heard the phrase "Derrick, Texas" from it, and looked up sharply. Imani's chair was facing away; she scooted it around backwards so she could see.

Two crisply-suited news anchors, one a man with impeccably-coiffed blond hair and the other a dark-haired woman with unnaturally knife-edged eyebrows, sat side by side in a studio. "And now," said the woman, with a well-rehearsed somber look on her face, "if you're just joining us, you're watching breaking news coverage of the convent shooting in Texas." Imani and Justina exchanged a glance, both of their eyes wide. Justina saw the same sick dread on her sister's face that she knew must be on her own.

"That's right, Sofia," said the male anchor, his face also carefully composed into an expression of utmost seriousness. "We're going now to Sally Hemphill, who is live in Derrick, Texas. Sally?"

The image shifted to a view of a woman in an elegant cream-colored jacket and sunglasses. There was a stiff breeze blowing: her perfect strawberry blonde blowout was tossing uncooperatively in every direction. Behind her was a cottonfield, and to most people it would have been indistinguishable from any other; but Justina and Imani recognized it. It was across the street from the commmandery-house.

Sally Hemphill nodded her head solemnly as she heard the two anchors in the studio turn the segment over to her. "Thank you, Brian. I'm standing now at the scene of this shocking crime, in which eight gunmen attacked a local convent here late last night. As you can see—"

The camera panned around, and showed the commandery at last. Both girls could recognize it. It was a scorched shell of blackened walls and vacant windows, charred rafters jutting like broken ribs where the roof had fallen in, and every windowpane lying in shattered half-melted fragments on the ground. Yellow crime scene tape stretched across what remained of the lawn, and smoke and puffs of ash still blew from the ruins. Both police and FBI moved over and through the scene, examining, collecting, and conferring with each other in voices far too low to hear over the moan of the wind.

Justina bolted to her feet, sending her chair crashing to the floor backwards behind her.

The camera panned back to the reporter. "—motive is yet to be determined, though the FBI is not ruling out the possibility of terrorism." She paused, and tucked a whipping strand of hair behind her ear. Then, after a moment, she continued, her face even more grim than before. "We have now learned that one of the five nuns present in the building at the time of the attack was declared dead at the scene, and the four others, along with the resident priest, have reportedly been admitted to the hospital in fair to serious condition. Names are being withheld pending notification of the—"

Imani sat motionless, frozen, feeling as if her body didn't quite belong to her, simply unable to assimilate what she had seen and heard. Then she became aware that Justina was standing rigid, her hands clenched white, her jaw locked, and she was shaking; not trembling, but shaking like an overloaded and overheating machine about to tear itself apart.

Imani jumped up, stepped quickly around the table, and took Justina by the shoulders, turning her away from the TV. Justina's face, when she turned, was terrifying. "It's okay, we're okay, just. . .dial it back now, all right?"

Justina closed her eyes and took several slow breaths, trying to regain control. When she opened her eyes again, her face was set like bedrock, and she turned and ran for the car without a word. Imani ran after her.

*

They drove out of town in complete silence. Justina had not said a single word since hearing the news report. Finally, Imani said, "Justina?"

Justina gave no sign that she had heard, but continued to stare straight ahead, her hands white on the steering wheel.

"Justina. . .come on, say something. Please."

Justina looked over at her, and Imani saw that her jaw was still clenched tight. Then she understood. Justina, whose singing had shaken the walls and burned out light bulbs when she was just a little girl, whose command had immolated a monster only a few hours ago, did not dare say a word, not now. At this moment, whatever power was in her, she did not believe that she could control it.

Imani sat still in her seat, her arms wrapped around her as if to keep a gaping hollowness from tearing her apart. She knew she had been afraid of her first mission, of failure, of the boo hag; but this new horror eclipsed that fear so completely that she could barely remember what it had even felt like. It seemed tiny and childish now, not even worthy of notice in the face of this deep, sick fear. Not when the commandery was a burned-out ruin, not when one of the sisters (*who?*) had been killed.

"We'll be okay," she said, barely even registering that she was speaking aloud. "God is still here. God is still good. We'll. . .we'll. . ." She stopped. After a moment, Justina heard her breath coming in jagged little hitches, and realized she was trying with all her might to cry silently, not to sob, so that she, Justina, would not be made more distressed than she was already.

Justina pulled over to the side of the highway and stopped the car. She reached for Imani, and all at once they were in each other's arms, clutching tight, and Imani did sob then. Justina held her until the storm of tears had ebbed, and Imani held Justina too, until her uncontrollable shaking finally stopped. When they drew apart at last, Justina's face also was wet, with a nephil's strange pearly tears.

They drove on. Imani took out her cell phone and started to call the sisters, but Justina reached out her hand and stopped her. "They would have called us hours ago if they could," she said. "It must not be safe." Imani acknowledged the wisdom of this, and put her phone away again.

When they reached the next town, Imani turned on the car radio and twisted the dial, until they found a station reporting the news.

"—latest on the Texas shooting," said the reporter. "All eight suspects are in custody, but there has been no report as yet concerning the motive for this shocking crime. We go now to Derrick, where the county sheriff, John Whitlock, is making a statement."

There was a pause, then a voice they both knew. The Order had worked together with the Sheriff's Department on several occasions, and the two organizations had often shared information with each other.

"This is a dark day for West Texas," said Sheriff Whitlock, with the stiff intonation that suggested he was reading a prepared statement. "Last night, around midnight, a group of eight gunmen broke into Saint Margaret's and began shooting, apparently with the intention of killing the nuns who were there. All eight men are in custody, but so far they have given disparate explanations for their motives, and at this point we still aren't sure why they carried out this heinous act. At this time. . ." He paused, and there was a sound of shuffling and muttering.

"You know what, ya'll?" he said, in a completely different tone. He had evidently decided to go off-script. "We don't know yet why they did what they did. But we *will* know. We'll know why they did it, and we'll find anyone who helped them. Make no mistake: I will see to it that the men responsible for this are punished to the fullest extent of the law. They will not get away with it. I know every one of the sisters at St. Margaret's personally, and I give them my personal word."

After a pause, he said, "I'll a take a few questions now."

After a pause and the sound of a microphone being passed to someone, a female voice said, "Sheriff, can you comment further on what you mean by the suspects giving 'disparate explanations'?"

John Whitlock cleared his throat, then said, "Well, you see they each told a different story. They don't seem to have coordinated their stories at all, so every one of 'em is different. We're trying to work out which story is the true one."

"Is there some reason for them doing that?" the same reporter asked.

He paused for a moment, evidently to think about it, then said, "Not that I know of. Seems stupid to me."

Again there was rustling and clattering as the microphone was handed off to someone else. "Sheriff," said a male reporter, "is it true that the sisters at the convent had an arsenal of weapons hidden on site?" There was a susurration of whispers and mutters in the background at such an inflammatory question.

Sheriff Whitlock sounded angry when he answered. "They did have an armory on site," he said stiffly, "but it wasn't a secret. The sheriff's department and the police department knew all about it, and the sisters had all the right permits and licenses. All fair and legal and aboveboard."

"Why—" the reporter began, but the sheriff went right on.

"You would have no trouble finding women in Derrick and surrounding communities, and men too, who took self-defense and martial arts classes at the convent," he said. "They offered classes for people who wanted to get a concealed-carry license, too. None of this is a secret. It provided some of the convent's income."

"But—"

"*And*," Sheriff Whitlock went on, raising his voice, "Sister Alana, their armorer, has placed highly in several national bladesmithing competitions. I understand she's got a Wikipedia page. Now, sir, if you could refrain from trying to turn this into some sort of scandal, I think we'd all be grateful."

There was a pause, just long enough to be awkward. Then the sheriff said, "I think there's time for one more question."

Another handoff of the microphone, and a different reporter said (in a noticeably respectful tone), "We understand there are other nuns at St. Margaret's, who were not present when the attack happened. Can you comment on where they are, and if they are safe?"

"Yes, I can. Communications have been restricted as a precaution, in order to protect the remaining sisters from possible attack." ("See?" said Justina.) "But we have word that all of them are safe, and we believe they are currently en route back to Derrick." He paused, then said, "Thank you. No more questions at this time."

Imani and Justina drove on. Between towns, radio reception sometimes broke up, but they were able to continue to follow the story in bits and pieces.

"—have been informed by the hospital in Derrick that the conditions of three the four injured nuns have now been reported as "fair". The condition of the fourth has been downgraded from serious to, quote, 'serious but stable'. The convent's priest is also in fair condition, according to a hospital spokesman. All are expected to make a full recovery.

"In related news, four of the eight suspects in the attack have also been admitted to the hospital under custody. None of their injuries are reportedly life-threatening, and doctors state that the nuns clearly defended themselves with skilled, but non-lethal, force—"

"They should've killed them," Justina muttered. "They could have. They should've killed them all."

Imani said nothing. They both knew perfectly well that the Sisters of the Holy Lance never, ever killed a human being except in the very last extremity, to save someone's life when there was no other recourse possible. But Imani understood Justina's sentiment, and agreed with it too much to say anything.

"—breaking news on the Texas convent shooting," said the anchor. "The victim, declared dead at the scene, has now officially been identified as Ella Marie Kirkpatrick, age thirty-six. Sister Ella joined the convent in 1999, and since then—"

Imani sat stunned in her seat. Later she would feel it, later she would grieve, but for the moment all she felt was blank unbelief. She tried to imagine a world without Sister Ella in it. Couldn't.

"I will kill them all for this," breathed Justina.

***

Counterpoint Four

The Sisters of the Holy Lance hunted and fought evil things. But they were not the only ones who did.

It would have been strange indeed if this had not been the case; if no person, having seen or been harmed by a dark creature, had ever decided to go on the offensive against them, to fight back. But in fact, there were many people who had devoted themselves, to one degree or other, to hunting down and stopping the things that lurked in shadows and on the edges of nightmares. Many people other than the Sisters of the Holy Lance did battle against supernatural or extranatural threats.

They were not an organization. Most of these people (the Order of the Holy Lance tended to call them "freelancers", as both a plain description and a satisfying pun) operated in small groups, loosely connected or not connected at all, having none of the tools of organization and research and wide communication that the Order enjoyed. News of attacks or threats spread far more haphazardly: whispered across tables or over pints in dozens of nondescript taverns and diners, described in ambiguous emails, mentioned obliquely in phone calls, discussed in dark corners of the Internet. Some modes of communication were older: glyphs scribbled in chalk or shoe polish or charcoal on walls and sidewalks and fences, indecipherable to anyone who didn't know the code, pointed to safehouses, motels and pawnshops and gun shops that didn't ask awkward questions, collections of books, clearinghouses for news, warnings, calls for help. The spread of information among the freelancers was organic and undirected, without a center or a real trajectory.

In spite of its diffuse nature, or because of it, the freelancer communication network was highly efficient. Within hours of the attack on St. Margaret's, word of it was spreading, and often provoking outrage: it was not uncommon for freelancers in danger, or in need of information or reinforcements, to go to a commandery-house of the Holy Lance for help, and over the years many of them had spent time at St. Margaret's. Over pints, over food, electronically or in person, and often by means of notes left at glyph-marked notice boards, word of the attack spread. News reports confirmed it.

There is, however, a problem with such an organic means of getting information: the information spreads untraceably, with no way to track its origins or sources or accuracy. From the beginning, reports about the attack were mixed in with hints of who had caused it, and where had those hints come from? No one knew.

Being widely believed has the ability to confer the appearance of proof, even without proof. By the end of the day, dozens of people who hunted monsters believed they knew who had caused the attack on the commandery: a nephil, the very one the sisters had so naively taken in as a baby. They believed they knew this, knew it positively, and they did what they always did: they prepared to hunt down the evil thing.

***

Twelve

At St. Luke's hospital, Sister Rebecca sat in the waiting room. She and Magdalena had returned from Amarillo a few hours before, and had braved the crush of reporters and journalists outside the hospital; they had not gone outside since. Sister Magdalena had folded herself awkwardly crosswise into one of the chairs, and had fallen asleep there; small wonder, as she was the one who had driven from Amarillo to Derrick, beginning at four o'clock that morning, as soon as they heard the news of what had happened. Even in sleep, her hand rested close to her gun.

Rebecca had tried to sleep during the drive, and had tried to sleep in a chair in the waiting room like Magdalena, but had been unable. Now she flipped restlessly through a worn and dogeared copy of *Texas Monthly*, picked up at random from a stack of magazines on a nearby end table, unable to pay attention to a single thing she read. She got up. Walked around the room. Sat back down, feeling no better. Picked up a copy of *Newsweek*, and flipped through that too, no more able to absorb anything from it. The waiting room TV was tuned to the *Food Network*, and the mundanity of the show was so incongruous that it almost made her angry: how could anyone possibly bake pineapple upside-down cake, without a care in the world, when St. Margaret's was a smoking ruin, and Brother David and the sisters were in the hospital, and Sister Ella was *dead*, with her blood splashed through the ashes? The mere existence of pineapple upside-down cake, in that moment, seemed almost a kind of desecration.

It was a relief when Sheriff Whitlock came in; if nothing else, his presence gave her something to focus on, something to do. He sat down beside her.

Sheriff Whitlock was a stocky, barrel-chested man, and he cheerfully embraced all the stereotypical accoutrements of a Texas lawman: sun-bleached Stetson hat, oversized belt buckle, well-worn but impeccably polished cowboy boots, elaborate tooling on the creased leather of his gun holster. His thinning hair was gingery, and his skin was weathered. "Sister Rebecca," he said politely.

She nodded at him. "Jack."

"What's the news?" he asked. "Anything?"

She shrugged. "Just more of the same, really. It looks like everyone will be okay. Even Sister Deborah is stable, and they say she'll be fine, but a bullet through the lung isn't something you just bounce back from all in a minute."

He nodded, and they sat quietly for a moment.

"Paloma and Katelyn should be here soon. And Justina and Imani."

"Do you know where you'll go, while the convent is being rebuilt?" he asked.

"There's another commandery-house in Lubbock. We'll go there."

There was another stretch of silence, but it was a comfortable silence. Neither of them was the kind of person who felt compelled to fill the air with endless words.

"How was your press conference?" Rebecca asked.

Sheriff Whitlock snorted. "Damned reporters—" he caught himself. "Sorry, Sister. *Darned* reporters, trying to stir up something, find some kind of scandal. Buzzards. Not a one of 'em gives a rat's a—" He cleared his throat. "A rat's *behind* about any of us, not really. Just ratings. We're a side-show to them, is all."

Sister Rebecca said nothing. She felt Sheriff Whitlock might be being uncharitable, but after fighting her way through a press of microphones and perfect hair-dos outside the hospital, she couldn't seem to make the effort to call him on it.

"Have you learned anything new from the suspects?" she asked instead. "Anything about why they would want to do something like this?"

Sheriff Whitlock crossed his right ankle over his left knee. "Well," he said, "I wouldn't mind running that by you, if you're interested."

Sister Rebecca leaned forward. "I certainly am."

"Well, you see," he said, "I get all kinds of excuses and explanations from suspects. I've heard it all. It's never their fault, they're always being framed, or misunderstood, or persecuted or whatnot. You know."

Rebecca nodded. "I can imagine."

"Well these guys, I've never seen anything quite like them. Every one of them is telling a different story, and on top of that, every one of 'em's sticking to it! Not a one has cracked, or contradicted himself, or made a mistake. If I talked to just one of 'em, I'd think he was telling the truth. Only problem is that none of them agree with each other."

Sister Rebecca tapped her chin with her finger. "That is odd," she said.

"Yeah. It's like they very carefully thought out their stories, and they're sticking to 'em, so I can't trip them up, only they missed the point. I don't need to trip them up when they all contradict each other. Even if they do contradict consistently."

"Could they be trying for an insanity plea or something?"

He shook his head. "I don't see how. None of 'em acts crazy at all. If that's their plan, they're going about it all wrong."

Sister Rebecca paused, thinking. "Can you tell me what their stories are? Maybe I'll notice something."

"Glad to." He shifted his position, putting both boots back onto the floor. "All of 'em say they were attacking something bad. Let's see." He counted them off on his fingers. "Two said they were attacking a terrorist cell: one Al-Qaeda, one ISIS. Two said they were attacking a drug cartel safehouse: one a Mexican cartel, one Colombian. One was going after a meeting of the KKK, one was going after a gang, one was breaking up a group conspiring to assassinate the governor—"

"Assassinate the governor?" repeated Rebecca, almost amused.

"Yep," said the sheriff. "Each one of the suspects had a different story to tell, and what they seemed to think was a valid and patriotic reason to go shoot up the convent. Only none of them seemed to believe it was a convent. Actually—" he wrinkled his forehead, pondering the weirdness of the whole thing. "Actually, not a one of 'em talked about attacking women. Some of them said they were attacking all men, and a couple said the group was mixed, but not one described attacking a group of women. Why would they lie about something that obvious?"

"Well, Father David was there," Rebecca said vaguely, not sure what point she was trying to make.

"I forgot that," said Sheriff Whitlock, equally vaguely.

After a pause, he went on. "I'll tell you what it's like," he said. "It's like they're all delusional. It's like they all really believe the stories they're telling. Suspects aren't usually master liars, you know. A lot of times you can tell when they're lying. Can't prove it, maybe, but you know. Not these guys, though. Every one of 'em, I think he thinks he's telling the truth."

Sister Rebecca thought about that. "Is that possible? I mean, is it possible that they really are all delusional? Could it be some kind of mass hysteria, or something?"

Sheriff Whitlock shrugged his heavy shoulders. "Don't know," he said. "You'd have to ask the doctors that one."

"I might do that." She tapped her chin with her finger again. "Of all the possibilities, it seems to be the one that makes the most sense. I mean, it doesn't make much, but more than the idea that they all decided, for some reason, to tell very internally-consistent stories that are all totally contradictory to each other."

"That's what I thought too."

"You know, it's funny," reflected Rebecca. "I'm used to dealing with monsters. And they can be genuinely horrible. But fighting monsters does have this going for it: when you get right down to it, most monsters are pretty simple. It's people that are weird and complicated."

*

Around noon, another of the attackers was brought to the hospital, by ambulance, and wheeled straight into emergency.

Soon thereafter Sheriff Whitlock, holding two steaming paper cups of hospital coffee and looking frazzled, returned to the waiting room; Sister Magdalena was not there, having ventured to the cafeteria in search of some kind of lunch for all of them, but Sister Rebecca was, and she straightened expectantly when she saw him. "What's happened?"

He sat down beside her again. "We just had to bring in a fifth suspect to the hospital. Code Three. Lights and siren and all." He held out one of the paper cups. "Coffee?"

"Thanks," she said, and took it. "What happened? Was it—"

"Was it something the sisters did?" He shook his head. "No, at least they don't think so. Though I wouldn't lose any sleep if it was.

"We would," said Sister Rebecca.

"Well," John Whitlock went on, sipping from his cup, "anyway, no. Seems it was a brain hemorrhage, like from an aneurism or some such. Looks like they'll have to airlift him out to Dallas."

"Huh." Rebecca took a slow swallow of coffee, thinking. "I wonder if that could explain his behavior? The delusions and everything?"

Sheriff Whitlock swirled his coffee. "Couldn't tell you. Maybe."

Rebecca sipped meditatively. "I need to talk to the doctor," she said. "This is a clue, it's got to be. There's no way something like that could be a coincidence, right?"

"Sure seems damned unlikely to me," he said; then, realizing his impropriety, he tried to cover his blunder by taking a huge gulp from his cup, which sent him into a coughing fit.

"Are you okay?" Rebecca asked, trying not to smile.

"Coffee just went down the wrong pipe," he said. Then he paused, and said, "What are you thinking? This might be something. . ." He gestured with his paper cup. "Something in your wheelhouse? I mean, the Order's wheelhouse?"

"I don't know." She finished her coffee, and stood up. "It's worth looking into."

∗

Sister Rebecca found Dr. Michaels in the on-call room, sprawled on the couch with his arm flung over his eyes, his scrubs creased, his white coat wadded in a pile on the seat of a folding chair. An open can of Red Bull, presumably from the on-call room's mini fridge, rested on the linoleum floor beside him. She knew well that he must need rest—he had been the attending physician through the entire ordeal—and so she made to sneak away. She could talk to him when he woke up.

Before she had cleared the door, he uncovered his face and saw her. "Oh, Sister Rebecca!" He started to get up, and came dangerously close to knocking over the can of Red Bull, which he had evidently forgotten was there.

She held up her hand. "No, don't get up. I'll come back later. I was just leaving."

"No, no! It's fine, I'm a master of the power nap." He rose to a sitting position, reached down for the Red Bull, and took a long swig. To Rebecca's relief, he then placed it on top of the mini fridge, rather than back on the floor.

"In that case," said Sister Rebecca, "why don't I come back in twenty minutes? Isn't that the accepted ideal length for a power nap?"

Dr. Michaels hesitated for a moment, then said, "That's a deal. See you in twenty minutes."

*

Twenty minutes later, Sister Rebecca returned to the on-call room, where Dr. Michaels was just finishing his Red Bull. She transferred his lab coat to a hook on the back of the door, then seated herself in the folding chair. He sat down on the couch, after tossing his empty can into the recycle bin. "What can I do for you?" he asked.

"What can you tell me about the suspect that was brought in a bit ago? The one with the brain hemorrhage?"

"Ah, right. Yes, he had bleeding in his brain, and not just in one place, either: he actually had *three* separate torn blood vessels." He paused. "He's being airlifted to UT Southwestern in Dallas now, and that's a solid place for neurosurgery, but I don't have high hopes for his prognosis, to be honest."

"What happened?" asked Rebecca. "Does anyone know?"

Dr. Michaels shook his head. "From what I understand from the sheriff, he was in a holding cell, and started to act strangely: delirium, talking incoherently, weaving when he walked, that sort of thing. Then he became unresponsive, and the sheriff's department called us. That's all we know."

Sister Rebecca tapped her fingers on the arm of the chair, thoughtfully. "Do you think the brain injury might have had something to do with him attacking us? Could it cause that?"

"Well. . ." Dr. Michaels made an equivocal gesture. "Brain hemorrhages, especially in the regions of the brain that these were, can certainly cause delirium, hallucinations, and aggressive behavior. That's well documented. If he'd acted alone. . ." he shook his head. "But brain injuries like this aren't *contagious*. It wouldn't have affected the other seven men."

Sister Rebecca propped her chin on her hands, thinking. "What if," she said slowly, "what if it did?"

"I don't think I follow."

"What if. . .all eight of them did have the same brain injury? Could that cause what we saw?"

He hesitated. "Are you asking if this could have been done deliberately?"

"Well, whether deliberate or not. Could the same injuries in all eight men cause them to have different delusions, but all the same *kind* of delusion, and then attack St. Margaret's together?"

He sat silent for a long moment, his forehead furrowed. "I don't know of any cases where that has happened, so, who knows? It seems to me that it could." Then he added, "But, that would be contingent on all of them somehow receiving exactly the same damage to the brain, which I don't really think is possible."

Sister Rebecca considered that. She knew of creatures that could do things to people that were normally medically impossible, though this particular kind of attack would be a new one for her. "Would you be willing to run an MRI on one of the other suspects here?" she asked. "Just to see if there's anything similar going on?"

He lowered his voice. "Do you think this could be something outside the normal? One of the things that you and the Order hunt?"

Rebecca hesitated. "I think. . .I think it could be."

Dr. Michaels swallowed hard. "I'll order the MRI," he said.

*

By the time the MRI results came back, Sister Katelyn and Sister Paloma had arrived. The four women sat together in the waiting room, picking at the food Magdalena had brought, making awkward and generally unsuccessful attempts to talk about what had happened. No words could heal the wounds of a grief so fresh, and so shocking; it was each other's presence that did the most good.

Dr. Michaels came into the waiting room, saw the sisters together, and waited respectfully until one of them looked up and saw him.

"I have the MRI results," he said. "And. . .I think you may all want to see them."

They followed Dr. Michaels into a vacant examination room, and he opened the MRI images on his tablet, propping it up on the counter against a jar of tongue depressors so they could all see it. He unwrapped a throat swab, to use as a pointer.

"Now," he said, pulling up the scan he wanted. It was a black-and-white rendering of a portion of one of the suspects' brains, viewed from above, and among the normal curves and folds of brain tissue they could all clearly see several white, irregular splotches. At the top of the image, in tiny white type, was the man's name: Elmer Preston. "This is what we found in the first man's brain, the man who collapsed," said Dr. Michaels. "See these light areas here, here, and here?" He pointed with the cotton tip of the throat swab. "Those are areas where significant bleeding has occurred. We took this scan after he had become unresponsive, so this represents a pretty serious hemorrhage."

With a couple of taps on the screen, he minimized that image, and pulled up a different one. The name at the top of this one was James Marquez, and it had light spots in the same places as the previous scan, though they were much smaller.

"On Sister Rebecca's request, I ran this MRI on one of the other suspects here. As you can see, he has bleeding in exactly the same three places, though far less severe." Dr. Michaels indicated the spots with the swab pointer. "He hasn't shown any outward signs of brain injury, not yet, but based on this, I would expect to start seeing some before long."

"How likely is it that both of them have the same injuries?" asked Sister Magdalena.

Dr. Michaels looked up from the screen. "It's not likely at all," he said. "Actually, it's impossible. But here we are."

"So it was done on purpose."

Dr. Michaels seated himself on the examination table, and twirled the throat swab restlessly between his fingers. "No, that's not what I meant." He paused. "I mean it's *impossible*. The best brain surgeon in the world couldn't have done this, not if he tried. It was so precise, and if we assume the end goal was the attack on St. Margaret's, so effective. The science of the brain is not capable of that, not now, maybe not ever. You can't just go in and reprogram someone's brain like a computer." His eyes slid back to the tablet, to the MRI on its screen. "Except it looks very much as if someone did it anyway." He looked at all the sisters, half hopeful and half afraid. "What could do this? Is there anything? Do you know?"

They all exchanged looks. The truth was, nothing came immediately to mind: none of them could think of a creature that attacked in this way, that actually manipulated a person's brain tissue to get a desired action, then just left the person to bleed. "We'll need to look into it," said Sister Rebecca. "*Something* made it happen, and we'll find out what it was. And stop it."

Sister Paloma moved over to the tablet, where it still sat propped up against the tongue depressor jar, and looked closely at the image. "Why are the two men in such different conditions?" she asked, turning back around to face Dr. Michaels. "I mean, why did the first man have such severe hemorrhage, and this second man hasn't even shown symptoms yet?"

He shook his head. "It's hard to say. But the man who collapsed —Mr. Preston is his name—he did have risk factors for brain hemorrhage. He had high blood pressure, and he was over sixty years old, and from what his family has said, he drank more than a little. Those things would likely have made it worse, made the damage apparent more quickly."

"What about the others?" asked Sister Katelyn. She was the youngest of the group, and this was her first contribution to the conversation. "I mean, the other suspects? Are you going to do MRIs on all of them?"

Dr. Michaels stared at the throat swab in his hand for a moment, as if seeking answers from it, then he looked up. "I think we'd better. Just to make sure. If the other six have the same injuries as these two, they'll all have to be airlifted out, since we're not equipped to repair something like this here at St. Luke's."

There was a moment of silence, then Sister Paloma said quietly, "If all this is true, that means those eight men were actually innocent. They were manipulated and forced into doing what they did."

Dr. Michaels looked uncomfortable. "I guess so," he said awkwardly. The thought that anything in the world could excuse shooting up a convent was not one he much wanted to entertain.

As the sisters left the exam room, he pulled Sister Rebecca aside. "You know, you very likely saved those men's lives," he said. "At the very least, you saved them from worse brain damage. We never would have tested them, so we wouldn't have caught it this early."

"I'm glad," she said. Then, seeing the look on his face, she emphasized, "Really, I truly am. If this was done to them, deliberately, then they're just as much victims as we are. They were used, and used by something callous enough to mutilate them like this, use them up, then just toss them away like. . .like empty toothpaste tubes." She stopped, surprised at the level of anger she felt. "They're not the bad guys," she said. "The real bad guys are the ones who did this to them, and that's what we're going to find out."

***

Thirteen

It was early afternoon before Justina and Imani arrived. When they entered the waiting room, Imani rushed at once to the sisters, and fell into Sister Magdalena's arms with a sob. Meanwhile, Justina just stood in the doorway, shaking. She had always, both by natural inclination and by self-discipline, been extremely self-contained, and now she was full of so many emotions, so powerful, that she didn't know what to do with them: fear and fury, grief for Sister Ella and a cold desire to see her murderer punished, guilt and confusion and a stew of emotions she couldn't even parse out. She felt a thick lump in her throat, as if something was trying to push its way up and out of her mouth, but whether it would come out as a scream or a battle cry or a sob, or all three, she was completely unable to tell. She was sure that if she just let go of everything that was in her, she would collapse into some sort of storm of hysteria, which would be shameful at best and potentially lethal for everyone in her vicinity at worst. So she just stood there, pulled in too many directions to do anything with them at all.

Sister Rebecca saw that her goddaughter was stranded. She got up and went to her, then, reaching up, pulled her down into a hard hug. Justina, uncharacteristically, clutched her tight, until Rebecca gasped "You're squishing me." Justina let go at once, embarrassed, as she always was by any show of weakness, but the hug had broken her paralysis; for the moment, her whirlwind of emotions condensed down into grief, and she fell into a chair, crying in gulping sobs, as she had not done almost since she was a baby.

In a few minutes, she recovered herself. Then, the others explained to her and Imani what seemed to have happened with the men who attacked the commandery: how something not yet identified had gotten to them, apparently twisting their perceptions and motives so severely that it caused major, potentially fatal, bleeding inside their brains.

"I should go and see them," said Justina.

Everyone looked up, surprised.

"I should go and see if I can tell. . .what it was that did it. Maybe it left a mark, or a sign of what it was."

No one had thought of that before, and as soon as she could get permission from the sheriff, she left the waiting room to go and see the suspects. Imani remembered what Justina had said in the car, and it occurred to her to worry that Justina might have more than just looking at them in mind; however, she knew Justina's keen sense of justice. She knew that Justina would never hurt an innocent person out of pure revenge, and would never lie to cover up the intention to do so, so she said nothing about it to the sisters.

*

The sisters were not alone in the waiting room. Several hours before, a young man with dark hair had taken a seat by himself , and since then had been fiddling vaguely with magazines from the end tables, just as Rebecca had been doing earlier. None of them paid any particular attention to him, or to his tense restlessness and watchfulness; he was in a hospital waiting room. Tension and vigilance were to be expected. Nothing seemed out of the ordinary. They did not notice immediately that, when Justina entered the room, he suddenly froze, then tapped furiously at his phone, and after that he stopped even pretending to pay attention to the magazines. When Justina returned from her visit to the suspects, they were all too focused on her words to notice that the man was listening just as intently.

*

When Justina returned to the waiting room, she looked shaken. "Did you see what it was?" Imani asked her, leaning forward.

There was a long silence, as Justina sat and tried to think how to phrase what she had seen. "I saw something inside each of their heads, curled up tight, like some sort of. . .embryo, or. . .more like a parasite. All settled in, like it had torn a hole in their minds and made some sort of nest for itself in there." She swallowed, feeling again the same mix of horrified anger and skin-creeping revulsion she had felt when she first saw it. "It was aware of me. It looked right at me. It had solid black eyes, like tar."

***

Counterpoint Five

Text Conversation

October 29

Group

Today 10:48 AM

In position.
Waiting room St. Luke's Hospital. Two of the sisters are here

Mr Lucky

Keep eyes on

Sheriff just arrived. Talking to sis R.
The attackers were delusional. Prob manipulated

Scary Bitch

??

Their brains were screwed around with
They thought they were attacking bad guys. KKK etc

Mr Lucky

All the same?

All different. KKK, drug cartels, etc

Today 12:05 PM

Sheriff is back
Another attacker is in the hospital now. Brain bleed
Looks like he passed out in custody.
They brought him in an ambulance

Viking Dad

Related to the delusions?

Sounds like
Sis R is going to talk to the dr

Mr Lucky

Can you listen in?

Not without being rly suspicious

Today 1:28 PM

Two more sisters just got here

Scary Bitch

The nephil?

No, others
No nephil yet

Today 1:37 PM

Dr just came back
MRI results
The sisters are leaving again to talk to him. FML

Mr Lucky

Did they do an MRI on a different attacker too?

Hard to tell. Looks like

Today 2:13 PM

NEPHIL JUST ARRIVED
Holy shit she's tall
The other girl is with her. Seems okay
She just stood there, no reaction at all
*the nephil
Now she remembered to cry and carry on

She left to go see the attackers
Shit she's going to kill them!

Viking Dad

Stay on task. The police will have to stop her

Scary Bitch

Describe her!

Today 2:20 PM
Ran back there. She didn't kill them. Not sure why

Scary Bitch
We need to know what she looks like!

Fkn tall. Like 7 ft
Black hair with white stripes, wavy, pretty short
Metal looking skin. Gold eyes

Kinda hot

Mr Lucky
WTF dude

Just sayin

Today 2:23 PM
She's back
Talking about something she saw

Do nephils have some kind of special sight?
She said she saw some kind of black eyed parasite in their heads
Viking Dad
Yeah, that'd be her!
Scary Bitch
Fkn A!

Today 3:02 PM
She's restless. Pacing around

She told sis R that she wanted to go see the commandery

Yeah that's not suspicious at all

Scary Bitch

Is she going now????

Not yet
I'll tell you.
GET AS MANY PEOPLE THERE AS YOU CAN!
We won't get a better chance to take her out clean

Mr Lucky

Tell us the second she leaves

Today 3:09 PM
Shit, the little girl is going with her!

Viking Dad

Has she left???

Yes, she just left!

But the little black girl went with her
Shit shit shit she has a hostage

Mr Lucky

Nothing you can do. Get to the commandery

On my way

***

Fourteen

Sister Rebecca first began to pay real attention to the young man in the waiting room when he, for no reason she could see, dashed out a couple of minutes after Justina, when she went to see the suspects. A couple of minutes more, and he dashed back in and resumed his chair. Not enough time to talk to a doctor, or see a patient; enough time to buy a snack from a vending machine, except that he didn't have one when he got back. Moreover, she began to notice that he was not just generally tense or vigilant; he was *watching*, in between bursts of rapid-fire texting on his phone. In particular, whenever she was in the room, he was watching Justina.

Rebecca supposed it was possible that he was simply thrown off by Justina's admittedly very unusual, and not a little intimidating, appearance. He hadn't done anything the least bit aggressive or threatening to any of them, so she saw no reason to approach him about it. But she did not forget.

Justina was restless. She could not sit still; she paced the room, she tried and failed to read a magazine, she tried and failed to occupy herself with looking at the blandly pretty framed watercolor prints on the walls, she picked at a leftover sandwich from the lunch Sister Magdalena had brought from the hospital cafeteria, she paced some more. Imani watched her with concern. Finally, she told the sisters that she was going to see what was left of the commandery.

Even Justina wasn't entirely clear on why she wanted to do this. Closure, the desire to try to apprehend the reality of it, even the mere compulsion to get *out* of the waiting room and *doing* something: all these probably played a part in it. She simply needed to see what had happened for herself, with her own eyes, and that was all there was to it.

Before she left, Sister Rebecca lowered her voice and said, "Be watchful. There's something going on here that we don't understand yet, and that man—" she indicated him with a small movement of her head— "has been watching us all morning, and especially watching you. I don't know what will happen when you leave here, or if anything will happen, but be on guard."

"I will."

"Stay in touch."

"Definitely."

Rebecca nodded, and swallowed a powerful sense of foreboding, of something about to happen. "The Lord bless you and keep you; the Lord make his face shine on you and be gracious to you; the Lord turn his face toward you and give you peace."

Justina looked nonplussed for a moment at the solemnity of the parting blessing. Then she said "Thank you", a little awkwardly, and left.

"I have to go with her," said Imani almost at once. "She needs me to go with her. It's not good for her to be alone." And she raced after Justina, catching up to her before she could leave. They drove toward the ruins of the commandery together.

*

When they arrived, for several long moments neither of them said anything. They sat in the car, staring at the ruins of the only real home either of them had ever had, watching the wind stir its cold cinders, motionless and wordless.

Imani started to open her car door, but Justina stopped her with a hand on her shoulder. "There's someone here."

Imani looked around, and saw only the desolation of the ruins on one side and the bleak stubble of the harvested cottonfield on the other. "Where?"

"I can't see them, but I can see that there are people here praying."

Imani relaxed. "That does make sense," she said. "The Order means a lot to a lot of people around here. I think it would actually have been weird if there *weren't* people here praying." Again, she made to get out of the car. Again, Justina stopped her, but without taking her eyes off the scene outside.

"So why are they hiding?"

Imani had no answer for that.

"Besides," said Justina, "those are not the prayers of people praying for peace, or comfort, or healing, or even bloody justice. I grew up with warriors, we both did, and I *know* what the prayers of someone about to go into battle look like. They look like that."

Again, as she had done so many times before, Imani wished that words existed to allow Justina to describe what she actually saw when she saw people's prayers. But no such words did exist; even the colors were things with no possible name. Calling them colors was, in itself, a stretch and a distortion. But she knew that Justina saw them (though probably the sense of sight wasn't really involved at all, at least in the usual way), and that, though frustrating, had to be enough.

"They could be sisters," offered Imani, "keeping watch in case of another. . ." she trailed off. What would be the point of that? The commandery-house was destroyed, Sister Ella was dead, what more was there here to protect? Besides, they would realize who she and Justina were. They would see that they were driving an Order car. They wouldn't just keep hiding. They would come out, talk to them.

"Uh oh," said Justina. "They've stopped praying now. Whatever it was they were preparing for, they're about to do it now."

"Is it *us?*" gasped Imani. "Were they waiting for us? Is it more people with. . .those black-eyed things in their heads?"

"I don't think so," said Justina, still scanning the ruins for movement. "I'm pretty sure I could tell. The manipulation would show."

Without warning, the windshield in front of Justina rippled and bulged in rings as the bulletproofing, modified onto all Order cars, caught a large-caliber bullet only inches from her nose. Both girls jumped, and Imani gave a startled yelp. A split instant later, they heard the shot from behind one of the refectory's remaining walls. Justina had to cross her eyes to focus on the bullet; the shot had been perfect, and might well have killed her. It would absolutely have killed anyone who wasn't a nephil.

It took only a heartbeat for the other people concealed in the ruins to realize that the first shot had failed. Guns opened up on every side, more bullets embedded themselves in the ballistic glass, the steel and Kevlar and ballistic nylon in the car's body caught still more, and they could both feel the impacts as ricochets hammered against the undercarriage. Justina slammed the car into reverse, whipped it around, and floored the accelerator, heading back the way they had come. Bullets continued to pepper the trunk and rear window until they were out of range.

As they turned to make their escape, Imani saw the faces of several of the shooters, who had stood up or broken cover to get better shots. She was quite sure that what she saw there was not rage or hate, but wide-eyed fear. They were afraid. And judging by the placement of nearly all the bullets, they were afraid of Justina.

*

"It was me," Justina said in a dazed voice, as they drove back to the hospital. "They were waiting for me. Why me?"

"They have to have been freelancers," said Imani. "They must have thought. . .they must have decided that you. . ." *That you were an evil nephil who needed to be killed.* She couldn't bring herself to say the words.

"I've never been a secret! I've broken bread with freelancers who came to the commandery, more than once! Why do they suddenly think—" She stopped, as all at once she understood. The car wobbled a little as her hands shook on the wheel. "They think I did it. They think I was the one who mutilated those men, who made them attack the Order! They think it was my fault!"

They reached the hospital parking lot. Instead of going inside, Justina sat still in the car, mind racing. "They won't stop," she said softly, and knew it was true. "I got away this time, but they'll keep trying until they get me. That's what any good slayer of evil things would do. It's what the Order would do. It's what *I* would do."

Imani said nothing. She was still processing what had happened, and what the people at the commandery evidently thought had happened. She was also shaking violently, as the adrenaline of being shot at ebbed away.

"Anywhere I go, I'll bring a target with me." Justina looked at Imani, her golden eyes more bleak and hollow than the burned ruins of their home. She was afraid, and Justina was never afraid.

"There's no way they would—"

"Come on. You've read Angelina di Genoa just like I have; you know what scale of nightmare is represented by a dark nephil on the loose. Even if freelancers don't know everything about it, they have to know that. They would do whatever it took." And Imani knew she was right.

"I can't put the sisters in danger. I have to run."

***

Interlude Seven

Excerpt from the Record Kept by the Sisters at St. Margaret's, About
Justina

Sister Magdalena. November 2.

I can't describe how I'm feeling right now. So I'm not even going to try. I'm going to write what happened and have done with it.

Last night, eight men under the influence of some creature we haven't identified yet attacked the commandery-house, and burned it to the ground. They injured Sisters Deborah, Alana, Aisha, and Katie, along with Father David. They killed Sister Ella. Shot her in the head. I know it wasn't their fault. The creature made them do it, and caused them serious brain damage in the process. But still there's something in me that wants to see them suffer for what they did. Wants to see them thrown into the deepest hole in the deepest dungeon where they'll never see the light of day again.

Bless me, Father, for I have sinned.

There was a man in the waiting room at the hospital. None of us paid very much attention to him. He was agitated, but in a hospital waiting room who isn't? But we noticed him. And it turns out that he must have been spying on us, or more particularly spying on Justina, because all the time she was there he was texting like mad to somebody, and when she and Imani went out to see what was left of the commandery, he followed after them. And when they arrived, a group of freelancers were waiting there to kill Justina. He has to have tipped them off. When they (Justina and Imani, I mean) got back to the hospital we all saw the car. Thank goodness for the bulletproofing and reinforcements, because the thing was shot to kingdom come.

Justina said they were gunning for her, and yes, most of the bullets were clearly aimed at the driver's side of the car. She said they believed she had been responsible for the attack that killed Sister Ella. We thought she must be right, because why else would the freelancers suddenly decide she needed to be killed?

She asked Sister Rebecca to switch cars with her, since the shot-up one wasn't really fit to drive. She said she had to go on the run, because if she tried to take shelter with the Order, she would just put us all in the crosshairs, and obviously the freelancers wouldn't be giving up.

I wasn't always a sister of the Order. I know as many swear words and blasphemies as the next person. I'm not going to write any of them. But I can't help thinking them.

Bless me, Father, for I have sinned.

Because none of us could argue with Justina. She was absolutely right. She said that the Order wouldn't give up, if they really believed there was a threat on the scale of a dark nephil, and it's true, we wouldn't. We'd hunt it down to the ends of the earth. We wouldn't shoot up a car with an innocent bystander (Imani) inside it, at least I really hope we wouldn't, but still, we'd hunt it to the ends of the earth all the same. And if they would disregard Imani's safety to get to Justina, would they also attack a commandery of the Order if they thought it was necessary? Probably. Would Justina's presence put us in danger? None of us were dishonest enough to try to deny it.

And what can Justina say to convince them? Nothing, she told us. And she's right about that, too. She's *half demon*. Anyone would expect her to have the same deceptive cunning as her father; if they didn't know her, the way we do, they couldn't believe a word she said. They couldn't reasonably be expected to.

Except I don't really care about *reasonable* right now. I don't think I want to be reasonable any more. I don't want to be merciful. I want to go after them, guns blazing, and show them who they're really dealing with, and what the Order is really capable of.

Bless me, Father, for I have sinned.

So Justina transferred all of her things over into Rebecca's car, and off she went. We didn't ask where. I don't think she knew, and even if she did, it's better if she doesn't tell us.

Our little is on the run, and none of us, least of all the little herself, have any illusions about how likely that is to end well.

I wanted to stop her from going, to tell her that everything would be okay, that everything would blow over and no one would hurt her and that we could all keep her safe. We all did. But we couldn't. We would have been lying. So instead, we had to bless her, and then watch her go, and know that there was nothing else we could do to save her.

Imani followed. We could not stop her, not without physically restraining her (which no one was willing to do), and they both left together.

We lost our sister already. Now we've lost our daughters, and we have no idea when we'll see them again.

Lord God, watch over Justina and Imani. Be their shield and bulwark. Guard them, before and behind. Bring them safely home to us.

***

Fifteen

Whenever she got into a car, the first thing Justina did was lock the doors after her. Imani knew this. Therefore, the younger girl jumped into the car beside her sister the instant the door was unlocked, and before Justina could do anything, she had settled herself into her seat, an obstinate look on her face. "I'm going with you," she said.

"You most certainly are not!"

Imani felt the force of the compulsion, the command, that always accompanied Justina's words when she said something like that. It was not a sharp strike, like a physical impact, but a measureless swell of overwhelming strength, like the smooth, immense power of a rising tide that lifted and drove everything before it. However, Imani had grown up with Justina, and was prepared. She had never known, not for sure, whether Justina always really meant to influence people the way she did; but whether she meant it or not, Imani had long since had to learn to work around it.

When she was younger, still training, Imani had often been instructed by Justina, and she had learned that something happened when Justina gave instructions. How to deliver a strike or block one, how to hold a sword, how to squeeze the trigger of a gun rather than jerking it, how to aim an arrow or a crossbow bolt: whenever Justina told Imani how to do these things, more happened than a simple transfer of information. It was as if Justina's knowledge, habits, instincts, and muscle memory soaked directly into Imani's skin and eyes and limbs, teaching not only her mind, but her body directly.

Imani had learned, over time, how to handle this transfer of skill, to ride on top of it instead of simply being swept along. She had developed the ability to actively open herself to Justina's orders. But in the process, she had grown to understand how the power actually worked, and, when necessary, how to allow it to roll over and through her and away, leaving her untouched. And on this day, outside St. Luke's, she let the compelling pull of Justina's command pass by her without doing anything at all.

"Get out of the car, Imani. You can't come with me."

Imani reached up to her shoulder, pulled down the seatbelt, and buckled it defiantly.

"This is too dangerous! You can't come!"

"Rule one!" Imani retorted. "Never go off alone."

Justina made a growling sound. "This is not the same thing," she said, exasperated. "This isn't a mission, where we stop the evil thing and then go home. I don't know where I'm going to go, or what I'm going to do, or where it will end, or *if* it will end—"

"That's right," said Imani, "and if you think I'm going to let you face that all by yourself, you've got another thing coming."

Justina sat quietly for a moment. Then, in a softer voice, she said, "At the commandery, most of those bullets would have hit me. But some of them would have hit you, and I'm a lot more durable than you are."

Imani said nothing, and did not move. *Irrelevant.*

"What would I have done?" Justina burst out. "What will I do, if they hurt you trying to get to me? Imani, *what will I do?*"

And Imani understood a second layer of meaning in the question. She knew that Justina was wondering, not only how she would cope, but what she, a nephil, a creature of immense power and potential danger, *might* do. Or might become.

"If they. . .if you. . ." Justina could not bring herself to put the possibility in words. "They are afraid of a nephil," she went on. "A dark nephil, that's powerful and homicidal and out of control. And if. . .anything happens to you, that's exactly what they might get. I think they probably would."

Imani looked straight at her. "They wouldn't."

"What?" Justina blinked at her, surprised.

"They wouldn't get a dark nephil, because you are never going to *be* a dark nephil." Imani pointed at her emphatically. "Whatever happens, you have a choice, and you've chosen the light over and over, ever since you were old enough to choose anything at all. There's nothing they can do to make you do anything else."

"But, I—"

"Also," Imani went on, "even if you did, there's nothing to stop you from turning back to the light again. Which you would."

"How do you know? I might not. And how can I do that to the world?" She swallowed. "How can I do that to the sisters, who would have to stop me?"

"I know because I know you. You are my sister. I know you aren't going to turn evil because you've fought against it all your life, and you aren't going to stop now." She crossed her arms with an air of finality.

"I still say it's too dangerous for you," said Justina, but she said it without much conviction. She knew when she was beaten.

Imani knew it too. "Now you're just wasting time. I'm not letting you out of my sight, and that's all there is to it."

Justina turned the key and started the car. "Where do you want to go?" she asked. "Shall we flip a coin?"

Imani took a quarter out of the car's console. "Heads we go north, tails we go south. Ready?" She flicked the quarter up with her thumb, caught it, and turned it over onto the back of her empty hand. Both of them leaned in to see what the coin had decreed.

"South it is," said Justina.

And with that, the two of them left the parking lot, left Derrick, and headed out into whatever might come next.

***

Part Three

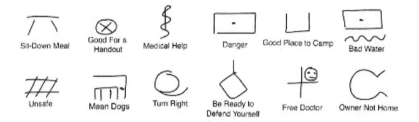

American Hobo Symbols, 20th Century.

"When any Knight-Sisters, in the defense of the innocent or for the destruction of evil, have been sent forth from the commandery, as we anticipate will often happen, they may be unable to hear the divine office. They should therefore say, in place of Matins, thirteen Paternosters; seven should be said for the Hours, and nine for Vespers. Or they may also, if they so choose and with their Commander's permission, substitute the singing of two hymns or Psalms, the reading or recitation of one Scripture or other holy text, and the saying of one Paternoster in place of Matins and Vespers. The singing of a Psalm and the saying of one Paternoster may similarly be substituted for the Hours, to give God his due. . ."

". . .After Sext Mass and the midday meal, the Sisters should busy themselves in repairing armor or equipment, sharpening weapons, practicing their skills at arms one with another (that 'as iron sharpens iron, one may sharpen the other'), or learning more of their evil foes, that they may not be found unready. . ."

"When Knight-Sisters are traveling, they may have occasion to stay in an inn, or in a private home not affiliated with the Order of the Holy Lance. Off consecrated ground, they may thus be vulnerable to attack by the evil creatures which are their foes. They must therefore take measures to consecrate these places, insofar as is permissible to secular dwellings, to protect themselves and their hosts. . ."

The Rule of the Holy Lance, approved 1139. Tr. from Latin c. 1387. Tr. to English 1798. Revised English tr. 1936.

Sixteen

By mid-November, Imani and Justina had begun to hope that after two weeks of meandering through West Texas, they might have thrown off their pursuers, as there had been no sign of them, and no attacks, since they left Derrick. Imani had even begun to access the Order databases again; since they were out in the field anyway, she reasoned, they might as well look into any attacks or incursions that happened near them.

Justina had been sleeping badly, often waking with a start from unsettling dreams she could never quite remember. The continued failure of their pursuers to appear had begun to wear on her nerves, and she knew very well that her vigilance was suffering for it, but there was no other option; after a while, though she knew it was a risk, she developed the habit of walking around and around any area she and Imani found themselves occupying, her long legs covering easy miles of streets and alleyways, looking for anything unusual.

"I've been thinking," said Imani one day. The two of them had just finished a series of sparring exercises (modified to accommodate the close quarters in the motel room), and, having changed out of her sweaty clothes, Imani was sitting on her bed doing stretches.

Justina looked up inquiringly. She was bundling their clothes together to take to the laundromat later; they had only taken a few changes of clothes with them to Mockingbird, and the rest had gone up in smoke with the commandery, so they had to go to the laundromat quite often.

"About everything that happened." Imani clasped her hands behind her and extended her arms back, stretching her chest muscles. Then she released the stretch and shook out her arms. "First, there were three pings in less than forty-eight hours: the ghost in Big Spring, the whatever-it-was in Amarillo, and the boo hag in Mockingbird. I checked the annals, all the way back to the founding of St. Margaret's in 1891—"

"I know when St. Margaret's was founded, Imani."

"Don't be rude. Anyway, ever since then, there have *never* been three cases all at once requiring sisters out in the field, until now. In the Commandery of Houston, sure, sometimes the Commandery of Lubbock even, but not the Commandery of West Texas."

Justina said nothing.

"Also," Imani went on, using one hand to bend the other back at the wrist, stretching her forearm, "look at the timing. Sister Ella *and* Sister Aisha were both injured and out of action at exactly that time." She switched hands, stretching the other forearm. "I don't think the commandery has ever been so vulnerable to attack before, in its whole history, with two sisters injured and six in the field."

"And it was exactly then that the—the brain parasite things, or whatever, compelled those men to attack it," said Justina, thoughtfully.

"And," Imani emphasized, "evidently the men were being prepared *before* everything started to happen. That's what the doctor said, right? That once they did all the scans, each man showed the exact same injuries, but some older than others? Going back weeks."

"That's what Sister Rebecca said last time we checked in." Justina tapped her fingers against her chin, considering.

"So this whole thing was one plan, all coordinated," Imani concluded. "The attacks to get as many sisters as possible out of the way, the eight men being manipulated beforehand, all of it."

After a pause, Justina said, "You know, I hadn't really thought about it before, but. . .why did the freelancers all come to the conclusion that the attack on the commandery was my fault? I mean, where did that idea come from in the first place? I wasn't even there, and they never said I was. Surely it wouldn't be the most obvious first assumption to make."

Imani nodded slowly. "Someone told them. We know they have a communication network, not organized, but widespread. Someone introduced that idea, as a known fact, and just let it filter through the grapevine, and here we are."

The two girls sat in silence for a minute.

"Turning a haunting violent, stirring up both a boo hag and the creature in Amarillo, directly manipulating eight men's brains via those black-eyed things, and planting false intel in the freelancers' network. . ." Imani looked scared. "What could *do* that? What could possibly coordinate and control all those different things? And why? They didn't take down the Order; they didn't really even take down St. Margaret's, since we're going to rebuild. All that effort. . . What was the point?"

"All we can know is what it actually did accomplish," said Justina slowly. "It drove us, you and me, out from the Order. Whether that was the goal of the whole thing or not, that's what actually happened."

And they sat in silence again, thinking about what that might mean.

*

On November seventeenth, Justina and Imani checked into a small motel in Odessa. They took the usual precautions enjoined by the *Rule*: anointing oil on all three sides of the door, salt around the foundation and on the windowsills, and a blessing read for the building. Imani stretched out on her bed and opened her e-reader. Justina, who had never found it so easy to lose herself in a book, went out for a walk.

The next morning, and every morning they stayed there, the two girls went to the nearest church that celebrated daily Mass. It was not the same as attending the Hours at the commandery, but the familiarity of it was enough to ease their loneliness and home-sickness, even if only a little. And Justina sang, with all her heart and all her voice, just as she had done at home, and it engulfed and lifted up every person in the building, and even some outside in the street, like an ocean swell.

It was not a large church, and those who attended weekday Mass and confession were very few in number. But it was enough. They told friends and family, they posted to Facebook and Twitter, and word of two young women in what looked like some sort of religious habit, one of them extraordinarily tall and with a beautiful voice, a voice that seemed full of some kind of supernatural or spiritual power, seeped out and began to spread. Before many days had passed, the information reached people who were looking for it, and who knew something of what it meant.

Less than a week after they arrived, Imani and Justina went outside one morning and found a graffito marked on their door with white shoe polish. It was a glyph neither of them had seen before, and did not look like the usual graffiti tag:

Still, it was only graffiti. The motel was hardly in the most prosperous middle-class part of the town; no barons of Odessa's oil industry were likely to live nearby. It was not the first piece of graffiti they had seen in the neighborhood. They told the front desk of the motel about it. The receptionist assured them that she would pass the word along to the manager, and it would soon be scrubbed off.

Cosmetic maintenance is not always the first priority in small motels. Three days later, the glyph was still there, and Imani was tired of looking at it; she decided to buy a pot scrubber from the nearby Walmart and clean it off herself. She slipped out after they returned from Mass, leaving Justina assembling their lunchtime sandwiches.

She returned half an hour later, the plastic Walmart bag containing the pot scrubber in her hand, and to her surprise found the door of the motel room ajar.

*

Tobias Hockley was what the Order of the Holy Lance called a freelancer. He himself had heard other terms: hunter or monster-hunter, most commonly, but some people half-jokingly referred to themselves as slayers (*a la* Buffy), which he supposed was legitimate enough. Anyway, he was one who had taken it as his duty to track and hunt down evil creatures.

He had been doing it for several years, since he was only fifteen years old, and he was good at it; if he hadn't been he would probably have been killed already. The fact was, no hunter could really expect to need much in the way of a long-term retirement plan; all but the very best, if they didn't give it up for a civilian life, would probably be killed by a vampire or a werewolf or a skinwalker or something before very many years passed. And this was even more the case with hunters who, like Tobias, did not often work closely with teams. He had a network of contacts, of course, and a number of friends he had often worked with, but for the last two years he had been fundamentally a solitary hunter. It was for that reason that Tobias, though he knew others were on the way and would arrive shortly, reached the marked doorway ("dangerous", said the symbol; "thinking creature, not a beast, demonic") alone.

His first intention was to stake the motel out, and wait for backup to arrive. He had been doing this, in fact: sitting quietly in his car and watching. But then he saw the other girl, the innocent dupe or hostage or familiar or whatever she was, leave the room with the nephil still inside.

Not catching the innocent girl in the crossfire, if it could possibly be avoided, had been a serious consideration for him and his compatriots when they discussed attempting a nephil-hunt. If she got in the way, they had to make every reasonable effort not to allow her to become collateral damage. However, they also acknowledged that this might be impossible, especially if the nephil was holding her by deception or misguided loyalty or naïveté rather than by brute force. The needs of the many had to outweigh the needs of the few. Though they all hoped it would not come to it, they were prepared to sacrifice the innocent girl's safety in order to stop the nephil.

Now she had left of her own accord. The fact that she was able to leave unaccompanied suggested that she was with the nephil willingly, and would therefore be nearly impossible to keep safe; however, if she was not present, there wouldn't be a problem.

Tobias watched her leave, walking briskly. She seemed tiny, though actually her height was perfectly average; it was only her proximity to the unnaturally tall nephil that gave the impression. She wore white pants, a white shirt with a red cross embroidered on it, white canvas boots, and a white jacket, and her hair formed a neatly-trimmed halo of close, dark curls around her head. He watched until she turned a corner and was out of sight, then hurried up to the door of the motel room. No time to waste: he didn't know when she would be back. It was an opportunity he might not get again, and he could not afford to wait for backup.

Tobias had taken all the precautions he could think of, and collected all the equipment or weapons he thought might help. Now, he snatched it all up from the car seat beside him: several small bottles of holy water, which he stuffed into the pockets of his cargo pants; a new box of Morton salt, which went into the larger pocket on his thigh; a finely-honed silver-plated Bowie knife (very much like Imani and Justina's ghost knives, though he didn't know it), which he sheathed on his belt; and his semiautomatic, loaded with silver-plated bullets, which he kept in his hand. He had memorized a rite of exorcism in Latin, and he wore both a crucifix and a St. Christopher medallion around his neck. He felt that he was as protected against a half-demon nephil as he could be.

He had a key card. He had gotten it when he first arrived the day before, to have it ready when everyone else arrived; the tired receptionist at the front desk had not been difficult to convince that he had perfectly legitimate reasons for needing access to the room, once he spun her a plausible yarn about being a friend of their Order. He took the card out.

Now that it came to the moment, though, he hesitated, standing on the cracked concrete before the motel room door with the key card in his hand. No one was completely sure of what nephils were actually capable of doing, or how powerful they really were, since there hadn't been one in living memory; all the sources he had seen did, however, agree that they were terrifyingly dangerous. He had a suspicion that attempting to engage one all by himself was, quite simply, an unusual method of suicide and nothing else, silver and holy water and crucifixes notwithstanding.

But she was alone, and not out in public, which would eliminate the problem of endangering innocent bystanders. She was on her own home turf (or what passed as home turf), and should therefore be as off-guard as she would ever be. The opportunity was the best any of them were likely to get, and Tobias could not pass it up.

Despite his resolution, his hand was shaking so much that he had to pass the key card over the worn, scuffed scanner three times before the green light came on and the door unlocked. He had secretly almost hoped that the receptionist had gotten it wrong, or changed her mind, and the card would not work, but it did. With his gun ready in his hand, he softly twisted the handle and pushed the door open.

It was the best possible circumstance, better than anything he would have dared to hope for. The nephil was there, and she was lying—not sitting or reclining, but lying down flat on her back—on one of the beds (diagonally, as it was the only way the bed could accommodate her long frame). She had one arm flung over her eyes.

But before he had time to really see her, certainly long before he had time to pull the trigger, she knew he was there, and that he was an intruder. How, he couldn't say, but even as he aimed, she whipped up and off the bed and onto her feet, with a terrible molten speed too fast even for his eyes to follow.

He pulled the trigger once.

It was an excellent shot; much better than he really had any right to expect. It hit the nephil near the center of her upper chest, surely very close to her heart, and the bullet went straight through, hitting the wall behind her in a spray of pure white blood. But she did not go down, and he fired again, wildly, in a kind of panic, driving more bullets into the wall and sending dust and chunks of wallboard flying. But none of these shots came close, except for one, and that one she actually dodged; he saw her move so fast she blurred, and that bullet, too, harmed nothing but paint and drywall.

"Enough," she said softly.

Tobias froze. A slow, sickening weakness spread over him, like the weakness of long hunger or high fever or many days without sleep. His arm drooped until his gun hung limp against his leg, and it was all he could do to hold onto it at all with his strengthless fingers. His shoulders sagged, and he swayed, hardly able to keep on his feet. He thought he still had at least two shots in the gun, but he couldn't even pull its trigger, much less lift it or take aim. The knife in his belt, the salt and holy water in his pockets; all were as inaccessible as if they were a mile away.

His next impulse was to turn and bolt. The still-open door was so close that if he reached back his hand—if he *could* reach back his hand—he could touch it. But at the first hint of tensing the muscles in his legs, they simply gave out, and he knew without a doubt that if he so much as lifted one foot to take a single step, he would fall.

The nephil stood and looked at him, her bottomless golden eyes narrowed, white blood trickling unheeded down her chest, with an expression of cold, almost emotionless contempt on her face. He felt a shifting and movement in the air, one that had nothing to do with the doorway at his back, and had a sense of something vast gathering itself, like the ocean pulling back from a beach just before a tsunami.

Only one option left. Tobias was not at all sure, now, that the rite of exorcism would work: the silver on the bullet, or even the bullet itself, for that matter, had clearly not bothered her particularly, and if the presence of the holy water or crucifix or St. Christopher medallion were having any effect, he certainly couldn't see it. But it was his last line of defense. He was gasping as if he'd just finishing running a race, spots swam in his vision, and he could not say the words as quickly or with as much authority as he would have liked, but he began to recite the Latin anyway.

"*Exorcizo te, omnis spiritus immunde—*"

The expression on her face changed from contempt to anger; her lip curled back from white, predatory teeth, and when she came toward him in long strides, he thought he could feel the air around him getting hotter as she approached.

"*—in nomine Dei Patris omnipotentis,*" he continued desperately, "*et in nomine Jesu Christi Filii ejus—*"

"How dare you," she said, her voice still soft, but nevertheless the fury in it was a physical blow that made him stagger. She stood almost in arm's reach now, towering over him, fire in her eyes and in her voice.

"*—Domini et Judicis. . .nostri. . .*" the words petered out. He tried to remember the next phrase, but could not; even the idea of the rite of exorcism itself took on an elusive vagueness, and he almost forgot what he had been doing in the first place. He had no more thoughts of remaining on his feet, and would later conclude that only the nephil's will was keeping him upright, or even conscious.

"That is a sacred rite," she murmured, "to be performed in faith, in God's name and with due reverence and full understanding. It is not some magic spell anyone can casually recite whenever they wish, and expect to make something happen." Her next words were brimming with fierce scorn: "Not even if you do try to recite it in Latin."

"You have come here, attempting to use the trappings of holiness to enable you to commit deliberate murder against one who has never offered you the least harm. How dare you. You have invoked Our Lord as Judge today, and you will indeed be judged for what you have done."

*

When Imani saw the door standing a few inches open, she knew something had happened. She put down the Walmart bag and pot scrubber on the cement doorstep. She had gone out wearing her gun in a shoulder holster, hidden underneath her coat; now she drew it, and, after half a second's hesitation, took off the safety.

From inside, she heard a voice. It was Justina's voice, without a doubt: Imani could recognize her sister's voice anywhere. But she had never heard it like this. It was full of a kind of icy anger, an exaltation of righteous wrath, and it had none of the harshness of a furious human voice; in fact, it sounded less human than Imani had ever heard it, a voice that she could hardly believe came from a mortal mouth and throat, something more like the sound of trumpets or the pounding of drums.

"You have invoked Our Lord as Judge today, and you will indeed be judged for what you have done."

Imani rushed inside, with some unformed idea of helping somehow, and nearly crashed headlong into a man standing almost in the doorway. Standing, but she had a sense that he wasn't standing under his own power; every line of his body drooped, and he was clearly wobbling on his feet as though on the point of collapse. A big, worn-looking gun lay on the colorless motel carpet beside his right foot, having apparently dropped from his hand.

Justina stood in front of him. Imani saw the bullet hole in her shirt, and the stickiness of her white blood around it, but it didn't seem to matter. She stood tall, showing every inch of her seven feet, and seemed to fill the room even more than she usually (inevitably) did. Her face was locked in an expression of pure, crystalline anger, some nameless species of anger that had been refined and distilled down until it was barely even an emotion any more. Imani had the strong impression that it was not human anger at all, but was drawn from the half of Justina's heritage that was angel. Something unbearably hot and bright gleamed far back in Justina's eyes, and Imani thought that if she turned off all the lights, they might glow with their own light.

Justina's fixed attention on the man shifted, as she realized that Imani was there. The moment this happened, the man, apparently released from whatever paralysis was holding him, simply collapsed. Imani, darting forward, managed to catch and support enough of his weight to keep him from injuring himself when he hit the floor, and he just lay there, eyes open and staring, his body shaking all over, in some kind of shock or catatonia. She found his pulse and made sure he was breathing, then she looked up at Justina.

Justina still looked as utterly inhuman as Imani had ever seen her. The alien, emotionless fury did not leave her face, and Imani realized all at once that she had arrived not a minute too soon; just a bit later, and the intruder might have been dead. Might even have been reduced to a handful of ash, as efficiently as the boo hag had been.

It might still happen. Imani got up and took Justina by both arms, looking her in the eye, trying to ground her. "It's all right," she said. "Let it go. Just let it go, it's over, everything is okay—"

"Look at him," Justina said, her voice thrumming with power. A light bulb in the bathroom burned out with an abrupt *pop*, and a few sparks snapped from an electrical outlet nearby. "He brought symbols and substance of holiness: holy water, a crucifix, sacred rites. He brought them to use to commit a murder. It's sacrilegious."

"How do you know he brought—"

"I know." Justina's tone allowed no doubt, and later, when Imani bent down again to examine the man's pockets (young man, she realized; if he was older than Justina, it wasn't by much), she found the bottles of holy water as predicted.

"Also," Justina continued, "he tried to use the rite of exorcism against me. Tried to use a holy rite of deliverance as a weapon, to do harm, and he used it without understanding, as if it was a magic formula he could recite without faith and get what he wanted, like putting a dollar into a vending machine."

Imani thought she understood, at least partly. Some portion of an avenging angel's merciless judgement and scorching righteousness were mixed into Justina's heritage, along with her persistent difficulty in seeing shades of gray, or allowing for human failings. She saw holy things being used for unholy purposes, and saw nothing else.

"He was afraid of you," said Imani. "He thought you were evil. He thought he was doing the right thing."

"What does that matter?" Justina demanded.

"It *matters*," retorted Imani, beginning to raise her own voice, "because you are not an avenging angel. It is not your job to inflict punishment on the wicked!"

Justina stopped short at that. She blinked rapidly, as if trying to clear her vision of something that dazzled her eyes.

"We belong to God," said Imani. "We act as God's hands, and God's hands stretch out in forgiveness a thousand times before they strike anyone down in vengeance."

Justina dropped her eyes, and swallowed hard several times. The last of the consuming supernatural fire ebbed away from her. For a moment she just stood collecting herself, then, without warning, she bent and pulled Imani into a tight embrace. Imani sensed how shaken she was.

"Thank you," Justina said softly. "Thank you so much. For stopping me."

*

Tobias came to himself slowly. His first impression was one of vague discomfort, as if he had fallen asleep in a awkward position. He tried in an aimless way to move his arms and legs, but met with resistance; he supposed, confusedly, that he must have gotten himself tangled up in his bedding somehow. Or was he in a sleeping bag? He couldn't seem to remember. After a bit, it came to his attention that he was not lying in a bed after all; was not, in fact, even lying down, but sitting in a chair.

His arms and legs still met with resistance when he tried to move, though he was able to turn his head from side to side. After verifying that he could do so, however, he stopped moving his head; it seemed to be spinning enough without that. Dizzy, so dizzy. . .he wondered, in passing, if he might have a hangover. He had no memory of doing any heavy drinking in the recent past, and on the whole he felt it was unfair that he couldn't remember having as good a time as he evidently had had, judging by the magnitude of the hangover.

It occurred to him that if he opened his eyes, it might clear up some confusion. With due deliberation, and cautiously, anticipating (on the hangover hypothesis) the icepick sensation of light shining into sensitive eyes, he did so.

He was in a motel room. That was clear; by and large, they all looked alike. All at once, he recognized the nephil's motel room, and remembered at least something of what had happened. Furthermore, he was sitting in a motel chair: aluminum frame, ugly indestructible upholstery on the back, seat, and arms. The fabric felt scratchy under his forearms, where they lay on the armrests.

202 | JENNY PAXTON

He looked down at his arms, and understood why moving had presented a problem. He was tied into the chair; he saw that his arms had been secured with narrow cords, padded by thin motel washcloths, and the job had been done properly. He knew several ways of escaping after being tied up, but an examination by eye, and a few experimental tugs against the cords, assured him that none were likely to work here. He tried to move his legs, and concluded that his ankles had been secured to the chair legs in the same way, though he didn't dare bend his head down to see for sure. He shifted his weight back and forth a few times, and found discouragingly little wobble in the structure of the chair; nothing that gave him hope of possibly being able to break any part of it.

On the other hand, he began to fully realize that in spite of all his expectations, he wasn't dead. As far as he could tell, he wasn't even injured; no particular new pains came to his attention, apart from general stiffness, and the dizziness was already almost gone. Even the cords: padded with washcloths to protect his skin. *What the hell?*

Only then, belatedly, did he realize that he was not alone in the room. The nephil was not there, but the small girl was; she sat quietly in another chair, the cushier one with the matching foot-stool, reading something on a handheld e-reader. She looked up from it, saw that he was now properly awake and alert, and laid it aside carefully.

"Listen," he said, "you need to let me go. I don't know what you think is happening here, but I'm not the bad guy."

The girl raised her eyebrows. "You broke in, using a deceptively-acquired key card, and tried to murder Justina without provocation." She paused, then added pointedly, "How exactly are you defining 'bad guy'?"

He wasn't quite sure how to answer that. He tried a different angle. "Listen, the nephil is dangerous. She's not even human! You're a sister of the Order of the Holy Lance, you're a demon-hunter! How can you try to protect one?"

The girl's dark eyes narrowed. "She is not a demon."

"She's half demon. That's enough."

"She's half human," the girl retorted. "*That's* enough."

Tobias began to have the terrible feeling that this girl was too brainwashed, or too innocent, to be convinced. She wasn't going to let him go. The nephil must have known it, too, or why would she have left her alone to go wherever she had gone? He jerked against the cords on his wrists, tried to slide his hands free, but he had no more luck than before.

He thought of a possibility, and felt a flash of hope. From where his chair sat in the middle of the room, he could see the time in big red numbers on the bedside clock radio. It couldn't be long before the others arrived. There was a chance they might get here before the nephil did. If he couldn't convince the girl, and he was doubting more and more that he would be able to, he might be rescued that way.

How much time could he count on? "Where is. . .she?" he asked. He couldn't bring himself to use the nephil's human name.

The girl fixed her eyes on him. "She went to confession."

He almost laughed. "You—" *You believed that?* he almost asked, but stopped himself awkwardly.

"You realize she almost killed you."

Tobias was quite aware. He said nothing.

"She was about to. I think she would have. But that's something the Order doesn't ever do if we can help it; our job is to protect people. I think. . .I think she actually scared herself a little. So she went to confession."

He couldn't help trying again to get through to her. "You realize there's no way she actually went to confession! She's half demon! She's off doing something else, but whatever it is, there's no way it's that!"

The girl leaned forward with an exasperated look. "How would you know?" she demanded. "What do you know about Justina, or even nephilim in general? Not much, clearly, or you would have realized that holy water and reciting the words of a rite of exorcism wouldn't have any effect on her. They wouldn't even have hurt a dark nephil."

That stung. As a hunter of dangerous things, he put a premium on knowledge, on intel, on knowing exactly what he was facing and how best to fight it, and clearly she was right: he had obviously come to this fight completely uninformed and unprepared. "Can she even go into a church?" he demanded, cuttingly.

For a moment she just stared at him, as though he had asked something unfathomably stupid. Then: "She was raised in a convent!" the girl yelled. "You wonder if she can go onto consecrated ground? For the first dozen years of her life, she never set foot *off* consecrated ground! She was taken to Mass every single day, beginning the day she was born! She and I went to Mass together just a few hours ago!"

He played what he figured was probably his trump card, if he was going to convince her that the nephil was an enemy. From all that he could figure, this girl was raised by the Order, and loved it. "She was responsible for the attack on the commandery! Whatever she was like growing up, she's showing her true colors now."

For a moment the girl just sat, disgusted. "What in the world gives you that idea?" she asked finally. "You know very well that she was a couple hundred miles away when it happened."

Tobias couldn't answer that. The truthful answer would have been "Everyone knows it," but what then? She would have asked why everyone knew it, and he realized, for the first time, that he wasn't sure. It was just something everyone knew. He had no idea where the idea had come from originally. The realization staggered him a little.

The girl sighed. "You've kind of got us over a barrel here, you know."

He was surprised by that. "I do?"

"You do." She paused, then went on. "We know that you're expecting backup. You have to be. You don't know much about nephilim, but you know they're dangerous; too dangerous to tackle all on your own. So you must be expecting help. Besides, I've seen you look at the clock about fifteen times in the last few minutes."

Tobias glanced away from it again hastily.

"We can't let you pass on information to your friends. But we also can't kill you, obviously. But we can't let you go, and we can hardly take you along with us, because you'd probably try to give killing Justina another shot. You see the problem?"

He admitted that he did.

"So when Justina gets back, we'll have to make up our minds what to do, and quickly, before your backup gets here."

For a few minutes they sat in silence. Tobias worked methodically at trying to inch his hands out of the cords, but made no headway. The girl returned to her book. Then, after a bit, she seemed to have an idea.

"You know how I said you don't know anything about nephilim?" she said.

He didn't see much point in replying. Obviously he didn't know anything about nephilim, hadn't he proven that?

"I'm not trying to be a know-it-all, but would you want to? Learn about nephilim?"

Tobias looked up, surprised. He had heard talk about the Order of the Holy Lance's archives—how they had books and books full of records and lore no one else had—but he had never been sure how true any of the stories were. Besides, he had always had the idea that if the archives really were as good as all that, the Order wouldn't let just anyone see them. Actually, his mental image had always been of some sort of medieval castle library, lit with drippy candles, full of weathered leather-bound tomes chained to their shelves, concealed behind a secret door or a revolving fireplace or something in a commandery-house cellar. Certainly he had never imagined the sisters being so free with their information, especially to an enemy who was currently tied to a chair.

The girl held up her e-reader. "I'd recommend that you start with Aldred's *Life of Myrddin*. If you want. It's about the life of the first light nephil—the first good nephil—that we know for sure really existed."

He couldn't resist the opportunity to have a look at the famous Order of the Holy Lance archive (even if it was in the form of ebooks, which just seemed odd; where was their sense of Aesthetic?). Neither, more importantly, could he resist the opportunity offered by the fact that she was evidently willing to untie at least one of his hands, so that he could read. If his backup didn't arrive in time, this would likely be his best chance to escape on his own, and he couldn't waste it. And if he could escape with that e-reader, too, so much the better; who knew what goodies were on there? "I'd love to read it."

The girl picked up a big Bowie knife from the desk beside her; from the pale, mellow shine of the blade, Tobias knew it must be plated in pure silver. She used it to neatly cut the cord around his right wrist, and from the ease with which she did it, he knew the blade must be lethally sharp. He felt a moment's pity for her; she wouldn't survive long as a hunter of monsters, as trusting as she was. No wonder the nephil had duped her so completely. But his pity didn't stop him. He was ready, and the instant the cord parted he made a lunge for her knife hand.

She flicked her arm out of reach and stepped back, as quickly and deftly as a magician vanishing a coin. "How have you survived?" she demanded, exasperated. "From the second you agreed to look at the book, I knew what you were going to do. You telegraph everything you're planning the second you think it; it's like you have a thought bubble over your head. I hope you never play poker."

He flushed.

"So, do you want to read the book or not?"

That was a surprise; he had expected her to withdraw the offer. "I. . .sure. Yes, I'd like to read it."

She tossed the e-reader to him without leaving her chair. It landed in his lap, and he picked it up with his free hand. "You'll like it," she said, "even if you are just passing the time. It's about Merlin."

"Merlin?" he echoed, sure she was pulling his leg.

"The first reliably recorded light nephil: the powerful magician who was born to a human woman and what the people then called an incubus."

"But. . .Merlin is just. . ."

"He's not just a myth. The Order has good sources, and Aldred wrote about him within living memory of his life." She poked her finger toward the book. "Read."

He read.

***

". . .Abode they stille in the towr a grete while, til that she was delivered of a sone, as God wolde. And when he was born it hadde the engyne and the witt of a feende, after the kynde of hym that begate hym. But the devell wrought so folily that our Lorde toke it to His owne use. . . And therfore, oure Lorde wolde not lese that shulde be His. And ther the devell was disseyved of his purpos, that he hadde ordeyned that childe to have his art and witte. . . And oure Lorde, that alle thynges knoweth, [when He] sye the repentaunce of the moder and that it was not her will that was so befellen, He wolde have hym on His parte; nevertheles, He gaf hym fre choys to do what he wolde, for if he wolde he myght yelde God His parte, unto the feende his also.

Prose Merlin, c. fifteenth century. Middle English.

Seventeen

Imani did not take her eyes off the man tied to the chair; with one hand free, he was much more potentially dangerous than before. He continued to try to twist and tug his left wrist loose (subtly, he thought, but she saw), though he wasn't making any noticeable headway. But in her mind, it was worth the risk. If she could convince him, if she could even create reasonable doubt in his mind, it would be well worth the attempt, and he seemed to be reading the book with interest. He didn't look up often to see if she was watching; he had even stopped glancing at the clock every few seconds. Maybe he would believe some of it. It couldn't hurt that he apparently had a degree of respect for the Order's historical sources; his eagerness to get his hands on the e-reader had been obvious.

Soon, Imani heard a car come to a halt outside, and purposeful steps striding up the sidewalk toward the door. The man in the chair heard, too; he looked up from the book, eyes wide, and began to pull frantically against the cords at his wrist and ankles, subtlety abandoned. He had been biding his time, hoping for an opportunity, but now he knew his time was up. He worked desperately with his free right hand at the knot securing his left wrist, but it was solid. He wrenched at the structure of the chair, but it only rattled a little.

Justina opened the door and stepped into the room, dipping her head under the lintel of the doorway. "I need to talk with you," she said to Imani. Then she turned her attention to the man in the chair, who was now nearly panicking. She could smell the fear oozing off his skin, slimily; it was so strong that she wondered if Imani could smell it too, even though she had always been told that humans couldn't smell fear the way she did. "Sleep," she told him, deliberately putting force and will behind it. He fought against it for a moment or two, blinking rapidly and shaking his head, but inevitably his head drooped and he slept.

It felt different than with the boo hag; less sure, more awkward, like trying to hold on to an object that had been oiled. She couldn't grip too hard, or she would lose her control; it took more delicacy and deliberation. But every time she tried, her control was better, and she was more able to feel precisely what she had done. This time, it had the effect of simple anesthesia, which would wear off shortly. It was enough to give herself and Imani privacy for a conversation.

Imani was still looking in surprise at the man, when Justina said "Catch," and tossed her empty duffle to her. Imani caught it. "We're leaving?"

"We're leaving." Justina unzipped her own duffle and spread the opening with her hands. "I've already checked us out of the motel."

Imani, who had been removing her clothes from a drawer of the battered chipboard dresser and piling them on the bed, paused and looked up. "What did you tell them about the damage? The bullet holes in the wall?"

Justina clapped her spare pair of boots together, shaking loose a puff of dust, and pushed them down to the bottom of her duffle. She did not look at Imani as she said, "Nothing."

"But—"

"What could I say?" Justina piled clothes into her duffle. "I wasn't going to lie to them, but how could I tell them the whole truth? It would be a mess, and cause delay and all kinds of problems."

Imani couldn't deny it. That would be a can of worms neither of them wanted to open.

"We've cleaned off the blood, so at least it doesn't look like a crime scene. Not a murder kind of crime scene, anyway. And since it's my blood, it never really looked like blood in the first place." She double-checked the safety on her gun, rolled it inside its holster and belt, and added the bundle to the duffle. "I think it's best to just let them come up with their own story. Maybe they'll assume someone came in after we'd left, and shot at the wall for some reason."

Imani fetched her small toiletry bag from the bathroom, and stowed it. She didn't like this; it felt like avoiding dishonesty by a pure technicality. But what was the alternative? Bring the police into it? That would be a mess. Hand the man in the chair (what was his name? They didn't even know his name) over to the police? For what? Attempted murder? That would hardly be fair, even though it was accurate; he had honestly thought he was putting down a dangerous monster, not murdering a person. And what if it went to court? What if she and Justina had to be witnesses? No, there was no way they could do that. They'd bring every freelancer in the state down on Odessa, and who knew what the collateral damage would be? She didn't like it, but she liked all the alternatives she could think of even less.

"So what do we do next? With him?" she asked. She pointed a rolled-up pair of socks at their prisoner. "Do we take him with us?"

Justina paused, staring vaguely into her duffle. Then she looked up and said, "Yes. He's coming with us. And, I've thought hard about this. . ." She paused again, framing her words. "We're going to let him go, free and clear. But not until he's worked a mission with us. You've been keeping an eye out; surely we can find one somewhere."

Imani, about to tuck her e-reader into her bag, dropped it. "You want him to work a mission with us? *Why?* And how can we trust him?"

Justina zipped her duffle closed. "We can't," she said. "But like I said, I've thought this through."

The window-mounted heater rattled to life. They both ignored it.

"Really," said Justina, "this whole 'on the run' thing, there's only three ways it ends. Either they kill me, or I kill them, or you and I, somehow, come up with a way to convince them that I'm not a bad guy."

Imani was shaken; she had never thought of it so bluntly before. "It won't be easy," she said. "I tried to convince this guy—" she pointed to him with the e-reader this time— "and he would not hear it."

"I know." Justina moved around the room, opening drawers, looking for anything that had been forgotten. "That's exactly why I think we need to do this. Would he believe what we *say?* Probably not. I don't think any of them would. The only thing he might believe is what we *do.* How we behave. Fighting evil things together, on the same side, protecting people together. . .there's not much that builds bonds more than that. There's no way it can not. And if we can convince him, then maybe he can help us convince the others."

Imani zipped her duffle closed too. It was dangerous, she knew that, though it probably wouldn't be dangerous to her, as the man still evidently thought she was an innocent bystander being duped by the evil nephil. And maybe it would be less dangerous for Justina than it seemed, since a bullet through the chest hadn't really hurt her; the wound was closed now, and looked as if it had happened weeks ago. By tomorrow there would barely be a scar. And she knew Justina was right. The only real way out of this was to convince the freelancers to leave off their hunt, and probably the only real way to do that was not with words, but with actions, actions eyewitnessed over a period of time by one of their own.

"Want me to get the bags?" Imani offered. "I'll put them in the trunk. You can bring our friend."

*

Tobias woke up facedown on the floor, with the faint mustiness of threadbare motel carpet in his nose. The first thing he noticed was that his wrists were now tied securely behind his back; the second thing he noticed was that his legs were free. Blindly, he tried to scramble to his feet, but without his arms to steady him he overbalanced and toppled over again. He fell flat on his back this time, jarring both shoulders painfully, and came to rest looking straight up at the nephil girl standing over him.

All at once, his fear boiled over into anger. "Stop playing with me!" he yelled at her. "Just do it already!"

"I'm not going to kill you," she said. "We're going to let you go shortly. But not here. Get up and come with me."

It did not even occur to him to believe her. How stupid did she think he was? Of course, he admitted to himself, going by the really pathetic level of credulity exhibited by the people around her, she probably thought he was very stupid indeed. Play along, he decided. Just go with it, play for time, and watch for any possible opportunity to escape.

He noticed the door, propped closed but not properly shut; he thought he could open it with his foot. He knew the motel's office was only a few doors down, just a short sprint. He shot a glance at the clock. Almost 5:00. There would likely be people around, in the parking lot or on the sidewalks. If he could just dash outside, maybe to the office, maybe to a group of people nearby, and shout or yell for help, make a scene. . . Surely the nephil wouldn't want to draw attention by kidnapping him in front of a lot of witnesses.

More carefully this time, he got his feet under him and managed to stand up, slumping his shoulders and trying generally to look appropriately subdued.

He had a clear shot at the door. All at once, never mind the awkwardness of his bound hands, he bolted for it.

At least, he tried to bolt for it. He had barely gone two steps when the nephil's long fingers closed on a handful of his shirt, and brought him up short with a jerk that rattled his teeth. He struggled for a moment against her grip, but all it accomplished was one thread snapping in a seam somewhere around his left shoulder. His shirt, a triple-stitched work shirt which he had chosen specifically for durability, otherwise didn't give an inch.

She spun him around, and he was only prevented from falling again by the nephil taking two big fistfuls of his shirt front in her hands. Then she lifted him up, right off his feet, with an awful effortless strength, until they were almost nose to nose. Sick fear coiled cold in his gut, the kind of fear that was nauseating, paralyzing.

"We are showing you mercy," she said, her voice quiet and controlled. The amber of her eyes seemed to prism back into bottomlessness. "Because it's the right thing to do, not because it is my personal inclination." She let him digest that, then continued. "You hunted us down. You tried to murder me in cold blood." She began to raise her voice at little as she said, "Do you have any idea how much Imani has lost in the last few weeks? How many times she's cried in her sleep? You would have had her come back here and find my dead body. It would have destroyed her."

All this time, she continued to hold Tobias up by his shirt, without any apparent particular effort. The seams under his arms and the fabric across his back strained, but the triple stitching and the tough cotton twill held solid.

"Don't mistake me. I could obliterate you for your misuse of holy things. I could kill you by inches for what you would have done to Imani."

He gulped. He had not the least doubt that she was entirely capable of doing exactly what she said.

"You hunted me down because you believed that I was not human. That I was a threat." She pulled his face a little closer to her own, and said softly, "Don't tempt me to prove you right."

Then, abruptly, she dropped him back down heavily onto his feet. He staggered and nearly fell, more from adrenaline than a lack of balance this time. The nephil propelled him out the door.

*

Justina had been right when she said that Imani had been keeping an eye on the Order databases, looking for a mission. In fact, when they set out from Odessa that day, she already had one in mind: rumors of wolves, along with several mauling deaths, in the town of Shinnery to the north. "From the descriptions, it seems likely that it's a werepack," Imani said, and Justina agreed.

They drove north, with their unwelcome guest tied up in the back seat. Justina had thrown a blanket over him to hide him from view.

Imani told him her name, and asked for his. Tobias, lying across the seats and squirming awkwardly (it had never occurred to him before how impossible it would be to find a comfortable position with his hands tied behind his back), thought fast. He had heard stories about certain creatures being able to gain power over a person by knowing his name; he didn't know if it applied to nephils, but he figured that it was better to be safe. On a whim, he chose his favorite gunslinger name from the *Dark Tower* series.

"I'm Jake," came his voice from under the blanket.

He was lying. Justina could tell, even without seeing his face. She thought about calling him on it, then decided it didn't really matter. They drove on in silence.

*

It was well after dark by the time they reached Shinnery and found a motel. The nephil girl and the younger girl—Imani, her name was Imani—left him in the car under the blanket while they checked in, then, after carefully making sure that no one was watching, they hauled him inside.

"I can put you under again," the nephil said, "and you won't wake up until morning. Or we can tie you into a chair again. Up to you."

Tobias weighed the two options. On the one hand, spending the night tied to a chair would be no joke; his back and butt ached at the mere thought. On the other hand, the idea of being completely insensible, of being involuntarily forced into sleep, and staying that way all night long. . .he couldn't think of any allies or friends he would want to be so completely vulnerable with, much less a nephil who was, not only an enemy, but also only half-human. Tied to a chair, at least he would know what was happening. He chose that option, aching body notwithstanding.

To his surprise, before they did anything, they had a kind of mini church service. He stood against the wall, awkwardly, enjoying having free use of his limbs for a few minutes. Imani told him that this was what sisters of the Order of the Holy Lance did when they were away from a commandery, and therefore not able to attend vespers. They read a passage out of the Bible (he noticed carefully that the book did not burn the nephil's hands or anything, and the words themselves did not seem to cause her any discomfort), said the Lord's Prayer in unison, and then they sang two hymns.

He had no explanation for his reaction to the hymns. He didn't know either of them—he had never gone to church, not since leaving home, and though he knew some monster-hunters who were very religious, he never had been, had never seen any attraction in it. But at the sound of the two voices raised in harmony, especially the nephil's soaring voice, more like a musical instrument than a voice, he was more moved than he had ever been by any piece of music he could remember. Exaltation warred with a bone-deep longing, a desperate loneliness for something he couldn't even name or identify, and the choking lump in his throat could have been triumphant laughter or tears of desolation, or both at once. Blinded by warring emotions he couldn't sort out, trying only to ride out feelings far too powerful to control, he realized only when the singing ended that his face was wet with tears. No one stopped him when he moved toward the bathroom; he grabbed a wad of toilet paper and smeared his tears away with it. He still had no idea what had triggered that kind of reaction.

The two girls began to get ready to sleep. At first, he anticipated the awkward, intrusive situation of seeing them in their nightclothes, but both of them apparently intended to sleep fully dressed, and they also left a lamp on. At the time, he supposed this was vigilance against anything he might do; he did not learn until later that sisters of the Order always slept fully clothed and with a light burning.

The nephil girl, Justina, tied him to his chair. He tried to clench his fists and position his wrists in such a way as to allow him to slip the cords later, but she evidently knew that trick, and tied him securely. Securely, but, as before, with flimsy motel washcloths padding his skin.

The small girl, Imani, curled into a ball in her bed, leaving only a rim of dark curls showing above the blankets, and apparently went to sleep without delay. Tobias waited hopefully for the nephil to do likewise; if he had all night to work at the cords, he might be able to get loose and make his escape. But she did not. She didn't even open her bed. She sat on top of the bedspread, hands folded, apparently deep in silent thought.

After a long time, he couldn't contain his curiosity. "What are you doing?" he asked her.

She looked up. "Reciting the Book of Psalms," she said casually, as if it wasn't any particular feat. "I memorized it when I was nine."

He just blinked at her, unable to come up with any response that wasn't idiotic.

"You should try to sleep," she told him. "I can go a long time without it, and I've been having bad dreams lately anyway. If you stay up all night, you'll be the sleep-deprived one tomorrow, not me."

He did try, but he was too uncomfortable, too full of conflicting thoughts, and too distrustful on top of it. A long time passed. The window-mounted heater rattled on and off a couple of times, puffing hot air into the room. Isolated cars drove past, and once a pair of headlights illuminated the drawn curtains from outside for a second or two. For a while there were muffled, indecipherable noises of TV through the motel's thin wall, but eventually they fell silent.

"I was reading one of your books," he said. The sound of his own voice was almost a shock. "The one about Merlin, by Al—Alfred or something."

The nephil looked up again. "Aldred," she said, smiling a little. "Good choice."

"I didn't get too far. But at the beginning. . ." He wondered if he would make her angry with his question, but decided it was worth the risk. She hadn't killed him before, and apparently didn't plan to, at least not right away. "It said that Merlin's mother died when he was born. That the mothers of nephils always die."

"Nephilim," she corrected.

"What?"

"The plural of 'nephil' is 'nephilim'. It's Hebrew."

"Oh," he said awkwardly.

"You want to know what happened to my mother," she said. "If I killed her."

He said nothing. That was exactly what he wanted to know, but he didn't want to admit it out loud.

The nephil girl paused, apparently deciding exactly what she would say. "No," she said finally. "She died in the delivery room on the night I was born, true, but I didn't kill her. The demon who raped her did that."

Tobias thought that was a pure technicality, but didn't dare say so.

"I was born in the dark, yes. But how is that different from any other child of Adam? Every human being is born in the dark. Every human being is born through blood, and suffering, and, historically anyway, often death. How many mothers dead in childbirth do you think are in your own ancestry? And how many rapists?"

He had never really thought about that before.

"The world is full of darkness. It's sick and festering with it. You have no idea how much darkness I see, how much I could see in this very room right now if I looked. How much I can see on you.

"We fight against the dark, myself and Imani and the Order, and apparently you do too. We're on the same side. I don't love it that we are, but we are, and I hope that if you work this one mission with us, and then we let you go unharmed, maybe our actions can convince you of it."

He had no idea how to respond to that, so he said nothing. He tried again to sleep, but he had too much to think about, and was still very reluctant to be unconscious in a room with a nephil. He couldn't help believing in what she said, couldn't help finding it plausible and believable, but wouldn't it be the same with a demon? Yes. Deceit and persuasion and half-truths were their stock-in-trade. He forced himself to remember that.

"Don't be afraid," the nephil said quietly, and, all at once, he wasn't. Finally, he slept.

***

Interlude Eight

From: imani.westtex@ohl.org
To: magdalena.westtex@ohl.org
Re: Adventures in Shinnery
November 28, at 9:17pm

Sister Magdalena,

I'm sorry I haven't written in a while. A lot has happened.

We're both safe, first of all, so don't worry about that.

We were in Odessa, and a freelancer tracked us down. Apparently he was part of a group, but nobody else had arrived yet, so he was by himself. I had gone out to run an errand, and apparently he thought it was the perfect opportunity to take Justina out without catching me in the crossfire. He'd talked the motel people into giving him a key card, so after I was out of the way, in he went.

He's safe too. Just so you know. But he almost wasn't. He attacked Justina with silver bullets, holy water, salt, and a crucifix, and he also tried to use the rite of exorcism against her. None of it worked at all, obviously. And when he did that, using holy things without faith, and to try to commit a murder, she sort of lost it, and I think would've killed him without even touching him. Her inner "avenging angel" just came out, I guess. Anyway, I got back just then and I was able to sort of snap her out of it. It's so hard for her to see shades of gray, and extenuating circumstances! I'm afraid that if this goes on much longer, and if there's some kind of confrontation, she may end up killing someone out of a desire for justice, and I don't want her to have to live with that! I don't think she will, but I'm afraid she might. She's afraid of that too. I'll take any advice you have for me.

We're taking steps that we hope will help stop all this from actually coming to a confrontation, anyway. We captured the one freelancer, the one who attacked us, and we also found a mission on the network in Shinnery. You may have seen it, too. That's where we are now. It's a werepack, maybe six or seven werewolves in all, and they've killed four people in the last month. The three of us, Justina and the freelancer and I, are working the mission together. When we're through, we're going to let him go. Justina thought that since none of the freelancers will believe anything she says, hopefully she can convince them with what she does. If she can show them that we're good guys, not just tell them, they might believe it. It seems like a good idea to me, and I hope it works so we can come home soon.

We split up today. I know we aren't supposed to do that, but I wasn't alone, and Justina thought it would be easier for me to get through to him without her around. Anyway, I went with the freelancer (he says his name is Jake, but I don't think it really is. He's an awful liar. We're just going with it though) to learn everything we can about the victims and how they were killed. Justina went out to where three of the victims were found, just on the outskirts of town, to see if she could detect any clues. She did, too: she found a trail they'd left, and said she should be able to follow it to their den. I don't really understand what the trail was like, because she said it wasn't exactly a scent trail or a trail of footprints. The local police or animal control or game wardens, or whoever would normally handle something like this, could have followed it if it was just that. But anyway, there was a trail, and she can follow it. So tomorrow we go on the hunt.

I'm still deciding how I feel about the freelancer. He doesn't do things the way we would. He lied his way into the morgue with fake credentials, and I didn't feel right about that. I guess it makes sense, though, since people like him don't have real credentials to get them into places like that the way we do. If they're going to fight evil things, how else can they do it? They have to lie. But I didn't like it. Anyway, he did that. Also, he talked about the were-wolves with hate, like he despised them and thought they were irredeemable monsters. They may be acting maliciously, but we don't really know that for sure yet, and anyway werewolves are still people. They're not like boo hags and things like that, that are just monsters. Only it's not a distinction he seems to make, and that concerns me.

But this guy is so damaged. I could tell after only spending one day with him. He didn't tell me his story, and I doubt if he will, but it's got to be a painful one. There's all sorts of pain and anger and suspicion and I don't even know what all in in him. He's reckless, but I don't think from overconfidence; I think it's mainly because he doesn't care very much what happens to him. I'm sad for him, and I wish that whatever things happened to him hadn't happened.

Anyway, I'll keep you updated. Tell everyone that I love them. Has the rebuilding started on St. Margaret's yet? Is Sister Deborah doing okay? We're thinking of you all the time.

--Imani

Sister Imani
Squire-Novice of the Order of the Holy Lance
Commandery of West Texas
Commandery-House of Saint Margaret of Antioch

From: magdalena.westtex@ohl.org
To: imani.westtex@ohl.org

Re: Re: Adventures in Shinnery
November 29, at 7:48am

Imani,

I'm so glad to hear from you! Everyone says hello, and Sister Deborah is doing great. Dr. Michaels says there shouldn't be any lasting ill effects, though she is having to have a program of physical therapy, which is very frustrating for her. (The sisters and I gave her a cane as a joke. She didn't think it was very funny! But how could we resist? We should get her one of those canes with a sword inside.) As for St. Margaret's, the crews are still removing the last of the rubble, but construction on the new buildings should start next week.

St. Ursula's, here in Lubbock, has made us very welcome, and they've been wonderful in general. But the truth is, it's just not the same. It's not home. It's so FLAT here! And EVERYTHING is about Texas Tech. I can't even tell you. I never fully realized the magnitude of it before! Tech is playing in a bowl game in football in a couple of weeks, and the whole town has gone completely Tech crazy! And you should have seen the town when Tech played U.T., their arch nemesis. It was quite something. It's crazy, and kind of weird, but here's the funny thing: you just can't help but enjoy that sense of community. On game days, EVERYONE is a Red Raider. Once I went to a grocery store on the opposite side of town on a game day, and they were actually playing the radio broadcast of the game over the P.A. Tech made a touchdown, and the whole store broke into a cheer. It was nuts, but oddly fun.

Anyhow, I'm sorry that you and Justina were attacked. But I'm glad no harm came to anyone! And I think that how the two of you are handling it is the best possible option. It's unorthodox, but in some ways that might work in your favor, by contrasting with the more pragmatic and ruthless treatment he probably expects.

"For then you will be seen as innocent, faultless, and pure children of God, even though you live in the midst of a brutal and perverse culture. For you will appear among them as shining lights in the universe."

We give people the benefit of the doubt. That's why we parley with vampires and werewolves and such: to give them every possible chance, and by expecting the best, we make it easier for them to live up to that expectation. Giving this freelancer the benefit of the doubt, and expecting the best of him, may be a little risky, but I think you're absolutely right to do it. Always be kind first.

You say it's a werepack that you're dealing with? That's weird. It's nearly always lone werewolves that go off the rails and start attacking people, as you know. Watch out; there may be something else going on. Maybe someone is even manipulating the werewolves, using them as a weapon, whether from inside the pack or outside it. There's a case of that described in one of the books (*One Soul in Two Bodies*, if I remember correctly; it might also be *A Study of American Weremorphs*).

We all love you and miss you. Be very, very careful! This sounds like it could be dangerous. All the sisters are praying for your safety and success.

Pax Vobiscum,
Sister Magdalena

Sister Magdalena
Knight-Sister of the Order of the Holy Lance
Commandery of West Texas
Commandery-House of Saint Margaret of Antioch

***

Eighteen

The second night in Shinnery, Justina conferred quietly with Imani. She trusted her sister's judgement, and her insight about people, and she and Jake had been working together for most of the day. Imani would have some sort of feel for his trustworthiness.

"What do you think?" Justina asked. "Can he be trusted to behave if we leave him free?"

Imani considered seriously, as she had been doing all day. "Yes, I think so," she said finally. "I don't think he'd just drop a mission in the middle, not if people were at risk, and even if he did, I think he'd just try to get away, not try to hurt us."

Justina concurred. She was able to see flickers of light and dark, temptations and principles, in people if she looked closely, and Imani's assessment agreed with her own. As Sister Magdalena would advise, when they read her email the next morning, they gave Jake the benefit of the doubt, letting him sleep without being restrained in any way. And though Justina allowed herself only a light, semi-conscious sleep, to keep watch just in case, their trust proved not to be misplaced. Jake, as they had hoped, lived up to their expectations of the best.

*

The books (which Imani had consulted, and had indeed found to contain the story Sister Magdalena had emailed her about that morning) all agreed that werewolves, like ordinary wolves, were least active around midday. The three of them therefore had several hours to kill before heading out.

Ordinarily, Tobias would have taken the opportunity to sleep in. But that was not an option in this case, because Imani and Justina were awake before sunrise for Matins. And though he tried covering his ears with a pillow, it could not keep out the bracing power of Justina's voice when she sang. After that there was no chance of going back to sleep.

After breakfast (toast, coffee, and cold cereal from the motel's complimentary spread), Tobias asked if he could finish reading *Life of Myrddin*. Imani pulled up the book on her e-reader, and handed it over.

It wasn't a long book. After he finished it, he moved on (at Imani's suggestion) to *An Account of the Birth and Childhood of Benjamin of Piedmont, or, The Light-Nephil*. Despite its unwieldy title, it was interesting; it described the early life of the most recent light-nephil known, before Justina. He had been born in the early 1600s in a village in the Piedmont, a region in the extreme northwest of modern Italy, and raised in a nearby monastery called the Abbey of Sant-Gilles; like Justina, the orphaned child, Benjamin, had been taken in by the monks before his demon-father could reach him, and he had been baptized within hours of his birth.

The book was apparently annotated by one of the Sisters of the Holy Lance, judging by the title page, but it had not been written by them. It had been written by the Benedictine monks who raised the nephil boy, Benjamin, and their perspective and priorities in writing the account were very different from what they would have been if he had been raised by a military order instead. Tobias didn't imagine the book had told the Sisters of the Holy Lance as much as they would have wanted to know about Justina. Still, it was interesting, and the monks clearly had no doubts as to whether their charge was inherently evil; they believed he was no such thing, and treated him as such. It was something to think about.

Tobias, too curious to pass it up, paused in his reading to check out what other books were on the e-reader, apart from the ones he'd seen. He wasn't sure whether he was allowed to do this, so he didn't ask, on the time-honored assumption that it was better to ask forgiveness than permission. The books, it turned out, were organized into "shelves" by topic: Black Unicorns (what in the world were those, he wondered), ghosts and hauntings, vampires, were-creatures, fae-creatures, energy predators, general compendiums of creatures, and more.

As he looked at all the books, he felt a sense of unreality, as if, on opening any one of them, he would find nothing but an empty file, or only a paragraph or two, like prop books that looked good but were really full of empty pages. He was used to making do with mere scraps and drips of information, gleaned from here and there, learned fourth- or fifth-hand from others, the kind of information you could only take and try and hope to God it was accurate. Of course, he had acquired a decent amount of tried-and-true intel of his own: this took the form of a tattered three-ring binder stuffed with photocopied pages, scribbled notes on notebook paper, clippings (well-annotated in the margins) from newspapers, photographs, lists of book titles, rough drawings and diagrams. . . Every monster-hunter he knew had a notebook like that. And of course he had contacts, people whose intel he trusted to be reliable. But still, it was nothing compared to this motherlode, this embarrassment of riches. He had known the Order of the Holy Lance had an archive. He had thought he was prepared for the scope of it. He had been wrong. When faced with the reality, he was floored anyway.

He came across the shelf called "nephilim", and stopped cold. He glanced up, checked to see if the coast was clear. It was: Justina had gone out for a long walk ("she does that all the time, she hates having to wait," Imani had said), and Imani was entirely absorbed in cleaning and oiling her disassembled gun. He looked down again, and opened the shelf. A list of titles appeared on the screen.

It was a short list, which wasn't very surprising, given how rare nephilim had apparently always been. Two he knew already: *Life of Myrddin,* and the one he hadn't finished yet about Benjamin of Piedmont. Two more were just general compendiums, which had probably been linked in every shelf; they wouldn't have more than a paragraph or two on the subject. The fifth book, however, was not one Imani had offered him to read: *A Brief Treatise on the Nephilim,* by Sister Angelina di Genoa. Had she been a Sister of the Holy Lance, he wondered?

He tapped the title and opened the book. The title page confirmed his assumption: Sister Angelina had been the *Comandante* of Genoa in the 1600s. He flicked through to the first page and started to read.

"Few supernatural creatures are so much Feared as the *Nephilim,*" it said. He felt a chill; this was the book they hadn't given him, that they didn't want him to read. This was the one that told the truth about nephilim. He read on. ". . .as if to demonstrate its foul Nature, the first act of a Nephil is the killing of its own Mother, for no woman has ever survived long—"

There was no way they wanted him to read this. It let the cat well and truly out of the bag. He glanced up again. Imani was still polishing her gun and paying no attention.

He read further. "Nevertheless," the book added, "it is possible to Break the demon Father's hold upon his Progeny. This may be accomplished by Baptizing the Nephil, and the Nephil may so choose to serve God rather than Satan. Few Nephilim have thus chosen, but those who have are named Light Nephilim, for they have chosen to walk in the Light and forsaken the Dark of their heritage."

Tobias stopped at that. The other books he had half-expected to be sugar-coating the reality of what a nephil was. One was written about a legendary figure (surely legendary even then, not long after his life), and the other was written by monks about a boy they had raised, and that they loved. This one was different. He flipped back to the preface, and learned that Sister Angelina di Genoa, and many other sisters, had not *raised* a nephil; they had fought and ultimately killed one, an evil one. The fact that she had nevertheless said that a light-nephil was possible (though it wasn't what she had faced). . .it made it harder to disbelieve.

What would Imani do if I asked to read this book, he wondered. Would she let me? He wasn't sure.

Better to take the opportunity that's presented, he decided, and read on. Better to ask forgiveness than permission.

*

By the time Justina returned from her walk, Imani had laid aside her gun (cleaned, oiled, reassembled, and loaded with silver-plated rounds) and was delicately stropping the edge of her ghost knife. Tobias, meanwhile, had read several chapters of *A Brief Treatise*, and when Justina opened the door he gave such a start that he almost dropped the e-reader. He had thought, after she knocked him cold without even touching him and then lifted him straight off his feet effortlessly, that he had at least some idea how scary she was. After reading what Angelina di Genoa had to say about the nephil she encountered, he realized that he hadn't known the half of it.

With shaking hands, he closed that book as quickly as he could, and reopened the one about Benjamin of Piedmont.

Justina was carrying a scuffed gray plastic footlocker under her arm. Tobias recognized it immediately, and wondered if it was empty; but when she lowered it to the floor, it hit the carpet with a solid *thud* that told him everything must still be in it. He knew how much that footlocker weighed, and couldn't imagine picking it up and carrying it like that, under one arm, as if it weighed nothing at all.

"Ready to suit up?" Justina asked Imani.

Imani put down her strop and slid her knife into its sheath. "All set."

"Good. Be right back." Justina turned to go back outside, presumably to the car.

Tobias bent over the footlocker. He opened the latches and threw back the lid, and everything was there: all his gear, all his weapons, even the tattered binder with his research in it. Even, he saw, his gun and silver knife, which he had been carrying the other day in his ill-advised (he was just now realizing how ill-advised, thanks to Angelina di Genoa) first attack on Justina. "How did you get this?" he asked.

"Ah," said Justina, pausing in the doorway. "I picked the lock of your car. Sorry."

Tobias stuttered a little, torn between relief at having his belongings back and outrage at the violation of his car.

He took out his shotgun and a torn box of silver deer slugs, and loaded it, putting the rest of the box of slugs in his pocket. He did not notice Imani eyeing these preparations with some concern. Next, he took out his knife, along with a silvered machete in a plastic sheath, and a small whetstone, and sat down at the desk.

Imani retrieved the e-reader, and he was very glad he had switched back to the first book before she looked at it.

"You have no idea how amazing it is," he said, sharpening his knife, hoping to distract her from looking at the "recently read" list on the e-reader, "to have all this information at your fingertips like this. You must be able to identify anything you come across."

She hesitated. "Not everything."

He tested the edge of the knife on the hair of his forearm, then continued sharpening, taking care not to grind through the silver plating to the steel.

"We still don't know exactly what it was that made those men attack the commandery," she went on. "It was something with solid black eyes, and it was clearly some sort of incorporeal construct, but apart from that—"

He stopped short. "Black eyes?"

"Yes, solid black eyes." She gave him a sharp look. "Do you know something?"

He turned the whetstone over in his hands a few times, then put down the knife and moved on to the machete. "There's an urban legend I've heard," he said. "A pretty new one, it doesn't seem to have been around that long. It started a few years ago, like in the '90s? 1995? Somewhere in there."

Imani leaned forward, her face intent.

"The first sighting that I know of happened in Abilene, outside a movie theater or something at nighttime. A man was in his car, and he was approached by two kids with solid black eyes. No pupil or iris, he said, just shiny solid black. And they tried to get him to let them into the car. They said they couldn't get in unless he gave them permission. He panicked and hit the gas, and when he looked back they were gone. Stories have been floating around about the black-eyed kids ever since."

Imani leaned back again. "Wow. That. . .might be it. It might be that this is some sort of construct that gets into your head, changes your perceptions, your memories, your motives, who knows. But it can't do it unless you give it permission, even if under false pretenses."

Tobias, continuing to sharpen his machete, said, "Is there a creature that can create constructs like that? I don't know of any."

"I'm not sure." Imani paused. "Maybe a demon could."

Justina pushed the door back open, this time with a black plastic bin under each arm. She put one down on each bed, and Imani opened hers and began to lay out pieces of body armor. Tobias stared at it: Kevlar and carbon fiber and high-tech ceramic, the best armor money could buy probably, and judging by the scratches and scuffs and dings, it had seen its share of action. Custom-fitted, too, it looked like. The mismatched, slightly ill-fitting secondhand motorcycle leathers he dragged out, in a very crumpled state, from the bottom of his footlocker suddenly seemed pitifully inadequate. The plastic zipper pull on the jacket had broken off last year, and he had replaced it with a big safety pin; the legs of the pants had been too long, so he had had to hem them up shorter by hand, to keep from being tripped. The hems were a little uneven. He put the leathers on anyway, feeling a bit like the homeless relative at a millionaire's Thanksgiving dinner. He put his hand in his pocket, and found an ancient cough drop, well furred with lint.

When the two girls had finished donning their body armor, and had checked each other over to make sure everything was secure, Justina turned to Tobias and said, "Would you go into the bathroom for a minute, please?"

"I. . .the. . .what?"

"We're potentially about to go into battle," she explained patiently. "Imani and I are going to say our confessions to each other, and it has to be done in private."

Feeling that things couldn't get much more surreal, Tobias did as he was told. He went into the bathroom, closed the door, and sat on the closed lid of the toilet. After a bit, Imani told him he could come out again.

"I'll be happy to hear your confession too, if you want," she offered, and he could tell that she genuinely meant it.

He avoided her eyes. "I don't really go in for the whole church scene," he said, feeling intensely awkward.

"Well," she said, "do you realize that God exists?"

He said nothing. The truth was, he had seen far too many supernatural and extranatural things to seriously doubt that God was out there in some form, but most of the time his policy had been to try to fly under the heavenly radar, and avoid attracting God's attention.

"And are you on God's side? That's really all you need to start out with."

He tried to dissipate some of the awkwardness he felt with a laugh, but it sounded forced and awful and only made it worse. "I'm a mess," he said. "I'm pretty sure I wouldn't get past the membership committee."

This weak attempt at wit seemed to distress Imani, more than he had expected. "That's not the way it works," she said. "You don't have to meet any requirements. They've already been met, God met them himself on our behalf, because we couldn't. It's about being on God's side, trying to live toward God, rather than away."

Tobias had never heard it put in those kinds of terms before. It was a strikingly different angle on the whole thing than any he had encountered before, and it would need pondering.

"I'll think about it," he promised. "I will. But I'm not. . .ready right now."

Imani accepted that, and didn't push. She said no more about it as the three of them got into the car and drove out of Shinnery into the scrubland outside of town, to take on a werepack.

*

"Can I ask you a question?" Imani said to Jake, as they drove out of Shinnery. The attacks had happened closer to town, but Justina had followed the werewolves' backtrail far enough to have an idea of where they had probably laired.

Cautiously, probably anticipating further awkward talk about God, he said, "Sure, I guess."

"How did you get into this gig? I mean, being a freelancer, or monster-hunter or whatever you call it."

For a moment, she thought he was going to refuse to answer. "It's not much of a story," he said at last. "I mean, I wish it was. I wish I could say it was a badass family curse, or my whole family was killed by a basilisk or an old god or something. I've even told people that's what happened. Girls mostly. It just sounds a hell of a lot cooler. But the truth is, it was really boring and ordinary."

He stopped, and Imani let the silence be, hoping that he would feel compelled to fill it.

He did. "My life sucked when I was growing up," he said. "My parents—" He seemed to remember, abruptly, to censor himself, and broke off. "Anyway, I ran away from home when I was fifteen."

"And something found you," Imani guessed.

"Something found me. Like I said, I wish it was something rare and impressive, but it wasn't. Just a run-of-the-mill vampire."

Justina turned the car off the highway and onto a rutted dirt road, which meandered deeper into the ranch land, past dry draws choked with mesquite and desert willow, and clumps of yucca and prickly pear. She was listening, but didn't say anything. Soft words were Imani's strength, not hers, and she knew it.

"They go after people who are isolated and weak. People who won't be missed." He looked up and added hastily, "You know that already, obviously."

Imani nodded, smiling a little. "I do."

"Well, anyway, I couldn't fight it or hold it off. I mean, now I could, sure, because I know what I'm doing, but then I couldn't even wrap my head around the fact that it was a *vampire*. I think I maybe got one punch in." He had dropped his gaze again, and was rolling one of his shotgun shells vaguely between his fingers. "Then it was holding me down and just drinking and drinking until I passed out."

"And someone saved you?" Imani suggested.

He nodded, continuing to twirl the shell in his hands. "Actually two people, a husband and wife team. I woke up in a sleeping bag at their campsite."

"Were they the ones who taught you? I mean, taught you how to fight vampires and things?"

"Yeah. At first, they were just going to take me to the hospital after I woke up, but I asked them to teach me." He looked up again, an echo of remembered anger in his eyes, and clenched the shotgun shell in his fist. "I never wanted to be helpless like that again, just easy prey. I wanted to be able to fight back."

Imani understood, and respected his determination. "So you've been at this since you were fifteen?"

He nodded. "Six years and counting."

Justina pulled the car to a stop in front of a gate across the road. "I just need to pick the lock," she said to the others. "Wait a minute." She took her lock-picking kit from the glove compartment, got out of the car, and began to work on the gate's heavy padlock. Jake stared out the window at the dry tumbleweeds caught in the barbed-wire fence, resolutely not meeting Imani's gaze. She supposed he thought he had shown weakness or vulnerability, and he clearly hated, *hated*, being or even feeling weak.

The truth was, though, that Imani felt great respect for him. At fifteen, Imani's own age, he had left whatever bad situation he was in and set out alone: maybe not the wisest choice, but it took courage. She knew herself well enough to know that she, Imani, would never have done that, not alone, and not if she had any choice about it. And then, when he was attacked and nearly killed by a creature he had never believed existed, he hadn't run as far and as fast as he could, the way a lot of people would have. He hadn't done his best to convince himself it hadn't been real, either. He had looked at the reality squarely, and decided he wanted to learn to fight it. If she, Imani, had been alone and completely unprepared, would she have reacted that way? She was not at all sure that she would have.

Through the windshield, she saw Justina get the padlock open. She unhooked the loop of chain from the gate, and swung the gate open, then returned to the car. They pulled through, jolting over the cattle guard, and after Justina had closed the gate again they drove on.

"You said it's been six years?" asked Imani.

"Yeah."

"Did you ever. . ." She stopped. "Just tell me if it's none of my business."

He looked at her, curious.

"Did you ever go back home? To see your parents again?"

He turned away again, and appeared to be addressing the window as he said "No."

She waited to see if he would add anything more, and though she was curious, she forced herself to respect his decision to keep silent if that was what he wanted.

"My dad was a bully, and my mother was a pathetic doormat. He beat on her, and she just tried to pacify him, and then wouldn't press charges when the police tried to help her. She just cried and apologized." He passed the shotgun shell between his hands in sharp, jerky movements. "And they thought they were so *righteous*. I'm telling you, they had their Bible reasons. They could give you the damn chapter and verse: 'the man is the head of the wife' when he beat her, 'he who spares the rod hates his son' when he beat me." Imani could see the muscles in his jaw clench, and felt sick for him. Sick for his mother; sick for his father even. She had been asleep two nights ago, when Justina told Jake that the world was festering with darkness, but she could feel that festering in Jake now, like a wound that just kept getting bigger instead of healing.

"And they were so damn sure that their shitty, tiny perception of the world was everything, the absolute. You couldn't argue, you couldn't question, you just had to swallow the bullshit they'd learned decades ago and never gave another thought to." Jake's gaze was turned inward now, and his fist was clenched white and shaking around the shotgun shell; he seemed almost to have forgotten anyone else was there. "They wouldn't know a new idea if it fucked them up the ass."

Imani flinched at this obscenity, and he saw it. All at once, he seemed to come back to himself, and he flushed. "I'm. . .sorry. I'm really sorry, I got. . .carried away there for a second. I'm going to shut up now."

Imani didn't know what to say. She wanted to change the subject, or ask a casual question that was perfectly natural and easy, or say something that would put him at his ease again, but couldn't think of a single thing.

"Have you ever gone after werewolves before?" Justina asked from the front seat. She was driving the car much more slowly now, scanning the draws and bluffs for signs of their quarry.

Jake caught the question like a lifeline. "Once or twice," he said. "Never a whole pack though. That's weird, right? A whole pack going rogue."

"It's really weird," confirmed Imani. "It's nearly always lones that get erratic and start attacking people."

"Wolves and people are alike that way," said Jake. "Recluses get kind of crazy. I know a guy who has this theory, that lone werewolves attack people because they're desperate for some sort of contact, but they're unbalanced so they figure attacking is the best way to get it."

"That's so sad," said Imani.

Jake shot her a look of surprise, as if it had never occurred to him to feel sorry for a werewolf. Then he shook it off, and said, with a kind of strained heartiness, "Some of us once tracked down a lone werewolf out in Arkansas. She'd killed a man who was out deer-hunting; maybe he was after the same deer she was. It wasn't easy, she really didn't want to be found, but finally we picked up her trail. That were-bitch led us a merry chase, I tell you! But we caught her, finally, and put her down."

"She wouldn't stop?" Imani asked.

"What?"

"You know, she wouldn't stop attacking people, so you had to kill her."

Jake stared at her. "She was a *werewolf*," he said. "She'd killed someone. So we ran her down and filled her with silver deer slugs. There wasn't a lot of negotiation involved."

Imani was appalled. "You didn't parley at all? You just hunted her down and killed her? Without even trying to talk to her?"

"A werewolf that's killed a person is just a rogue animal," he said, his voice flat and hard. "You have to put them down, the same way you do if a bear starts attacking people. If you try to be nice, they'll just attack someone else. You have to take them down first." Imani saw casual mercilessness on his face, and thought it made him look like a different person, one she didn't like at all.

"Like you tried to do with me," said Justina mildly from the front seat.

After a very awkward moment, Imani said firmly, "We always try to parley. We never take a life unless we have to. Werewolves aren't human, but they're still *people*: what C.S. Lewis called *hnau*. We treat them as such, and never attack them until we've tried talking to them first."

"If they go out and attack someone else then, because you didn't deal with them when you had the chance, that's your fault. The blood is on your hands."

"That's what the Order does," Imani said. "We protect human lives first, but we protect the lives of all people. We would rather convince a werewolf, or a vampire, or whatever, to repent, rather than see them dead. That's our duty. To be kind first."

"You should be glad it is," Justina added, still in a perfectly mild voice. "It's mostly the reason you're still alive."

Jake seemed to be working on some sort of rebuttal or argument. Then, all at once, his eyes focused on something outside the window opposite him, behind Imani. "Stop! Stop the car."

Justina hit the brakes, and brought the car to a halt beside the road in a swirl of dust. She looked back, alarmed. "What is it? What's wrong?"

"Look over there to the right," he said, pointing. "See that old house?"

Both girls looked. They saw a tiny cabin, clearly abandoned for many decades, perched on a swell of ground above one of the draws. It was tiny, probably only one or two rooms, and its clapboard walls were faded to a colorless gray-brown by sun and wind and dust and time. Its walls sagged, showing daylight in the spaces between planks, and most of its roof had drooped and fallen in. Mesquite scrub and prairie grass crowded close. Abandoned houses like it were not uncommon along roads in rural West Texas, and all three of them had seen them often. The only remarkable thing about this one was a large graffiti glyph, fresh and unfaded, spray painted in fluorescent orange across the colorless boards facing the road.

"This is the place all right," said Jake. "See that symbol? It means there's a dangerous werepack in the area. There are seven were-wolves in it, or at least there were when whoever it was drew the sign. It must have been pretty recent, too; look how bright the paint still is."

Imani squinted at the glyph. "It says all that?"

"Yeah." Jake started to get out of the car. "The symbols we use are based on the old Depression-era hobo signs. The originals were so hobos could keep each other informed about safe places to camp, whether the police were active, where you could get a good meal in exchange for work, if the water was bad to drink, stuff like that."

Imani and Justina got out of the car too, and moved around to the trunk to get out their gear. "We still use some of those old signs," Jake said, following them, "and we've built on them. That one combines the symbol for mean dogs with the symbol for a mean man, so it means 'werewolf'. The number shows how many there are. If there wasn't a number, it would just mean one lone werewolf."

Justina paused in the act of opening the latch of the trunk. "That is extremely handy," she said, impressed. "The Order doesn't know anything about those symbols. Is there a list?"

"I'm. . .not sure," he admitted. "Everybody just. . .sort of knows. I could try to write them down for you."

"Please do," said Justina. "It could be important information." Then she threw the trunk open.

*

Tobias had always kept his gear in that battered footlocker in the trunk of his car. He had expected something fancier from the Order of the Holy Lance, but even so, he couldn't help but stand open-mouthed, wondering if he would ever stop being blindsided by the Order's resources.

In the trunk of the car, flush with the edge and filling the entire width, was a kind of carpet-covered tray. The items it held were not jumbled together, but organized neatly and carefully, with each thing tucked into a little shaped and padded compartment made for it, like the compartments for picks and capos in a guitar case. On the right was a first aid kit: not one of those dinky plastic things made to fit in a glove compartment or a bathroom cabinet, but a metal box the size of a small crate, worn and scratched and obviously well used. Beside it was a gallon jug of holy water, neatly labeled, and a box of salt, the kind you could buy at a big-box store, enough to last a household for about thirty years. Next, tucked in their respective padded compartments and uniformly labeled, were a bottle of anointing oil, an engraved metal box of holy incense, a canvas bag of purifying herbs, a basket of blocks of cedar wood, and two books: a Bible and a thick missal and liturgy. There was also a small metal firepot or brazier, which he supposed they must use (along with the cedar wood and herbs and whatnot) to smoke out ghosts, and a rectangular metal can of lighter fluid.

Toward the left side of the tray, a row of ammunition boxes sat in their compartments, along with a compact gun maintenance kit in a hard plastic case, and four long canvas-wrapped bundles, which he guessed to hold arrows, crossbow bolts, or vampire stakes, or all three. Two compartments, obviously for two handguns, were empty.

"Right," said Justina. "Are you good on ammo?"

Imani patted her gun, already holstered on her hip, and said, "Fully loaded and ready to go."

"Here," said Justina, opening one of the ammunition boxes, "better take a spare magazine." She handed it to Imani, who took it and stowed it in one of her pockets.

Then Justina turned to Tobias. "How about you? Do you need any more ammunition? We have plenty."

"Oh. . .no. No thanks, I think I'm good," he said, feeling more than ever like the homeless relative at Thanksgiving.

The carpet-covered tray had two canvas handles, one on each side. Justina used them to lift the tray up and out and place it carefully on the ground outside the car, revealing another tray underneath. The neat, padded compartments on this level contained a set of throwing knives, gleaming with oil; two machetes (in leather sheaths, not plastic like Tobias's own); two well-polished shotguns; and a crossbow, one of the state-of-the-art kind, made of fiberglass and aluminum and high tech materials and with all sorts of pulleys and gears and things attached to it. Tobias knew a guy whose preferred weapon was a crossbow (he was a little too smug about it, actually, in Tobias's own opinion, and seemed to snub guns as being beneath him), and he would've given his eyeteeth for one like this. There were also two compartments for Bowie knives; those spaces were empty as well.

"Machete?" asked Justina, lifting one of them from its place for herself, and offering the other to Imani. Imani took it, and threaded its sheath onto her belt opposite her knife.

This tray also had canvas handles on either side, and Justina lifted it out too, and placed it on the sandy ground beside the first one. Tobias saw the two plastic bins that had held the body armor, nested neatly down into the trunk, as well as another bin containing shields. They were made of transparent plastic, like police riot shields, but they were smaller and more maneuverable, and round instead of rectangular. Each of the two girls took one, and fastened it to her left forearm.

"Okay," said Justina, beginning to lift the two trays back into their places. "I think that's all we need. She lifted the last tray into place, and said, "Oh! I almost forgot. Jake, do you want a hat or gloves or something? It's cold, and we have extras."

Tobias hated to have to accept. But it was cold, and they might have to walk a ways to find the werepack, and, dammit, he hated being cold more than he hated needing help. Already his ears were beginning to hurt. "Thanks," he said unhappily. But when he pulled on the woolen cap, which came down well over his ears, and the knitted gloves, he was too relieved to worry about it.

Justina made sure the car was off the road enough that it wouldn't hinder any other car trying to drive through. Then, one by one, the three of them slipped carefully between the strands of the barbed wire fence, and set off into the brush.

***

Nineteen

It was Justina who led the way. She seemed to have some idea of where they were going, and every now and then she would stop and peer around her, or stand still with her eyes closed, or make small weaving motions with her hands, almost as if she was actually feeling her way along a trail neither of the other two could detect.

"What is she—"

Imani grabbed his arm and shushed him, shaking her head. Tobias filed away his questions for later and continued to follow in silence.

Twice, Justina turned them a little to the right, back toward town. Once they took a long detour around a dense thicket of false willow in the bottom of a gully, and twice they had to stoop and carefully worm their way through a tangled stretch of mesquite, stopping every minute or two as someone got clothes or equipment snarled in the thorns. Tobias, warm with exertion, began to rethink the woolen hat and gloves. Cottontail rabbits sometimes dashed across their path, and Imani took a moment to poke an owl pellet with a twig, interested.

Tobias was glad for his well-worn cowboy boots—he had bought them secondhand, and their cowhide was scraped, scuffed, and stained, but they were as tough and indestructible as ever, and had shaped themselves to his feet until they were as comfortable as a favorite chair—and wondered why the Order didn't adopt them. Justina and Imani were wearing canvas hiking boots, which were fine, but after his boots fended off an unpleasant encounter between a yucca and his ankle for the dozenth time, he felt they ought to see the advantages of a different type of footwear. He decided to bring it up later.

All at once, in an open area between mesquite thickets, Justina stopped. The others rushed up to see what she had found.

It was a deer, a big whitetail doe, or what was left of one: practically all of it had been eaten, even much of the hide. Leg bones had been smashed open for the marrow, and the skull for the brain; flies droned heavily around the carcass, but there wasn't much left for other scavengers. The marks of gnawing on the bones had clearly been made by sharp teeth, and the paw prints around the kill site were canine; the legs and skull, though, hadn't been broken open with teeth, but with a jagged rock, which still lay beside them where it had been dropped, smeared with blood and with deer hairs still sticking to it. Beside the rock was one single bare human footprint, almost obliterated by the wolf prints on top of it.

"Werepack kill," said Tobias. Justina nodded.

Without another word, they all moved closer and examined the carcass. Tobias picked up the rock and hefted it in his hand, noting its weight.

"This hasn't been here long at all," Imani observed, her voice trembling a little. She spoke almost in a whisper, and imagined she could feel wolf eyes glaring at her from every direction. She imagined wolf tongues licking eagerly over long bloody teeth. "Some of the blood isn't even dried."

"They'll be resting now, probably," said Tobias, in the same low voice. "Sleeping off the meal. No better time to find them and take them out."

Justina got up. "This way," she said, and strode into the scrub without the slightest hesitation. Whatever trail or track she had been following, it was now very, very fresh and clear. They were close.

Soon they began to follow a thin, winding track through the scrubland. It wouldn't have caught anyone's attention, but once they knew it was there, it was easy to see. The center of the werepack's territory must be nearby; clearly they traveled this route often. A few of the overhanging mesquite branches had caught wisps of fur, and in one lower spot, where there was a moist patch of sandy ground, a big canine paw print stood out clearly. Imani bent down and spread out her hand over it; her fingers could only just span its width. She realized that she hadn't really understood, in her gut, just how big a werewolf in his or her wolf phase would actually be. Suddenly feeling very exposed, body armor or no body armor, she rushed to catch up with the others.

The trail abruptly turned and dipped down into a narrow gully with a trickle of creek running down it. On the left was a ragged limestone bluff, its lip ten or fifteen feet above the gully's gravely floor; the sandy patches between the gravel and flat stones and clusters of false willow were thick with huge paw prints like the one Imani had examined, and at one point they found a pile of gnawed bones, much heavier than the deer bones they had seen before. There was one skull intact enough to identify: a steer. The werewolves must have had some opportunities to go after the cattle on this rangeland, and, a whole steer being too much for them in one sitting, they had brought leftovers back to their lair. Then, when they had stripped the bones, they piled them here, out of the way, almost as humans would do.

The three of them moved more carefully, watching their steps, screening themselves behind the false willows, looking for a den. At last, they saw it: a sandy-floored, roughly triangular gap in the bluff, deep enough to give shelter, high enough in the center that most werewolves in human phase could stand up.

They could see the wolves inside, lying comfortably around and beside each other, leaning against each other casually, sleeping or drowsing after their meal. It was impossible to count them from outside the den, though the opening was only fifteen or twenty feet away from where they crouched behind the false willows, but it clearly was a pack of decent size; the "7" posted beside the road seemed accurate.

Tobias unslung his shotgun from his back and, with great care to avoid noise, prepared to fire.

Justina grabbed his wrist and stopped him. He gave her a furious look, and tried to jerk his hand loose. She shook her head.

"This is the perfect opportunity!" he hissed, with all the fierceness he could muster in the lowest possible whisper. "We can do this with minimal risk!"

"We parley first," whispered Imani. "We don't want them dead if it's avoidable. They're people."

"There are seven of them at least, and only three of us! This bleeding-heart bullshit will get us killed. Or bitten."

At that point, the whispering apparently finally reached the werewolves, or perhaps they had slept long enough anyway. One or two of them began to stir. A pointed ear flicked. Paws stretched. One wolf gave a long yawn, disclosing gleaming teeth and a warm pink gullet. "Shit, that's done it," Tobias breathed. "I hope you're happy."

Justina ignored this completely. Instead of replying, she stood up, no longer bothering with stealth, and stepped out of the thicket onto the stretch of pebbly ground and stones in front of the cave. Imani, despite being shaking and obviously afraid, did not hesitate to follow. Tobias did hesitate for a moment, as it occurred to him that he could take this opportunity to make a run for it, and he struggled with himself for a few seconds. But they were his teammates, his hunting partners, even if only temporarily (and not actually voluntarily), and he had enough self-awareness to realize that he would despise himself if he ran out on them now. Very unhappily, he also broke cover and followed Justina.

The wolves in the den came fully awake, with low snarls and flashes of sharp fangs. Two emerged from the den, all the fur in their manes raised into hackles, their legs stiff under them, their tails bristling and ears flattened to the sides, their lips twisted upward to reveal all their white teeth. They vibrated with low, heavy growls, and when their eyes met Tobias's, as if staring him down, he saw a disturbing awareness there that was not animal at all.

The rest of the pack emerged after the two first wolves, all growling and baring their teeth, all with hackles raised: there were eight of them now, not seven, and three of them, to Tobias's surprise, were in human phase.

He had never actually seen a werewolf in human phase before. The one he had hunted in Arkansas had kept in her wolf form the entire time: the form that could run for miles and had fangs and claws. He had always supposed vaguely that human-phase werewolves just looked like ordinary people, and only now did he realize that he had been wrong.

Wrong, but only just. They looked close to ordinary. With a little care, they could probably easily pass as human if they needed to. But standing there now, no more clothed than their wolf-phase packmates, apparently unconcerned by the chilly wind (which Tobias was starting to feel again, now that they were no longer walking briskly and fighting through mesquite thickets), they were obviously, disturbingly, inhuman. Their similarity just made them more disconcerting, more threatening; close to ordinary, but just wrong enough to make his skin crawl.

The first thing he noticed was the way they stood. Though all three were naked, they stood openly, without a trace of either shyness or seductiveness. They neither flaunted nor hid their bodies; he had the feeling that if someone had offered them bathrobes or something to put on, they would just have stared blankly. They obviously felt exactly as comfortable in their bare skin as they would have in their bare fur.

All three of them were solid with muscle: not the gleaming, showy muscle of bodybuilders, but the lean, sinewy, tough muscle of hard and varied use. They had more hair on their bodies than a human would. The chests of the two male werewolves bristled with it, and even the one female had a wide patch of hair over her breastbone. The hair on their heads was heavy and thick, and it seemed to actually be standing up around their foreheads and necks and shoulders, in a more human version of wolfish hackles. They were staring down Tobias and the two girls, just as their wolf-phase packmates were, and their eyes were the buttery amber color of wolf eyes. Even the shapes of their faces were slightly wrong: cheekbones a bit too sharp, eyes a bit too large, canine teeth just a touch too long and pointed.

Sure, they could pass as humans, if they wore clothes and maybe colored contact lenses, but humans that would make you uneasy if you looked too close, uneasy without really knowing exactly why. Humans who looked, and behaved, just a little more animal, a little more predatory, than they should.

The fact that they were naked clearly bothered the three human-phase werewolves not at all. But it made Tobias much more uncomfortable than he would have expected. This was mostly because the female werewolf, despite the hair on her chest and legs, actually had quite a sexy athletic body, and her small, firm breasts, nipples tight in the cold, were very nice indeed. She did not seem to notice or care at all that she was standing there completely naked, but Tobias, to his discomfort, noticed very much.

One of the two lead wolves turned back, facing the rest of the pack, and seemed to communicate by eye and posture with several individuals. Then, without warning, she galloped off to her right, and three other wolves peeled off and followed her. Justina held up her hand to check both Imani's and Tobias's immediate impulses to react defensively to what looked very much like a flanking maneuver.

At the same time, almost too quickly to see, the three human-phase werewolves stretched, bent, folded, and dropped to the ground on four paws, as easily as changing out one shirt for another. Tobias was both relieved and disappointed at this development. He knew objectively that he would be much better off not distracted by the naked werewolf girl, but that didn't make the distraction itself less enjoyable.

Justina addressed the remaining alpha werewolf, her ringing voice cutting sharp and commanding through the cold air. "We speak for the Order of the Holy Lance," she said. "We have come here because your pack has ended human lives, and we would like to resolve this situation peacefully. Would you be willing to parley with us? We will not attack you in any way if you act in good faith." To emphasize this, she held out her long hands, open and empty. Imani did the same, then jabbed Tobias with her elbow until he also (very much more reluctantly) followed suit.

A couple of the wolves made small whining noises, and averted their eyes. One tucked his tail down and flattened his ears, nervous and unsure.

The alpha wolf did not stop growling, but it diminished from a vicious snarl to a low throb, and his lips relaxed to almost (but not quite) cover his teeth again. His ears lifted into a slightly less aggressive position, and the fur of his hackles smoothed out a little.

He paused, apparently thinking. The wolf beside him whined, ears and tail tucked, and nosed at his jaw appealingly; that seemed to decide him. In a fluid motion, he stretched, reached, lengthened, and stood up on human feet.

*

This werewolf was older than the others. In human phase, he looked as if he might be in his thirties, instead of a teen or young adult. He had probably been strongly built, even when he was human, but not especially tall; he was nowhere near being able to look Justina straight in the face, but that didn't stop him from continuing to stare hard into her eyes.

"I understand the humans," he said. "But you—" he narrowed his eyes, but did not break his gaze. "You've never been human. The smell of you burns my nose. You're less like them than we are. Why are you taking sides?"

His observation threw Justina off her stride for a moment, and she said nothing.

"Take your pets with you," said the werewolf, and his voice was full of the absolute and unshakeable surety of a man accustomed to being followed and obeyed. "Go now, and we'll let you go unharmed."

"No," said Justina. She still held her own stare into his eyes. "Your pack has killed people. Your pack has turned people. That has to stop today."

The werewolf began to growl again, a sound nearly as inhuman it had been before, when he was in wolf-phase. "Every one of those we've turned has wanted it," he said. "And every one of those we've killed deserved it." He lowered his voice until the word itself was a growl. "Richly."

"No person has the right to decide that."

"We are not people."

"You aren't *human*," Justina emphasized. "You are people. You're responsible for your actions. How else would you be standing there talking to me?" She paused. "If you were just animals, we would've killed you all by now."

He made the low, almost completely inhuman growling sound again, and shifted his weight slightly forward. The three wolf-phase packmates grouped behind him snarled through their gleaming teeth, stiffened their hackles, leveled their ears. Justina heard Jake unsling his shotgun from his shoulder and prepare to fire, but she did not turn.

It was Imani who realized the problem. Justina had never been much of a diplomat. And the alpha werewolf needed a way to save face: he needed the option of giving in without looking weak, looking as if he couldn't defend his pack. So Imani, looking anywhere except at the werewolf she was addressing (she had grown up in a convent, and never saw anyone naked, least of all a man), took her courage in both hands and piped up. "You said you've never turned anyone against their will?"

"No," he said. "Every one of them is in the pack right now. We take care of our own." He kept his eyes on Justina, apparently regarding Imani as an extension of her.

"And you've never. . ." It was hard to bring herself to say it. "You've never killed anyone who didn't. . .deserve it?"

Without looking down, the alpha dropped one hand to rest on the head of the wolf standing at his left. She kept her eyes on the intruders, kept growling, but she also leaned slightly into the touch. "Julie's father bullied her. Hit her. Tongue-lashed her. Manipulated her. Locked her up. She lived in fear and bruises. Now she will never need to fear a man like him again, and she tore out his throat with her own teeth." He said this casually, not as a threat, but as a simple explanation.

"That must stop," said Justina. "Take all the deer and rabbits you want. Take cattle. But you must not attack a human again."

"Please," Imani added. "If you agree to that, we'll go, and you never have to see any of us again. You can live in peace."

"Also," said Justina, still looking the alpha werewolf in the eyes, "you can't outflank us. I smelled and heard your packmates behind us as soon as they arrived."

Both of the others, who had smelled and heard no such thing, whirled around, Jake with his shotgun already leveled and searching for a target, Imani with her buckler raised. The four wolves were close; probably close enough to be on them in a single lunge. They were standing quietly, however; alert, tense, but not on the point of attack. Imani retreated a step, until her back touched Justina's, but otherwise she held her ground.

The nearest of the four flanking wolves lifted and stretched into human-phase. She was also older, close to the age of the male alpha, and was clearly the second half of the alpha pair. In contrast to the werewolf girl they had seen in human-phase before, who must have been just a little wisp of a person before her transformation, this woman looked as if she could pick up a car and throw it. "We will refrain from attacking humans," she said, "unless they seek us out to attack us first. And we will not turn anyone who is unwilling. Is that satisfactory to you?"

Justina turned to face her in turn. "If you all agree to that, the three of us will leave you in peace."

The two alpha werewolves looked at each other, past Justina and Imani and Jake, communicating in a way that had nothing to do with words. Apart from the sound of the creek and the wind, the clearing between the bluff and the false willows was entirely silent. Huge wolf paws shifted over pebbles. Jake held his shotgun ready; if things went south, he would be able to fire without a second's delay.

"We agree to your compromise," the male alpha said.

Justina smiled then, but without showing her teeth. "In that case, we will leave you in peace." She deliberately broke eye contact: not by dropping her eyes, a gesture that would have had submissive overtones, but by drifting her gaze to one side. She started to leave, and Imani hastened after her, almost gasping with relief that it had not come to fighting.

"You can't leave it at that," Jake hissed, grabbing Justina's arm to try to stop her. "You can't—wait!" She didn't stop walking, and he didn't have the strength to physically bring her to a halt. He rushed to get in front of her. "You can't trust them! They're not human! You heard what he said: that one girl killed her own father! With her *teeth*!"

"We negotiated terms, and they agreed," Justina said. "We have nothing more to do here." She kept walking.

Jake trotted to keep up. After a moment, Justina heard him mutter under his breath, "Maybe *you* don't."

*

Tobias hadn't really believed, in his heart, that the two girls were actually going to let the werepack just get away with everything, despite all their talk about "parley". There was no way, he had reasoned, that they could possibly be so stupidly naïve, especially since the werewolves themselves actually bragged about their kills! It was a shame, sure, but they were too dangerous to leave alive. At the very least, the alphas ought to be killed; that might be enough to bring the others in line. But nothing less than that would do any good at all.

And then! The male alpha agreed to their terms, and that was supposed to be that. There wasn't a chance in hell of the werewolves actually living up to their end of the deal; why should they? Justina had just clearly demonstrated to them that the Order or the Holy Lance was all talk and no action, and that they, the werewolves, could literally get away with murder as far as the Order was concerned. He wondered whether they would bother to wait until he and the girls were out of earshot to shift into human phase and start laughing at them.

Well, he thought, the Order was going to do nothing about this. Fine. But the mission was over, as far as Justina was concerned, and according to their deal (well, *her* deal; she made the rules), he got to go free now. He knew where the werewolves were laired. He knew how many there were. He could get up a hunting party of his own, and come in and wipe them out. If fact, he not only could do that, but it was practically his duty to do it, and Justina and Imani could do nothing to stop him.

"Maybe *you* don't," he muttered. Justina probably heard him, though Imani almost certainly didn't; he found himself not caring in the least whether she heard or not.

What he had failed to consider was whether any of the werewolves would hear.

One did.

The first thing he felt was the heavy impact of a large body hitting him from behind, throwing him forward onto the pebbles and sand and knocking his breath out. Then came an intolerable, agonizing pressure on the back of his neck, just where the collar of his motorcycle leathers left skin exposed, followed by blazing agony. His vision almost disappeared in flashes of red and black.

Then, abruptly, the pressure was gone, leaving only the blinding, screaming pain.

I've been shot, he thought disjointedly. *I've been shot in the neck, I'm going to be paralyzed.*

Then, with a stab of sick horror in his gut, he realized what had actually happened. He had been bitten. By a werewolf.

He was going to turn. He was going to be a lone werewolf. Until someone killed him, which probably wouldn't take long.

The gray and red in his vision merged and closed in, and then everything was gone.

***

Twenty

When the wolf closed his jaws on the back of Jake's neck, Imani involuntarily threw her hands over her ears, to avoid hearing the horrible meaty *crack* of vertebrae being broken. But it didn't happen. Too quickly for her eyes to follow, Justina lunged at the wolf, and dragged his jaws back open with her hands. Then, before the wolf could try again to bite, or flee, or do anything else, she dug the strong fingers of her right hand down into fur and skin and muscle and picked up the massive creature by the scruff. He thrashed and snapped and yelped, but Justina took no notice. She turned her hot, furious eyes back on the rest of the pack.

They stood frozen, the two alphas still in human phase. The werewolves all seemed torn between attacking in defense of their packmate, and backing down in the face of the overwhelming power Justina clearly brought to bear.

"We had an agreement," she said, and though she spoke softly, the air shivered with her words. "We had an agreement for less than five minutes, and already it has been broken. But I won't hold all of you responsible." With her free hand, she drew her silvered ghost knife from its sheath. "Just this one. Maybe now the rest of you will see fit to abide by it."

The captured werewolf squirmed and struggled more wildly than ever, but with no more effect. Justina got a good grip on the handle of her knife, and Imani stood frozen at what she was obviously about to do. She reached out a hand and touched Justina's back, but whether to stop her or just to reassure herself, she honestly had no real idea.

"Wait!" the male alpha took a step forward, his eyes averted, his arms and shoulders down, his back stooped. If he had been human, he would have been on his knees. "Please don't. He's. . .he's new. He was only turned a couple of months ago."

"If he can't control himself, or won't bother, all the more reason." Justina's voice was as hard and cold as granite bedrock.

"I was near him. I should have stopped him," said the female alpha, her posture also submissive, her eyes also averted. "Hold me responsible."

Justina thought about it for a few seconds, weighing the risk, deciding what would be the right thing to do. Then, all at once, she dropped the werewolf from her hand, letting him land hard on the pebbled ground with a sharp yelp. He cringed, tail tucked tight under his body, his belly half-exposed.

"I may be able to stop my friend from turning," she said. "If I can, I will. But if he turns—"

"We will take responsibility for him," the male alpha said hastily.

Justina narrowed her eyes. "Do you really think he would join *this* pack? He would rather your packmate had killed him, as he intended to do."

Justina drew herself up to her full seven feet. "If he turns, I will come back here. I will cut *that one's* head from his shoulders, and then I will decide whether to do the same to the rest of you."

She turned, and picked Jake up in her arms as if he weighed no more than a toddler. Then she left at a run. Whatever she could do for him, she needed to do it quickly, or the turn would begin and she could do nothing more.

All the sisters of the Order trained in running, as part of their regimen. Imani could run for miles. But she had no chance of keeping up with Justina's huge, loping strides, and by the time she reached the car, Justina had already lain Jake down carefully face-down on the ground, with his head and shoulders cushioned and elevated with folded-up towels, and his bloody shirt removed. The first aid kit was out of the car's trunk and sitting open nearby. "How bad is it?"

Justina looked up. "Not as bad as it could have been; just a soft tissue injury. Another half a second, and the werewolf would have crunched his vertebrae like popcorn. As it is, the werewolf serum is the main thing we need to deal with at the moment."

"Do you really think you can do something?" asked Imani. "Everything I've ever read says that there's no way to stop a person turning after a werewolf bite."

"I don't know for sure," said Justina. "But there are records of Benjamin of Piedmont healing people, and I can *feel* the serum in his system. I think, I *think*, I may be able to draw it out before it takes effect."

"What can I do?" asked Imani.

Justina pointed. "Sit there, in front of his head." Imani moved to obey. "This is going to hurt, and he might start coming to. If he does, you'll need to hold down his shoulders to keep him still. Brace yourself."

Imani leaned forward, put the heels of her hands on Jake's shoulders, and braced herself. "Ready."

"Here goes." Not roughly, but firmly, Justina pushed her long fingers down into the jagged-edged wound, and into the deep punctures where fangs had gone in. She could sense the werewolf serum, not as something evil, but as something *foreign*, like a transfusion of the wrong blood type. She could feel it in her mind and in her fingertips. She touched ragged muscle and sticky blood and hard bone, and with her mind and her fingers she caught the foreignness. Then, with concentration so complete she barely noticed when Jake began to wake up, began to move, began to struggle, she carefully drew the foreignness to her, like playing a fish on a line. She withdrew her fingers from the wound, slowly, and when she did there was a clear, viscous fluid clinging to her fingertips. Imani, after making sure that Jake was calm again, let go of his shoulders and tore open the paper packet of a sterile wipe from the first aid kit. She handed the wipe to Justina to clean the fluid from her hands.

"What are you doing to me," Jake asked, his voice almost expressionless. It was also harsh and raw, and Justina realized only then that he had been screaming while she worked.

"Would you please hand me some gloves, and the bottle of saline?" Justina said to Imani. Then she answered Jake: "I extracted the werewolf serum from your wound, so I don't think you'll turn. Now I need to dress the bite, so it won't get infected."

Imani handed over a pair of nitrile gloves, which Justina pulled on, and then gave her the squeeze bottle of saline solution.

"No you didn't," said Jake, his voice still dull and dead. "Nobody can do that. People who get bitten always turn, that's just the way it is."

"I'm a nephil. I did it. Now hold still, this saline will sting."

Justina rinsed the wound thoroughly for several minutes, making sure to force the water down into all the punctures, and while she was doing this Jake just braced himself and said nothing.

Imani unwrapped a pad of sterile gauze and passed it to Justina, who positioned it over the wound. Then she taped it to his skin, sealing the edges carefully, and peeled off her gloves. "There." She stood up and stretched.

Jake did not get up. "You shouldn't have done all this," he said. "I'm going to be a werewolf. A *lone* werewolf. If you don't kill me, other people like me will."

"It's been long enough that if you were going to turn, it would have started by now," Imani said. "It was. . .a pretty serious bite, and lots of serum got in. But you aren't turning, and we don't think you will."

"We'll keep a close watch on you tonight," said Justina, closing the first aid kit and hoisting it back into the trunk. "If anything is going to happen, it will have happened by morning. Then, when you get a clean bill of health, you can be on your way."

Imani crouched beside him, and offered a hand. "Here, can you stand? We'll take you right back to the motel, and then we can all get some supper in us. All right?"

Jake said nothing, but he took Imani's hand and managed to get to his feet. She gave him some pills for the pain, and before they reached Shinnery again, he was sound asleep.

*

That night, Justina did not intend to sleep. She planned to keep an eye on Jake; after all, though she was sure she had removed all of the werewolf serum, it wasn't a procedure that had ever been done before. She didn't know whether to expect complications, and anyway, she wanted to watch for fever or other signs of infection.

But, without meaning to, she dropped off in her chair, something that very rarely happened to her; her control over her sleep was usually far greater than a human's. But on this night, it happened. And after she fell asleep, she dreamed.

It was an uncomfortable dream, like many she had been having of late; uncomfortable and unsettling. She saw a man walking, relaxed, swinging his arms, whistling. She saw a wolf, the same one she had had in her grasp yesterday and, contrary to her own reason, had allowed to live. He growled, low, and drool ran in strings from his teeth. The man who was walking noticed nothing.

Justina rushed to stop the wolf, but a hand on her arm stopped her short. You told him not to, said a voice, and it was Sister Rebecca's voice, perfectly unconcerned, even cheery. You talked to them, and they agreed not to attack anyone. See? Everything is fine.

The wolf pounced. Justina struggled, but her feet wouldn't move from the spot. The wolf clamped his jaws around the back of the man's neck, and crunched down, grinding through meat and gristle and bone and spine, just as he had been stopped from doing to Jake. When he was done, he turned back and looked at Justina, his tongue lolling and his eyes squinted in a smirk, his tail gleefully up. Thanks! he called out to her, and then laughed, a gloating human laugh, and kept laughing until she covered her ears against it.

See? said Sister Rebecca, her voice still cheery. You did exactly what you should have.

We didn't do any good at all, Justina objected, watching the werepack eat the man who had been whistling, all of them still looking back and laughing at her between bites, fangs flashing white and red. People died before, and people are still dying.

It's such a shame, said Sister Magdalena, her voice full of syrupy fake sympathy. But it's not our problem, is it?

We might have to go and talk to them again, Sister Rebecca added. That should take care of it.

You never should have tried to attack them, sighed Sister Magdalena, like a self-righteous false mourner at an alcoholic's funeral, telling the bereaved family that he never should have started drinking in the first place. This never would have happened.

That's not what happened at all!

Sister Rebecca patted her head, as if she was a pet or a toddler. Now, now, child, you can't expect to know as much about it as we do.

Maybe *you* don't, said Jake, his voice sneering and superior. He raised his shotgun, and grinned with white teeth. Behind him, other men and women raised shotguns too, raised machetes and knives and handguns. The werepack lay resting in the sun, content, unaware. The sun flared on silver, so bright Justina had to look away, and the men and women fell on the wolves, their mouths twisted with fury and malice. The wolves went down, riddled with silver slugs, chopped by silver blades. The alphas tried to protect. Failed. The silver sneered in the sun, brighter than ever through red and red and red.

Justina tried to go to help. No! cried Imani pathetically, clutching at Justina's arm. No, don't leave me alone! Don't leave me! I'm scared! I'm scared! Her voice was thin and weak, full of whiny, childish demand.

I told you I wouldn't, said Justina, and when she turned back, all the wolves were dead. Thanks! said Jake, the machete in his hand clogged with blood. He threw back his head and laughed, and kept laughing until it turned into a wolf's howl.

Sister Rebecca stood there, her arms and hands drenched with blood to the elbows, blood spattered in shocking red across her habit and smeared on her face. See? she said virtuously. We never hurt anyone. We talk to them. It's the best way. Her clothes were soaked solidly with blood now, her hair drawn into sticky strings dripping with red. We are always *kind*.

We are always kind. . .

Justina slept late that morning. Imani had to wake her up for matins, which she did with some concern; she had never needed to wake Justina up before. Ordinarily, Justina had the ability (which

Imani envied but didn't really understand) to wake up at exactly the time she wished, fully rested and alert. And after she was awake, Justina continued to seem rattled and unsettled, a circumstance Imani found even more concerning. But she did not press; there would be time later to find out what was wrong. She would give Justina every chance to come clean on her own, and if she did not, then she, Imani, would insist that she talk about it.

She knew that Justina had not been sleeping well. Justina hadn't discussed it, but Imani had seen her stirring and restless, even sometimes distressed, in her sleep, which had never happened in the commandery in the eleven years they had shared a cell. Whatever she had dreamed about this time, though, seemed to have made an even stronger impression, and Imani decided enough was enough. Justina was going to talk about whatever was going on.

***

Interlude Nine

From: imani.westtex@ohl.org
To: magdalena.westtex@ohl.org
Re: Shinnery Again
November 30, at 9:07am

Sister Magdalena,

A lot has happened since yesterday morning, and there are a couple of things I want to run by you.

First of all, we went and confronted the werepack, and there were actually *eight* werewolves in it. We found their den. And I hadn't really realized—not *really*, in my gut—how *big* they actually are when they're in wolf-phase! Anyway, Justina and I talked to them, and we convinced the two alphas to stop attacking people, and to not turn anyone who didn't want to be turned. After they agreed to that, we left.

I'm not going to lie: it felt weird to do that. The pack had killed people; they told us so, straight out, and they weren't sorry for it, either. The male alpha said that every person the pack had killed had really deserved it. But the Order gives second chances. We do, and we *should*. And I don't see any real reason they *wouldn't* live up to their end of the deal. But we don't know for sure, do we? What if they do kill someone else, and that's our fault? Jake said it that way, that if we let the werewolves off, and they kill someone, that's on us. But we can't kill people (even people who aren't human) *just in case*; that would be all kinds of wrong!

Anyway, that wasn't even what I wanted to run by you. Apparently the werewolves were thinking kind of the same thing I was, and one of them decided to deal with a future problem permanently. I guess they figured that Jake wasn't actually part of the Order, so he would be the most likely to change his mind, come back, and try to take them out. Well, one of the werewolves jumped on him as we were leaving, and bit him in the back of the neck. Justina grabbed the wolf, pried his mouth open, and pulled him off Jake before he could kill him (which was what he apparently was planning to do). But he'd been bitten, obviously, and he was going to turn.

Here's the interesting thing (yes, this whole story had a point!). Justina got Jake back to the car and the first aid kit, and then she *extracted* the werewolf serum from the bite. She put her fingers down into the wound and concentrated hard, so hard I don't think she even realized it when he woke up (he'd passed out after the wolf attacked and bit him, unsurprisingly enough) and started squirming and screaming. I don't blame him, he had a big chomp out of the back of his neck, and Justina's fingers were pushed down into it! I was holding him down, and he nearly threw me off, even though I was braced and had all my weight on his shoulders, and he was face-down and didn't have any leverage. But I don't think Justina noticed any of that. Also, there was a weird change in the air as she was working. I don't know how to describe it, exactly, but I could feel heat coming off her, as if she had a roaring fever. Then she pulled her fingers out, and the werewolf serum was stuck to the ends of them, like a clear, sort of syrupy stuff, like Karo syrup. And Jake didn't turn. We kept an eye on him overnight, but nothing happened, except for a little redness and swelling at the wound, and that just needed antibiotics. So that means Justina did something nobody has *ever* done, at least that there's any record of: she reversed a werewolf bite. There's nothing about that in any of our accounts of nephilim.

So that's the first thing: Justina beating a werewolf bite. The second thing is that Justina has been having bad dreams. She's had them for a while now, but last night, she had a particularly vivid and troubling one. It took some convincing to get her to tell me about it. But it sounds like it was all about bad things happening because we restrain ourselves (werewolves eating people because we don't kill them, the freelancers and Jake going back and slaughtering the werewolves because we don't stop them, that sort of thing). She said that she saw you and Sister Rebecca, and you were covered in blood, but all pious and unconcerned.

It could all come from her own subconscious. I'm sure she's troubled by the idea of letting dangerous creatures go their way, just like I am; just like I guess we probably all are sometimes! But at the same time. . .I wonder. I wonder if there's more to it. I wonder if the dream might come from outside herself.

Here's the thing. We haven't heard from her demon father, really since she was born. But surely he wouldn't just let her go without a fight, would he? And I was thinking about the black-eyed things in those men's heads, and the violent haunting and the boo hag and the chupacabra (isn't that what you said it was, in Amarillo?) all happening at exactly the same time, and there's no way that could all be a coincidence, right? That would be crazy. But what kind of creature *could* orchestrate it all, except a powerful demon? And we know from Scripture, and from tradition and historical sources too, that angels can visit people's dreams, so obviously a demon could too, right? He doesn't have any direct control or influence over Justina, because she's been baptized, but surely he could tempt or manipulate her the same way he could anybody else, right? What if it was never the commandery he was attacking? What if it was really Justina all along?

Anyway, that's longer than any email needs to be.

TLDR: Justina can stop a werewolf-bitten person from turning. Justina had a weird, unsettling dream that really cast the Order in a distorted, bad light. I wonder if her demon father might be involved in all these goings-on?

--Imani

Sister Imani
Squire-Novice of the Order of the Holy Lance
Commandery of West Texas
Commandery-House of Saint Margaret of Antioch

***

Twenty-One

On December first, not long after sunrise, Justina and Imani dropped Tobias off at a Texaco near the middle of town. They had offered him a lift back to Odessa, to pick up his car, but he declined that; the mere thought of sitting in a car with the two girls for several hours, talking about the whole werepack thing and his own bite (or trying not to talk about it), was more awkward then he could stand. Anyway, he could easily bum a ride to his car with someone later. For right now, he just needed someone in his group to pick up himself and his footlocker of gear. The Texaco was a fine place for that.

They gave him his cell phone back, and after their car had pulled out of sight, he made the call. He had expected disbelief; he had expected everyone to assume he was being controlled or manipulated or that some other deception was afoot, and in that he was perfectly right. It took a good fifteen minutes of grilling, as he walked around and around the dusty gas station parking lot, before they believed him enough to send someone to pick him up. And when the car pulled in a couple of hours later, the driver, a beefy man named Ryan who Tobias had never particularly liked, had brought two other hunters as backup. They watched without helping, guns drawn, as he heaved his footlocker out of the gas station, where he had been waiting, and into the trunk, and they both covered him as he got into the car and buckled his seatbelt. The car smelled like stale corn chips and long-gone fast food, and Ryan had a pair of fuzzy dice hanging from his rear view mirror; Tobias had never been able to decide whether that particular adornment was meant to be ironic or not.

When Ryan had last been in contact with everyone, back in Odessa, there had been eight people from the network gathered to hunt the nephil. More had arrived now, several of them people who had been involved in that first abortive attempt to kill the nephil at the ruins of the commandery (the attempt that had failed thanks to the Order's scrupulous attention to security measures in their cars, not to mention their deep pockets to fund automotive bulletproofing). Now, at last count, there were seventeen people gathered in Odessa, ready to take the nephil on, said the passenger sitting beside Tobias in the back seat. His name was Cassius, and he was a skinny, wiry kid who always wore wifebeater shirts, even in the dead of winter, for reasons best known to himself. He must have fifteen of the things.

No one said much during the drive, and that was fine with Tobias. He was thinking.

He knew they would want to know what had happened to him, and how he had survived a nephil for several days, when everyone had assumed he must be dead. They would want to know what he had learned, and how they should proceed with attacking Justina. He knew all this; the one thing he didn't know, though, was exactly what he would answer.

Imani had told him that they were not leaving right away, as they wanted to keep an eye on the werepack for a bit to make sure they lived up to their end of the deal. He also suspected they wanted to be able to protect the werepack if need be, from freelancers like himself, and that Imani had diplomatically omitted that. She had also said that it was a gesture of good faith; she and Justina were not running. They trusted him. He would have felt much more comfortable if they had not; his decision would have been easier if he knew that, whether he told everyone where they were or not, they would be gone by the time anyone arrived to attack them. And he still hadn't decided whether telling everyone was the right thing to do.

The truth was, Tobias had not discounted the possibility that he actually was under some sort of external control. He might be, for all he knew; he wasn't sure whether anyone could know that, if they were the ones being affected. And Justina *was* a demon's daughter; neither she, nor Imani, nor any of their books had disputed that, and demons were more slyly deceptive than any other creature. Maybe the whole thing *had* been a setup to trick him, or maybe his perceptions really were being meddled with somehow. How would he know?

But he kept running up against one question: what would be the point? Why would she go to so much trouble? If she really was capable of taking all of them in a straight fight—and after reading Angelina di Genoa, he was pretty sure she was—why would she bother with deception?

And there was this, too. He knew that he, and the rest of his fellow freelance monster hunters, didn't have much information about nephilim. Imani had pointed that out right from the beginning, and as much as it stung, he knew she was right. But the Order of the Holy Lance had *three whole books* of it, not to mention the fact that they had raised Justina from a newborn. Could he really assume that his people knew more about her nature than the Order did? Just framing the thought, it sounded stupid. What did he really have to go on? What actual evidence, even assuming he could trust himself at all?

What he had seen. More than anything else, that. What he had actually seen and witnessed.

His hand strayed to the thick gauze dressing taped over the wound in the back of his neck, the one that would have turned him into a werewolf by now if not for Justina, and he had the depressing feeling that he was going to have to disagree with all the rest of his people before long.

*

They had all taken rooms in a scruffy motel near the oilfield, and also set up in a vacant warehouse across the street. Every few minutes, eighteen-wheelers and tankers rumbled past, or dirty trucks which, judging by their faded and peeling decals, were from oilfield supply companies, or even dirtier pickups which, for some obscure reason, were nearly always white. A refinery nearby was flaring; Tobias could see the plume of smoky flame whipping in the West Texas wind on top of its spindly stack, and whenever a gust of wind blew from just the right direction, he could catch the sour, oily smell of it.

"Nobody will notice us here," Ryan commented. "Oilfield workers are coming and going from this motel at all hours."

They did not go into the motel, however, and no one offered to give Tobias a lift to go and pick up his car. Instead, he was ushered immediately into the warehouse, where a back room (a break room once?) had been furnished with a couple of wobbly folding tables and a mismatched collection of folding chairs. It looked like the most ghetto of all conference rooms. A metal filing cabinet, one side of it bashed in, sat in a corner, one drawer sagging half open.

A conference room was, in fact, more or less exactly what it was. Tobias was directed to a chair, and over the next few minutes all seventeen of the others came in, by ones and twos, and crowded around the tables too. He knew most of them, but not all, and some that he did know he knew only slightly; by freelance monster-hunter standards, this was a regular army. He wasn't sure he'd ever seen so many gathered together for one hunt before. They were leaning together, whispering, shaking their heads, darting curious glances at him.

He was glad they had set things up here the way they had. He imagined what it would have been like if he was sitting in front with all of them facing him, or worse, in the center of the whole crowd, like a suspect being grilled, or a Duck-Duck-Goose player in the mush pot.

He realized he was fidgeting, and that each time he did his chair squeaked against the floor. He made himself stop.

"Okay everybody, listen up," said a stocky, bearded man. Every-one always called him by his last name, Hill; Tobias had always sup-posed this was because his first name was something unfortunately unimposing, like the guy in "The Great Escape" whose first name was Virgil. Hill looked like a middle-aged Viking who, having mostly retired from a life of fighting and plundering, had devoted himself instead to eating as many wild boars and drinking as many barrels of beer as he could. In a sense, this impression would have been deceiving, since he was still very much in the fighting busi-ness, though he did drink a great many beers and eat a great many pulled pork sandwiches and racks of barbecued ribs.

"Toby here was the first one on the scene in Odessa, after the nephil was verified to be around. He didn't wait for help from any-one else, which I'm sure he has a *fascinating* explanation for—"

A tiny murmur of chuckles rose and died, almost before anyone could hear it.

"—and then something happened. That was three days ago. Today, we get a call from Toby his very self, from up north in

Shinnery, and here he is, ready to give us the intel we need to bring this nephil down."

Everyone looked at Tobias. He squirmed uncomfortably, feeling abruptly put on the spot. His chair gave a groan, as if in commiseration.

"I attacked her," he said. "The girl she's with, Imani, had gone out and I saw the chance to keep her out of the crossfire—"

"I don't care what Hill said," interrupted a dark-haired woman with a sleeve of tattoos covering her right arm. "We don't care *why* you did any of it. Is it really true you've been with the nephil for the last three days? She took you prisoner?"

"Yes," said Tobias.

"And you got away? *How?*"

"I didn't get away," said Tobias. "She let me go."

"Right," said a man on the opposite side of the table, very drily. Tobias didn't think he'd ever met him, though it was hard to be sure; he had one of those utterly nondescript faces that you could see a hundred times and never really remember very well. "And what kind of deal did you have to cut to get her to do that?"

"I didn't make any *deal*," snapped Tobias, beginning to feel nettled. "She let me go because she wanted me to be a. . .a witness."

Hill leaned forward, squeezing his meaty belly against the edge of the table. "A witness to what?"

Tobias looked down at the tabletop in front of him. The imitation woodgrain was peeling back from a deep gouge, revealing the deteriorating particle board underneath; he picked at the broken edge of the imitation wood with his thumbnail, almost without noticing he was doing it. After a moment he looked up again, feeling that he had made some kind of choice.

"To her. . .not being a monster."

Murmuring, hissing whispers, stares. "She's a nephil!" said the man with the forgettable face. "She's a monster by definition!" Several others voiced agreement.

"Does that mean you don't have any *useful* information for us? About how to fight her and take her down?" This was said by a tall woman named something like Carrie or Cassie, who was wearing a "Rage Against the Machine" concert t-shirt faded almost to oblivion. "My god, what fucking good are you?" This sentiment was echoed from several other corners of the table, and even those who said nothing wouldn't meet Tobias's eyes.

"I have plenty of information!" Tobias retorted, suddenly angry with the whole lot of them. "I've been with Justina, the nephil, and Imani for three days, and yes, I know a lot. Do you want to hear it or not?"

"Everybody settle down now," said Hill, and Tobias felt that he hated the man's calmness. "Of course we want to hear whatever Toby can tell us."

Tobias took a second to collect himself. He had the momentary impulse to just get up and walk out, but he controlled his temper and took several deep breaths.

"I know this, first of all," he said. "We don't actually have a clue about nephilim. I mean, what have we got? A few bits and scraps of hearsay, and the *Book of Enoch* that everybody knows is mostly bullshit. But the Order of the Holy Lance has books, multiple whole books, about nephilim, and from actual eyewitnesses, too, not hearsay."

"And do you know that because the *nephil* told you?" asked another man Tobias didn't know, snidely. He wore a flat cap and a plaid work shirt, and had a flourishing mustache, like some sort of threadbare hipster. "You seem pretty friendly with, what's her name? *Justina.* You sure *witnessing* was what she wanted you for?"

Tobias flushed, mainly from anger, but also from unexpected embarrassment. Somehow, even the suggestion of something like that with the sisters—nuns, effectively!—made him feel like a shy virgin accidentally walking into a room where someone was watching hardcore porn. He felt strangely ashamed, as if he'd been caught doing something inexpressibly dirty.

"I know because I saw the books," he said, coldly. "I read them."

"Sure you did," said the snide faux-hipster, "because obviously she would have brought *those exact books* along for your convenience. Right, that's plausible."

The nondescript man gave a short snicker, and rolled his eyes for the benefit of anyone who happened to be looking at him.

"They had them," said Tobias, "because believe it or not, the Order of the Holy Lance is more interested in practicality than aesthetics. They have their whole archive digitized, and sisters in the field take it with them on a Nook." He glared at the snide man, then, pouring on some snideness of his own, added, "Is that plausible enough for you?"

"All right, now, let's all settle down," said Hill. "We're getting off topic. Toby here isn't our enemy, so let's all be civil." He paused, presumably to give everyone a chance to become civil. "Now then. Toby, what can you tell us?"

Once again controlling his temper, Tobias said, "First of all, just what I saw with my own eyes. When I first sneaked into her motel room, she was lying down with her arm over her face. She didn't see me, but she heard me come in, and she knew I wasn't Imani. I'm still not sure how she knew. Then she was up on her feet so fast I couldn't even see it. I fired one shot, and it may have been the luckiest shot I ever took, because it hit her right in the chest and went through-and-through. But she didn't even seem to feel it. It didn't hurt her at all. Then I saw her actually *dodge* another bullet, from only a few feet away."

He paused, then clarified, "They were silver-plated bullets, by the way. Turns out, silver and salt and holy water and those sorts of things don't do anything to nephilim. I tried the rite of exorcism, too. No effect, except it made her mad."

"It made her mad?" said the woman with the tattoo sleeve, hopefully.

"Well, yeah, but because she thought it was sacrilegious, not because it hurt her."

The woman sat back in her chair, looking faintly disappointed.

"Right, you emptied your gun at her and it didn't work," prompted Hill. "What then?"

"I actually didn't empty my gun. Before I could, she said one word, like 'stop' or 'enough'. One word, anyway. And I just. . ." He foundered for words, for some sort of description. "It was like. . .like I had been awake for three days straight, or I hadn't eaten in a week. Just, all of a sudden, it was like my arms and head suddenly weighed a million pounds. I couldn't even take a step. I would have fallen down. At some point I dropped my gun, but I don't even remember doing it. I was only conscious because she wanted me to be, then when she let go, I just collapsed, out cold. She didn't even have to lay a finger on me." He shivered, surprised by how disturbing the memory still was, even in light of everything he knew about Justina now.

"What then?" prompted Ryan. He had been sitting in the back of the room until now, just listening and watching everyone.

"I woke up tied to a chair, with Imani watching me." He thought about mentioning that Justina had gone to confession, but decided to leave that out; it would only have invited ridicule and disbelief. "She let me start reading one of the books about nephilim to pass the time." He also elected to edit the fact that the book was about Merlin. That would have invited ridicule too. "When Justina got back, they had a consultation, and decided that they would let me work one mission with me, then let me go. We were in Shinnery to work that mission."

"So you could be a witness," said Ryan.

"Exactly. So I could be a witness. So I could have something *to* witness."

"Okay," said a skinny man named Jorge. "So what did you witness? She's fast and has powerful senses, she can take a bullet, and she can effect your perceptions, or whatever it was she did to knock you out. So, either we would have to surprise her, or else just out-number her."

"Or find some sort of pressure point," added the nondescript man. "Some sort of leverage."

"You're missing my point," said Tobias. "I told you already what I witnessed. I witnessed her *not being a monster*. That was the whole idea. I witnessed her not killing me when she could have. I witnessed her treating me with respect. I witnessed her stopping a pack of werewolves that had already killed several people, and I wit-nessed her *letting me go*. She and Imani even stayed in their motel in Shinnery, instead of running again, as a show of good faith."

The nondescript man snorted. Several people rolled their eyes, or exchanged skeptical looks.

"For god's sake, don't you realize that all of that was just a show? To trick you into calling the whole thing off?" demanded Carrie (or Cassie). "What a fucking idiot!"

"Of course I thought of that, but what would be the point?" retorted Tobias. "Why go to all that trouble? Why bother? Just kill me and leave. That's all she needed to do, if she just wanted to go about her business."

"She didn't do anything we didn't already know," said Kyle. "Whatever reasons she had, she didn't actually give you any real intel."

"She cured me of a werewolf bite." Tobias had been waiting for the moment to drop that on everyone.

He was not disappointed. For a moment, there was dead silence in the abandoned break room.

"Say that again," said Hill.

"I was bitten by one of the werewolves. It jumped me from behind, and was going to crunch right through my spine. She could have let it do it. She could have just stood there and done nothing, and the problem I represented would have gone away. But she didn't. She hauled the werewolf off me and saved me. And she could have left it at that! I could be a werewolf right now! Nobody has ever cured a werewolf bite; she could have done nothing, and I wouldn't have thought a thing of it. But she didn't. She reversed the process and I'm still human. The only one that's happened to, ever."

"Bullshit," said Kyle with simple, certain finality.

Tobias, furious, yanked the gauze dressing from his neck, tearing the tape loose from his skin, and turned around, letting them all see the bite. "Look! Look at it. Tell me now that I don't know what happened. Tell me now that I wasn't really bitten. Tell me, I dare you." He paused, letting everyone get a good look at the deep fang punctures, the huge bite radius, far too big for a coyote. Letting them remember that ordinary wolves had been extirpated from Texas many decades ago. Then he turned back around, tossed the blood-spotted gauze onto the table where everyone could see it, and sat down again, glaring. No one said anything.

"It was her plan," said a slim, unassuming man named Jamie. He had mousy-brown hair and a smoothly-shaved face, and looked more like a librarian than a hunter of dangerous things. He spoke kindly, but the implied pity only infuriated Tobias more. "She wanted to convince you to call off the hunt, *and she did.* You believed exactly what she wanted you to believe."

"Or maybe, *maybe,* the Order of the Holy Lance, who has all the reliable source materials and who also raised Justina from a newborn, *maybe* they know more about it than we do!"

Most of the others looked a little uncomfortable at that. They all knew, if they were honest with themselves, that they had practically no hard data about nephilim at all, and if the Order really did have three whole books about them. . .

Tobias was on a roll now. "And what the hell! Let's just say, for the sake of argument, that all of this was some pointlessly elaborate scheme to make me believe that Justina isn't an evil monster that it's our duty to hunt down. Again, what would be the point? Let me tell you something. I read one of the books, where the author describes an evil nephil that she and dozens of other sisters had to fight and kill back in the 1600s. She described what it could do, what it *was.* It took *dozens* of well-trained, well-armed, fully prepared sisters to kill it, and a lot of them died in the process. It was unimaginably powerful, a certifiable fucking nightmare."

No one said a word. Several people wouldn't look him in the eye.

"I realized something. We all assumed that Justina ran from us to protect herself, because she didn't think she could take us in a straight fight. But she can. She absolutely can. She didn't run to protect herself; she ran to protect the sisters, and innocent people in the crossfire, and us! She ran to protect us! She had no fucking need in the world to go to all that trouble to deceive me, then send me back as a witness, because she would be completely capable of killing every one of us, right now!"

There was a long silence. The man with the nondescript face murmured, "Something as dangerous as that..." and then he trailed

282 | JENNY PAXTON

off. After a moment, Jorge said slowly, "What about the other girl? The human one? Imani, is that her name?"

"Yes," said Tobias. "We all thought that Justina took her along just as a hostage, or kind of a pet or something, but that's not true. They were raised together at St. Margaret's, and they're sisters. Justina loves Imani, and would protect her at all costs. She is not a demon; she's human too, in every way that really matters."

There was another long, uncomfortable silence. Everyone looked at each other, but no one looked at Tobias.

"We were afraid of this," said Hill, his voice full of genuine regret. "She got to you. We were afraid she might."

Tobias had not thought anything of the fact that the two biggest, strongest men in the room had taken the seats immediately to his right and left. Now he realized that they had positioned them-selves there on purpose, and realized why, as they both pounced on him at once and started hauling him out of the room. No one moved to help him, and he saw that everyone, the whole group, had been in on it. Most had the decency to look ashamed, or at least embarrassed. The man with the nondescript face, though, just looked smug.

He thrashed and fought, and (both his arms being clamped behind him) kicked and even tried to bite. "Stop! What the hell are you doing? You don't know what you're doing! Let me go!" It was no use, though. The two men hauled him to a smaller room in the back (an office, probably), heaved him inside, and locked the door. He hammered at it with his fists, and tried throwing his shoulder against it, but it was made of steel (damn places with good security measures in place, he thought), and all he did was hurt his hands and shoulder.

Through the door, he heard Hill say, "We know it's not your fault. Once we get the nephil, you should be okay. And you did tell us what we needed to know: we need to focus on the little girl,

Imani, and use her to draw the nephil out. You'll thank us, you really will. I'm so sorry about all this."

Tobias had never been very concerned for Justina. He knew she was more than a match for a scrappy bunch of freelancers. But the thought that he had put little Imani in the crosshairs now was horrifyingly unexpected. "Don't you dare!" he yelled through the door. "Don't you fucking dare!"

But there was no answer from outside, and though he pounded some more against the door, all he got for his trouble was bruises.

***

Twenty-Two

Again, Justina had no of intention of sleeping that night. Dreams, she felt, had become an attacking enemy, and she could easily do without it; once she had gone for a week with no sleep, just to see if she could, and it had been easy. She had learned, during that week, to love the commandery library in the deadest hours of the night, when herself, her chair, her book, and her lamp seemed to make up all the waking universe. But tonight, sleep descended upon her irresistibly, the way it always did for humans, but as it had never done for her before the last week.

In her dream, she stood out on the open rangeland at twilight. A heavy, pewter-colored overcast covered the sky, and she could see its surface rolling briskly before a sharp winter wind. The mesquite and live oak trees near her tossed, the gale moaning and howling in their winter-bare branches, and the same wind pulled at her hair and clothes and pushed at her body until she had to brace herself against it. It caught up dead leaves and whipped them around her, hissing, their brittle edges scratching against her skin. She heard booms of thunder, once and then again, not near, but from every direction. Blue pulses of lightning illuminated the clouds near the horizon.

It was a wild dusk, the kind of weather Justina had always gloried in, without sun or shadows or anything but naked, unchained elements. She drew in a deep breath, tasting rain and ice and cold earth in the air, and wanted to add her own voice to the glory of the storm. But no words came to her.

Behind her, a voice sang a single, ringing note. It said no words —at least, no words she could grasp—but it was like the triumph of all the trumpets in the world, like the triumph of crashing waterfalls and the crashing thunder that underlined the voice. Sharp blue webs of lightning flared across the sky, then vanished again.

She turned.

Her father stood there.

He was a creature of fire and power. Even in the blue-hued overcast, his wings were brass and bronze and burning gold, fire and ember and lightning, stretching and stirring, untouched by the wind. His body blazed like molten bronze, and his eyes, in the sunless twilight, were brighter than the sun, too bright even for Justina to look at. The tips of his wings, so many wings, seemed to reach for the horizon to his right and left, and the incandescent silver of his hair almost seemed to meet the steely sky. She closed her eyes, but the fiery image of him remained, blazing through her eyelids and into her brain.

I know who you are, said Justina. She shouted the words, but the wind caught them away, so they made no noise even in her own ears. She shouted still, though she could not hear herself. You are my father. You are a demon. You are more powerful than I am, but not more powerful than God.

She stretched out her hand against him, and it also glowed like hot metal under the scudding clouds. In the name of Jesus Christ! In the name of God, leave this place, and leave me!

Nothing happened, and the fallen angel looked at her with pity. My poor child, he said. That magic will never work for you.

Thunder cracked, and instead of lightening in the sky, the tracery of veins under Justina's skin flared fierce blue-white for an instant. She looked away, half-blinded.

You cannot banish your own blood, he said, his voice gentle.

I am dedicated to God, said Justina, but she was shaken and no longer shouting. I have been dedicated to God since the day I was born.

You have been dedicated to me since the day you were conceived, he said, more harshly. You are what you are, and the Order of the Holy Lance cannot force you to become something you are not, however hard they may try.

I am a light nephil, said Justina, but her voice was thin and uncertain now. It was true that she had never been called on to try to combat a demon. Perhaps the sisters had known she could not do it, or worse, had been afraid of what she would realize and understand about herself if she tried.

You are a nephil, said the fallen angel. Light and dark have no bearing on the matter. You are what you are, and the sisters lied to you when they claimed to believe otherwise. The Order has known from the beginning what you are, and what you will become.

The storm was gone. Instead, Justina saw an unfamiliar chapter room, with a group of women in the habits of the Order of the Holy Lance assembled around a table. She didn't recognize most of them, but one was Sister Deborah; definitely Sister Deborah, but obviously years younger.

I move that precautionary measures be taken against this child, said a sister with dark blonde hair. Second, said another.

She should be kept under constant supervision at least, and possibly restrained, continued the first woman. Her eyes and smile burned with malice. The purpose of the Order of the Holy Lance is to protect people from supernatural or extranatural threats. That is our duty and our vocation. A nephil is a very significant threat, and this child should therefore be kept under careful watch and fully controlled. Her comfort must not take precedence over the safety of all the people she will hurt when she does become a threat. There will be far less collateral damage, and far less loss of life and limb for the Order, if she is controlled now, rather than when she has come into her full powers.

They feared you, said Justina's demon-father. They feared you then, and they fear you still. They have tried to tame you, to hamper you, to crush you down into something they could control and comprehend.

On the rangeland again, under the roiling sky and the thrashing wind, he reached out one hand to touch her face, gently, as a real father would. Though the air around his hand shimmered with heat, his touch did not burn her. His skin was the same temperature as her own.

They were capable of no better, he said, and there was no scorn in his voice, but only a simple, objective surety. They are bound and blinded by a weak, mortal body, made of dust, and the inability to see the reality of things around them. They are afraid of violence, afraid of harshness, afraid of taking a firm stand on anything lest they cause harm.

For an instant, Justina saw the dream-figure of Sister Rebecca again, drenched in blood, eyes piously closed against unpleasantness, while the consequences of her attitude ran in sticky streams from her habit, her hair, her hands.

They have never understood you. They have never understood what you see. They have never understood that your judgements are righteous and just, and should not have been constrained.

Images, scenes, broad strokes of form and emotion swirled around her, as if driven by the roaring wind.

You know she has trouble being patient with anyone who isn't up to her level, which if we're being honest, is nearly everyone, fretted Sister Deborah. You know she can be harsh. Impatient with weakness or stupidity.

And why should you not be? her demon-father whispered. Why should you tolerate less than yourself? Should you stifle your own excellence for the sake of indulging human inadequacy?

Flickers of Imani. Imani afraid, shaking, wide-eyed outside the boo hag's house, her body small and breakable, her senses weak, the stink of fear-sweat oozing off her. Then Imani in the werewolves' territory, staring wide-eyed at the wolf-killed deer, the feel of her small body shivering against Justina's back. Weak. Weak. Made of dust.

Staring down the male alpha of the werepack. Hearing him admit, casually, even proudly, to murdering human beings. Having him agree to stand his pack down, to refrain from further deaths. Then, mere moments later, a snarling wolf lunging, jaws gaping, white teeth gleaming, with the full intent of killing again.

Feel of dense, warm wolf fur in her hand. Weight of the wolf on her arm. Thrashing, squirming, like any evil creature trying to escape its rightful fate, like the boo hag.

She saw herself letting the werewolf live, and turning to go.

More flashes. Flashes of white teeth, bloodied jaws and fur, a human body with wolf-crushed bones, wolf-torn skin and flesh. The wolf she had spared looking up from the kill, feral, full of animal glee.

You were right, said the fallen angel. You were right, and you knew it all along. You knew that sparing the werewolves was foolish, yet you did, because the Order forced you to think that you must. They tried to cumber you with restrictions fit only for humans, not for anyone with immortal blood.

Now the motel room in Odessa. Jake sneaking into the room, gun in hand, believing he had taken her by surprise, but she sensed him the instant he entered, smelled his unfamiliarity, saw the darkness of him behind her closed eyes.

She saw his face, grotesque with a mix of abject fear and blind hate. Saw the dark scum of paranoia, self-hatred, mistrust, deceptiveness, and old, stale bitterness. Then, out of that, she heard him fumbling at the words of the Latin rite of exorcism, tainting its holiness with his own nastiness even as he said it. She felt again the clean, white heat of her own righteous wrath in response.

You knew the justice of it then, her father said. You knew he deserved to be struck down. Yet you were stopped. You were restrained and cumbered from doing what you knew must be done.

A blur of unfamiliar faces, angry, bitter, lawless, hiding lies just below the surface of their skin.

A sneaky-looking man with colorless hair and a nondescript face: She's a nephil, she's a monster by definition!

A tall, bitter-looking woman: My god, what fucking good are you? For god's sake, don't you realize that all of that was just a show? To trick you into calling the whole thing off? What a fucking idiot!

Jake himself, smug, describing everything he had seen, giving them information, telling them that she, Justina, and Imani were still in Shinnery.

They taught you not to kill, not to act on your desire for righteous destruction of the wicked, the fallen angel whispered. They were wrong. They ever understood you. You have grown up hampered, weakened, sickened with guilt and empty piety and endless, endless laws. But you were never made for that. You are a nephil. You are made for power and freedom. You are made to bring wrath. You are made to right wrongs with the edge of your sword.

It took all Justina's strength to remember who she was, and who he was. She closed her eyes to the images of human weakness and human betrayal and human stupidity. You are a demon. You are a demon, and I will not serve you or do your work! I will never! I refuse.

Oh my child, he said, cupping her face in his hands, hands that seemed strong and solid to her, in contrast to the fragility she could always, always feel in human hands. I would never ask you to go against your nature. Only the Order demanded that of you. I want you to be free, free to follow your own purpose. If bringing wrath on the wicked is what you desire in your own heart, I would never try to prevent you. I would even help you. The sisters were entirely unable to help you learn to use the power you have; even now, you have barely begun to touch it, and that only outside the Order's influence. But I know your power. I know what you can do. I will teach you, and you can bring about all that you desire in the world.

I've read about dark nephilim, said Justina, still fighting. I've read about what they have done, what they are. I want nothing to do with that.

The fallen angel's wings, so many wings, fire and ember, bronze and gold, drew back slightly, in what she interpreted as a recoil. You know of the nephil killed by the Order many years ago, he said, his voice full of disgust. My brother was a fool, and encouraged his son to destroy wildly and thoughtlessly. Pointless. He did not rise above humanity, as you will do; he sank below it, and became nothing but a rabid animal. The Order was quite right to kill him. He was a monster. I would never allow that for you, even if you wanted it.

I belong to God, said Justina, trying to make herself believe it. I will never side with you.

I will never force you to, unlike the Order, who forced you to take a side before you were five hours old. I will only hope that you will come to me, my daughter. If you call me, I will be here for you.

*

The instant Justina woke up, Imani knew something was wrong, drastically wrong. She knew it by the shocked, lost look on Justina's face; it was as if the foundations of her life had cracked, as if things she had known with bedrock certainty had turned out to be as unstable as dry, sliding sand. She looked afraid, and Justina was never afraid. She looked desperately uncertain, and Justina always knew what to do. Just seeing it, Imani felt sick with fear herself; she was used to being afraid, and it was as familiar to her as an unwelcome friend, but if *Justina* was afraid. . .if Justina was afraid, there was truly something to be afraid of.

Justina sat on her bed, knees drawn up to her chest and her arms wrapped around them; again, this body language was all wrong. Justina rarely intimidated people on purpose, or deliberately filled a room with her presence, but she never made herself small. She made herself small now. Imani got up on the bed next to her, and felt her shaking; not with that terrible, out-of-control shaking she had done in Mockingbird, after finding out about the attack on the commandery, but the way a human might shake after hearing terrible news.

"What happened?" asked Imani, and resolved not to take any excuses or delays this time. This time, Justina would really tell her what was going on.

Justina raised her head and looked at her, golden eyes full of a terrible desolation, but she said nothing.

"It was your. . .your demon-father, wasn't it?"

Still Justina said nothing, but she did flinch slightly, and Imani knew she had been right.

"You know that whatever he told you, whatever he showed you, it was a lie. You know that, right? He's a demon. Lies are what he does."

"They weren't, though. Lies." Justina's voice was terrible, worse than when it had been inhuman with power. "He showed me things, and I know they were true. I saw them happen. And. . ." She stopped, apparently unwilling to give voice to something even deeper.

Imani ignored that for the moment. "It doesn't matter," she said. "If he told you things that were true, it was with a deceptive purpose, so it was the same thing. He did it so you would believe the other things he told you. He did it because he's a master liar, and the strongest lies are half-true. You know that."

"I couldn't. . ." The desolate, lost look was back in Justina's eyes. "I couldn't make him leave. I told him to go, in the name of Christ, and he didn't even blink. He said. . .he said it wouldn't work for me. God couldn't work through me that way, because I have demon blood. I'm. . .tainted."

Imani straightened up at that, feeling more fierce than she could ever remember feeling. For a moment, she was too angry to do anything but stutter.

"And it wasn't a lie!" Justina cried, and the anguish in her voice knocked the breath out of Imani, leaving her gasping. "It wasn't a lie, I really *couldn't* order him to go! It didn't work, even though I called on God's name in faith!"

"Stop that right now!" ordered Imani, and Justina looked at her in surprise. "He wanted to convince you that you are cut off from God, that you're destined to be evil, but it was a *lie*. He was manipulating you."

"But I couldn't—"

"It was a dream! Who knows what the rules are in dreams? Normal rules don't apply to anything else, so why should they to that? For all you know, he planted this whole thing in your brain years ago, just waiting for the right moment! Who knows what he did? But you can be sure he lied. He wants to get you back, and he can only do that now by deceiving you. Were you expecting him to be bad at it?"

Justina swallowed several times. "I don't know," she said.

"God doesn't work like that, just writing people off. What does the Book of Deuteronomy say about allowing Moabites into the Israelite assembly?"

Justina blinked at this abrupt non sequitur. "What?"

"Come on, what does it say?" Imani knew very well that Justina had it memorized.

"They couldn't be admitted in, even after ten generations."

"*But*," prompted Imani, "who was actually the great-grandson of a Moabite woman?"

Justina didn't answer for a long time. "It was King David," she said reluctantly.

"It's about *choice*," Imani emphasized. "Which side you *choose* to be on, whether you *choose* to serve God. It's not about bloodline."

Justina stood up. "I think I need to go for a run," she said. "A long run. I just. . .need to think. About everything."

"Don't believe anything the demon said," Imani told her. "Remember that he's a demon, and remember that he wants you, and remember that he's a liar and good at it."

Justina, pulling her running gear out of her duffel bag, looked up and gave her a weak half-smile. "I'll try to keep that in mind."

***

Interlude Ten

(Unread) From: magdalena.westtex@ohl.org
To: imani.westtex@ohl.org
Re: Re: Shinnery Again
December 1, at 9:57am

Imani,

I have consulted with the sisters, and with Brother David, and we all agree that the situation is concerning. If Justina really is coming under attack by her demon-father, the danger from the freelancers pales in comparison. We can be in Shinnery later today, and we'll decide then what the best thing to do is. Email me back with which motel you're staying in.

TLDR: Hang tight, we're on our way.

Pax Vobiscum,

Sister Magdalena

Sister Magdalena
Knight-Sister of the Order of the Holy Lance
Commandery of West Texas
Commandery-House of Saint Margaret of Antioch

(Unsent) From: imani.westtex@ohl.org
To: magdalena.westtex@ohl.org
Re: SOS

Sister Magdalena,

Justina's demon-father came to her in a dream again last night, this time openly, and it really shook her. I think

***

Twenty-Three

Imani was writing an email to Sister Magdalena when, only a couple of minutes after Justina had gone, someone knocked on the motel room door. She put aside her laptop and got up.

Through the peephole, she saw an unassuming man with light brown hair and an amiable face. Imani took her gun out of her duffel and held it down beside her leg, just in case, then opened the door a crack. "Can I help you?"

"Are you Imani?"

No one should know that. Not even the sisters knew more than which town she and Justina were in. For a moment she tried to push the door closed again, but he held it open with all his weight, and he weighed more than she did. So she let go of the door and rushed back into the room, putting her back to the wall to avoid being flanked.

Three men walked in, and closed the door behind them. All doubt about whether their intentions were good disappeared. Imani raised her gun, a fist of fear clenched in her gut, but her arm steady. "Stay back."

The man she had seen at first held up both his hands, placatingly, and said, "We're not here to hurt you. We're the good guys. Just put the gun down."

Imani did not.

"There's no point in that," said one of the other men. "She's under the nephil's influence too. She's not going to cooperate." With that, he started toward Imani.

With a quick prayer that she was doing the right thing, Imani pulled the trigger, shooting the nearest man in the leg. With a spurt of blood, he went down with a hole cleanly through the muscle.

The other two lunged at her. She managed to shoot one of them in the shoulder, but after that they were grappling with her, and she dared not fire again for fear of killing one of them accidentally. She reversed her grip on the gun, and smashed the butt with all her strength across the face of the man she had winged, and he fell back with a snarl of pain, his hand to his face and blood dripping through his fingers.

The third man was behind her, trying to get a grip on her arms. She threw herself backwards, slamming him between her body and the wall, and used her elbows. With a gasp, he lost his hold, and she wriggled free.

She seemed to have broken the nose of her other attacker, and possibly also knocked loose a tooth or two. He aimed a punch at her with a huge fist, but it was a clumsy, obvious attack, and she slipped it easily. She let her gun drop and caught his wrist in both her hands, and, with a grunt and a twist of her body, redirected his momentum, sending him crashing headfirst into the wall. He howled with pain at the impact, and more blood from his nose and lip flew in big, wet drops onto the carpet.

A weapon. She was outnumbered and outweighed, and needed a weapon.

The chair. She dived for it, but when she passed the man she had shot in the leg, he reached out one big hand and caught at her ankle. He didn't get a good grip, but it was enough to trip her up, and she fell against the chair with all her weight, throwing it back into the wall and gouging a deep gash out of the drywall.

For a moment Imani saw stars, after striking her head against the aluminum tubing of the chair's frame.

Before she could recover, one of the attackers threw her to the floor facedown, and held her there with a knee in her back. She thrashed like an eel, but could not throw him off.

"Feisty little thing, isn't she?" said someone.

Hands pinned her wrists to the floor, holding them down with his weight; she threw her head back, hoping to strike his nose or mouth, but he moved out of the way.

Up to that point, Imani had fought more or less in silence; screaming for help was not usually very high on the Order's list of options, and it hadn't been part of her training. Now it occurred to her, and she screamed with all her strength, surprising herself with the volume of it. Despite the closed door, maybe someone outside would hear. She kept screaming until someone grabbed a handful of her hair and pulled her head up, then a rolled-up hand towel from the bathroom was tied around her mouth as a gag. She clenched her teeth, but a pair of fingers pinched her nose until she had to open her mouth or suffocate. Scratchy terry fabric pulled tight against her teeth and tongue, muffling her screams.

Big hands dragged her wrists behind her back and secured them with what felt like handcuffs. Someone pulled a white hotel pillow-case over her head. Then they hauled her to her feet.

She did not cooperate, but kept squirming and kicking. She hoped that, if nothing else, she could make them drop some sort of clue: someone's belt buckle or earring or something, something that would point the sisters, or the police, in the right direction. There would be DNA already: she knew at least two of the men had left blood, and all three had surely left hair and probably fingerprints. There were the two bullets, too, and they would trace to her gun. People would know that she had been here, and that she had been attacked.

She kicked something unyielding: furniture. Then, blindly, her foot connected with something more helpful. From the meaty sound, and the scream of pain that followed, she guessed it was someone's knee.

"Little *bitch*!"

With the pillowcase over her head, she didn't see the blow coming, and if they had not been holding her by the arms, it would have knocked her down. She saw stars again, and only heard dimly as a different voice said, "Stop! Stop it. We need her."

The door opened. "All clear," said someone, and they hustled her outside. Of course they would check out the area first; wouldn't do to have any passerby see such a blatantly obvious kidnapping in progress.

She expected them to throw her into a car trunk. In fact, she counted on it, figuring that if the drive lasted any length of time, she could work the pillowcase off her head and the hand towel out of her mouth. Then maybe she could pick the lock on the handcuffs; there should be a paperclip in her pocket. She could definitely kick out the taillights, and signal other cars for help. But apparently the kidnappers knew that too, because they didn't put her in the trunk. Instead, they wrestled her (still fighting, though she was tiring quickly) into the back seat.

"It's like trying to get a cat into a carrier to go to the vet," someone muttered.

Two of the men got into the back seat with her, one on each side. She heard them buckle their seatbelts. Then the third man climbed into the driver's seat and started the car, and off they went.

"Pull over," said someone after a few minutes. "Little bitch broke my nose, and I've got a bullet in my shoulder and a busted knee! Kyle's got a hole through his leg!"

"Nope," said the driver. "We can't afford the time. The nephil is bound to be back soon. Here." He opened the glove compartment, took something out, and tossed it back. "Patch up as best you can, but unless someone's bleeding out, we don't stop."

A box opened: glove compartment first aid kit, Imani guessed. Scissors cut through fabric, probably to get to the one man's leg wound; paper packages tore open, and she caught the sharp smell of antiseptic. Then the ripping sound of fabric tape being unrolled to hold down dressings, and the hisses of pain and muffled swearing as antiseptic was applied to open wounds.

"Have we got an ice pack in the trunk?" asked the man to Imani's right. From the sound of his voice, Imani gathered he was the one with the broken nose; it must be swollen enough now to her to be able to tell.

"We should," said the man to Imani's left. "One of those single-use chemical ones."

The car began to decelerate and pull over. "I'll give you two minutes to find it," said the driver. "After that you'll just have to tough it out until we get to Odessa."

While they were looking for the ice pack, the driver pulled the pillowcase off Imani's head and the gag out of her mouth. She had been working quietly at the gag all along, and thought she would have been able to get it loose soon, but nonetheless she was quite glad to let him help her out.

She saw that he was the smallest of the three men, the one who had knocked on the door, and also the least injured, probably because he had attacked her less aggressively. He would undoubtedly have some nice elbow-shaped bruises, and probably some bruising down his back and maybe a lump on his head where she had slammed him against the wall, but not much more than that.

She stretched her mouth, and spat some bits of terrycloth fuzz off her tongue. "Thank you," she said, and meant it.

He got out again, and back into his own seat behind the steering wheel. "Like I said before, we're not the bad guys."

The other two men got back into the car on either side of her. One was bending and squeezing a blue-and-white chemical ice pack between his hands, and when the chemicals inside had activated, he folded it in a towel and applied it gingerly to his cut and swollen nose. He glared at Imani while he did this, and she looked away, shivering. He was much bigger than she was, and she was hand-cuffed. If he really decided to hurt her, she couldn't stop him. She wasn't sure the other two men could stop him, at least in time to keep her from being badly injured. He was the one whose knee she had kicked (it was wrapped in an Ace bandage now, she saw; she might had dislocated the kneecap or something), and likely also the one who had hit her before. She couldn't reach up her hand to check, but her right eye was beginning to feel sore and puffy. I'll have a black eye, she thought.

"We're sorry about all this, we really are," said the man who was driving. "We just didn't have a choice."

Imani snorted. "You always have a choice. And you keep on saying you're the good guys, right? Well, did you know that there's a place in the Bible that actually gives clear instructions about how to tell if someone is a good guy?"

No one answered.

"'You will recognize them by their fruits,'" Imani recited. "'Are grapes gathered from thornbushes, or figs from thistles? So, every healthy tree bears good fruit, but the diseased tree bears bad fruit.' Jesus was using fruit trees as a metaphor. You know what kind of tree you have by what kind of fruit is on it. So if a tree has peaches, it's a peach tree, but if it says it's a peach tree and it has crabapples, it's not a peach tree, no matter what it says. People aren't good because they say they are: they're good because they choose to do the right things."

She tried to catch the driver's eye in the rear view mirror, but could not.

"You broke into our motel room," Imani went on, beginning to be angry. "You attacked me and kidnapped me, in order to use me as bait to draw in my sister, who loves me and will come to my rescue. So that you can kill her, even though she's never harmed you in the least, or harmed any person. Right? Isn't that your plan? So in light of all that, tell me again that you're the good guys in this situation. I dare you."

For a while they drove in silence. A winter landscape of bare cottonwood trees and stubbled cottonfields, railroad embankments that looked as if no train had ever run on them, and last autumn's windblown tumbleweeds caught in barbed wire fences rushed by. The wind picked up, buffeting the car, and when they passed farms or towns, every banner and flag and plume of pampas grass whipped in sudden, jagged gusts. A dull khaki-colored dimness began to rise on the horizon to their right, as the freshening gale caught loose dust up into the air.

"Cold front blowing in," said the driver to no one in particular.

"You need to let me go," said Imani after a while. "I'm serious, you really do. I'm not just saying that because it's the right thing, even though it is. You don't understand at all what you're bringing down on yourself."

The man with the shot leg made a sound of exasperation. "Oh, for god's sake, shut up! We're not going to let you go. You're going to bring the nephil to us, and we're going to kill her, just like the Order of the Holy Lance would have done years ago if they had any balls, and then you'll be free to go on your merry way. That's what's going to happen."

"That is not what's going to happen!"

"Listen, bitch," said the man with the broken nose. "If you don't shut up, I'll shut you up. I may do it anyway. Just give me an excuse."

Imani ignored this. "Justina is so far out of your weight class that. . ." She struggled to find an analogy. "Never mind it not being a fair fight. It won't even be a fight. She could obliterate every one of you if she thought she had to, and doing this, kidnapping me, might very well convince her that she has to."

The man on Imani's left, the one with the shot leg, said, "Okay, that's enough. Back in with the gag." He rummaged around in the floorboards of the car for it, and while he did, Imani made a last try to get them to see their danger.

"Do you know what the first thing is that angels usually have to say any time they encounter a human?"

"Hello?" offered the man to her right, facetiously.

"'Do not be afraid'," said Imani. "And why? Because people *were* afraid. People were terrified. We have records of angels leveling cities and wiping out armies in a single night."

"Justina isn't an angel," said the driver.

"No! No, she isn't. She's half human, and you're banking on that. You're banking on her responding the way a human would. I have no idea what would happen if someone kidnapped a person an angel loved; I don't even know if angels experience love in that way. But I know what a human would do. A human would charge to the rescue, guns blazing, and that is exactly what Justina will do. And no, she probably isn't capable of wiping out an army, but she won't need to, will she? There are probably what, a dozen of you? Two dozen maybe? This is not a fight you can win, and you don't have to fight it! Honestly, you don't! Justina is not evil, and she's not your enemy! Just let me out, give me my phone back so I can call her, and you can get on with your lives with a clear conscience!"

The man to her left found the hand towel at last. "I'm trying to save your lives!" Imani insisted desperately, and then he stuffed it back into her mouth and knotted it behind her head.

"Thank *god*," said the broken-nosed man, in exaggerated relief. "So, Jamie, you think we could have some music or something?"

*

Sisters Rebecca and Magdalena arrived in Shinnery in the late morning, and canvassed the motels in town, trying to find the one where Justina and Imani had been staying. It was midafternoon before they found the right one, and Magdalena, fitfully checking her emails on her phone every few minutes and chewing her lip, was becoming seriously alarmed.

"Hell yeah they were here!" said the receptionist behind the desk. She looked frazzled, and a smell of cigarette smoke hung around her. She had apparently been trying to paint her fingernails when the sisters walked in—a bottle of fire engine red nail polish sat on a paper towel beside her—but making a mess of it, and no wonder; her hands were visibly shaking. "The tall one checked out this morning. I don't know what's wrong with her, but *something* sure as hell is. Look."

They looked where the stickily botched crimson fingernail pointed, and stared, struck silent. It was a handprint, actually burned into the Formica countertop, black and charred in the middle and fading to sickly yellow-brown around the edges. It was placed where a person might rest her hand as she was talking to the receptionist, and the size and the long fingers suggested it must have been Justina's hand that left the mark.

"Please tell us everything you can," said Sister Rebecca, endeavoring to speak more calmly than she felt. That handprint. . .

"Look," said the woman, "all I know is, the tall girl came in here around eleven o'clock, eleven thirty, and wanted to check out. She was in a hell of a rush, and I don't think she even realized she left that burn on the counter. She paid up, with that Order of the Lance or whatever credit card, and then she just lit out. Got in her car and screamed out of the parking lot; probably burned rubber and marked the blacktop all up."

"Did you see the younger girl? Imani?" asked Sister Magdalena.

"Not today," said the receptionist, fidgeting with the nail polish bottle. "Maybe she was in the car."

The two sisters exchanged a look, both looking sick. Something seriously wrong had obviously happened, just as Imani had feared.

"We need to see their room, if we could," said Sister Rebecca. "We have credentials if you need to see them."

The receptionist put the nail polish bottle down on its paper towel again, nearly knocking it over as she did. "Housekeeping probably hasn't gotten to that room yet, so everything should be like they left it. Just let me get someone to cover the front desk, and I'll take you over there."

The room, when they entered, was a mess. The desk chair had been thrown against the wall violently enough to take a gouge out of it, and lay on its back on the floor. Another large dent (this one noticeably head-shaped) had been bashed into another wall and sprinkled with thick drops of what could only be blood; more drops, and one bigger splash, had soaked in to the carpet in several places. The desk was knocked slightly crooked, and one corner had a wide scuff across it, as if it had been kicked. In the middle of the room, a dark, tacky stain clearly marked the place where someone had bled while lying on the floor.

The receptionist took one look at all this and screamed, clutching at her shirt front and leaving nail polish stains (far more red than the blood now) on the fabric. "Ohmygodohmygodohmygod," said said, making it all one word. "Holy shit, she murdered her! She murdered that poor little girl!"

"No, she didn't," said Sister Rebecca, "but something bad certainly happened."

"I'm calling the police," said the woman, her voice rising with encroaching hysteria.

"Yes," said Sister Rebecca, deciding that was probably the best thing for her. "That's a good idea. We appreciate it."

The receptionist ran for the office.

The two sisters began to move around the room, methodically. "There was obviously a fight," said Sister Magdalena, "but there's no way Justina was involved. There would either be a lot more damage than this, or none."

"Agreed."

Sister Rebecca searched the carpet near the largest bloodstain, and finally said, "Aha!" She held up the misshapen bullet. "Looks like one of ours. It's the right caliber, anyway."

"It's one of ours, all right," said Sister Magdalena. She pushed aside the bed skirt, and withdrew a handgun from behind it. The grip was imprinted with the seal of the Order.

"So what do you think?" asked Sister Magdalena, sitting back on her heels. "Justina was out for some reason, and someone attacked Imani? She defended herself with her gun?"

"Looks like it. And Justina was so upset because she came back to *this*." Rebecca stood, gestured to the state of the room.

"I wonder where Imani is, then. Injured? Maybe she was in the car, like the receptionist said?"

"I doubt it. Justina would have called us. As it is. . ." Sister Rebecca trailed off, noticing a scrap of something in a corner. She picked it up. It was a sheet of paper from a motel notepad, the kind with the motel's logo and contact information printed on it, and it was browned and crisped from heat. Its edges were curled and charred, and black cinders flaked off onto Rebecca's hands when she touched it. The only thing written on it was an address, in Odessa.

She handed it to Sister Magdalena. "Someone must have abducted Imani," said said quietly. "They're using her as bait to draw Justina in, and this is the address where they have her. Justina saw the state of the room, read the note, and—"

"—And next thing you know her hands are burning everything she touches," Magdalena finished.

"Right."

"We need to get to this address," said Magdalena. "Like, now. We may already be too late to help deal with whatever's going down, and if Justina's demon-father really is behind all of this—"

"I'm thinking more and more that he must be," said Rebecca. She had the sick feeling that they were already too late to try to thwart whatever his endgame was. If he was to be defeated in his efforts to get Justina back under his influence, it would have to be Justina who did it, without their help. The thought was terrifying.

"Back to the car. The police can handle things here." Magdalena put the scorched note back down where they had found it. "You can drive; I'll get on the phone to the commandery in Lubbock. We can't physically intervene, but we can pray. We can all pray."

*

Tobias sat on the concrete floor in the stripped-down office, bored out of his skull. He was also tired, but not tired enough to take a nap; the floor was no more comfortable now than it had been last night, and if he tried taking off his shirt and wadding it up for a pillow, it was not only hard but freezing cold as well.

A wobbly metal desk, painted in several peeling layers of battleship-gray paint, stood against one cinderblock wall. He had throughly examined its contents for anything he might be able to use to escape; even a forgotten paperclip would be useful for trying to pick the door's lock. But there was nothing but dust in the desk. He checked all the joins between the desk's parts, thinking that if one screw was loose enough to let him grab it, he could wrap his fingers in his shirttail and twist it free. If several screws were loose, he might be able to get a leg or a drawer track or something else that he could use. It would take time, but he had nothing but time.

Not one screw was loose enough to do anything with, unless he happened to find a forgotten screwdriver lying around. Fat chance.

Next, he had examined the walls minutely for nails, left behind after pictures or calendars or diplomas had been taken down. He found plenty of nail holes, but the nails themselves had been pulled out, either when the warehouse was emptied or more recently, by his own people. Had they taken that much trouble to make sure he had no way to escape this room?

It certainly looked like it. No paperclips, no nails, not so much as a thumbtack.

He had examined the door. That hadn't taken long. The lock was solid, the door was metal, and the hinges were on the other side, where he couldn't get to them. Even if they hadn't been, he had no tools to work on them with anyway.

He had examined the two walls that weren't cinderblock, thinking that if they were flimsy partitions, he might be able to work an edge loose enough to squirm though. But they were solid; too solid, at any rate, to break without tools. Even if he had tools, trying to break through them would make enough noise to bring everyone down on him before he could make a dent.

He had paced the room until he got tired of it. Then he had tried to find a halfway-comfortable position on the floor that would allow him to sleep, but that was no good for more than a few minutes at a time. The desk was worse, if anything; its vinyl surface was less cold than the floor, but no softer, and the desk was so small that his feet and legs stuck out far beyond the edge. Also, it apparently had one short leg, or else the floor was uneven; anyway, it wobbled every time he moved.

They had brought him breakfast that morning. At any rate, he assumed it was morning; he had no windows to see out, and there was no clock. It wasn't a bad breakfast, either: a styrofoam bowl of Cheerios and milk (only slightly soggy), a blueberry muffin, and a cup of mediocre coffee (mediocre, but hot). He was pretty sure it had all been smuggled out from the motel's complimentary breakfast, and the thought of his fellow freelancers (those who hadn't drawn the short straw of having to babysit him, anyway) getting to spend the night in beds, getting actual sleep, frustrated him almost enough to start hammering on the door again.

Instead of that, he had tried the plastic spoon from the Cheerios on the desk screws that seemed the loosest. It only snapped and splintered, and the screws didn't budge. He flung the spoon ferociously at the wall, but it was too light to do anything satisfying; it only made a little *tap* against the cinderblock and fell to the floor pointlessly. The styrofoam bowl and coffee cup were even worse; it was like trying to throw a handful of feathers.

Tobias had lost his temper then. He took it out on the only other thing in the room, by flipping the desk over forward with a crash. Then he heaved it over again, and sent it crunching against the wall; all the drawers fell open, but there was no use in that, not so much as a paper clip.

He flipped the desk several more times, accomplishing nothing, but when he had tired himself out he felt a little better. He went to sit on the floor against the wall.

That was where he was sitting when he heard someone unlocking the door again. He perked up a little; maybe it was lunch. That would give him something to do for a few minutes, anyway.

It was not. Instead, Jamie came inside, hauling Imani beside him, gagged and handcuffed. He untied the gag and unlocked the cuffs, and as he did this, Tobias jumped up, furious (furious, but not as dramatic as he had hoped to be; his butt had gone numb from sitting on the concrete, so it was more a case of staggering to his feet than jumping).

"You idiots!" he yelled. "You *fucking* idiots! You have no idea what you've done! You've killed us all!"

Jamie said nothing. He left Imani in the room, and as he closed the door, Tobias screamed after him, "Do you hear me? *You've killed us all!*"

Imani just stood there for a moment. She looked at the desk, piled crookedly against one wall, its drawers sagging open. She looked at the bleak walls, the lack of furniture. She looked at Tobias. He couldn't meet her eyes. She looked scared, scared and only fifteen years old, and one of her eyes was bruised and nearly swollen shut. They hadn't just kidnapped her; they'd hurt her. He felt sick, half-blinded by a mix of fury and deep shame.

She crossed the room and sat down on the floor beside him.

"I'm sorry, Imani, I'm so sorry," Tobias said. He hadn't planned to say anything, but now that he had begun, he found himself babbling on. "I swear to God, I had no idea what they were going to do. Believe me, I never wanted anything like this to happen."

She glanced at him, surprised. "I know," she said, as if anything to the contrary had never even crossed her mind. "You didn't have anything to do with this. If you had, it would have been better organized. And if I didn't know before, I sure would now. You wouldn't be locked in here too, if you'd been in on it."

"It's my fault, though," he insisted, feeling an obscure need to convince her to blame him as much as he was blaming himself. "I told them you and Justina were still in Shinnery. That's how they knew where to look for you."

"Jake—"

That was more than he could stand. "My name isn't really Jake!" he burst out. For the first time, he turned his head to look at her, nakedly, ashamed.

"I know," she said again.

He blinked at that. "You. . . Wait, what?"

Imani smiled a little. "I told you before, it's like everything you're thinking is over your head in a thought bubble. We knew from the beginning that you were using a fake name, but we figured, if it made you feel safer, what harm? We let it go."

Everything she said made him feel worse, more like a traitor. She had no business being so nice to him; she ought to be screaming at him, ripping him a new one, and the fact that she wasn't doing that made him feel even more guilty. He smacked his fist backward into the cinderblock wall at his back.

"My name's really Tobias," he said.

For a few minutes they sat in silence. Imani felt it was her duty to pray, and she tried, but found it hard to focus; she knew she should pray blessing on the men who had kidnapped her ("Pray for your enemies, and bless those who curse you"), but it was hard. She could barely see out of her eye. She ached: her shoulders ached from the hours in handcuffs, her jaw ached from the gag, her foot ached where she had kicked the piece of furniture, she ached in various places without even being able to identify why. She was afraid, afraid that the angry man with the dislocated knee might come in here and do more to her than just give her a black eye, afraid that she would never get home, afraid that everything would fall apart and there would be lots of deaths today. She was also angry, and tried hard to bring to heel the part of herself that wished she had shot her kidnappers in the head rather than in the leg or shoulder. She tried to pray for her kidnappers, but also couldn't help praying for vengeance and justice in the manner of some of the Psalms, and she strongly suspected the result was mainly just incoherent. That was all right, she supposed; an incoherent prayer was still a prayer.

"Did you put up a good fight?" Tobias asked. "When they came for you? Did you give them some good bruises to remember you by?"

"Yes," she said, and was fiercely glad that she had. Well, she thought, there were plenty of Scriptures of people exulting over the defeat of their enemies. At least she was in good company. "One shot in the shoulder, one in the leg, a broken nose, and I think a dislocated knee."

Tobias gave a short laugh, full of vindictive glee. "Three of them against one, and you're a fifteen-year-old girl! They'll never live it down! Serves them right."

They were silent again. Imani stood up and walked around the room, stretching her legs.

"I checked the desk," said Tobias. "Not even a paperclip to try to pick the door lock with."

"I have a paperclip in my pocket," said Imani absently.

Tobias got up quickly. "You do? Let me see it!"

She took it out and handed it over. "I thought about picking the handcuffs, but I was squished in the back seat of a car with two other people, so I couldn't do it without them noticing. And any-way, we were in a moving car on the highway; there didn't seem to be much point."

Tobias examined the paperclip, then the lock on the door.

"I don't think there's much use in that, though," said Imani. "I counted ten people outside, all armed, building barricades around the door and whatnot. We wouldn't get far."

Tobias knew she was right, but still, it was intensely frustrating. He threw down the paperclip, but it was no more satisfying than the plastic spoon had been earlier that day.

"I think we'll just have to sit tight here, until Justina arrives," added Imani, and bit her lip.

Tobias sat down again, and leaned his head back against the cold cinderblock wall. He realized then that the wall was vibrating a little, and when he held his ear against it, he could hear the rising wail of the wind outside.

"Sounds like a hell of a cold front blowing in," he said vaguely, just for something to say.

To his surprise, Imani's eyes snapped sharply in his direction, and when she also pressed her ear to the wall, her eyes widened.

"What? What's the matter?"

"It might just be a cold front," she said. "It might also be Justina making this happen."

He swallowed hard. "Really?"

"You've read the books," said Imani. "You know some nephilim have had the ability to influence the weather, and I know for a fact that Justina's demon-father did."

"Wait." Tobias tried to process that. "Justina's what now?"

Imani squinted at him. "You've known all along that Justina is a nephil, and you're saying her demon-father never once crossed your mind?"

For a moment, Tobias just sat, his mouth open. Now that he actually thought about it, it seemed like a spectacularly stupid thing to have forgotten. "No," he admitted finally.

Imani sat down on the floor beside him again. "The night Justina was born," she said, "the hospital in Derrick called St. Margaret's to come and pick her up. They didn't have any idea about her being a nephil; she was just an orphan baby who needed a home."

Tobias nodded, understanding, but said nothing.

"Sister Rebecca was the one who went to get her, and as soon as she saw her she knew. She grabbed baby Justina and rushed for the commandery as fast as she could. She was *just* ahead of the demon-father. Apparently it was quite a race, and the demon attacked her in all sorts of ways to try to stop her. One way was hitting her with a windstorm powerful enough to blow down streetlights, break windows, and knock out all the power in Derrick for most of two days."

"So you think this is. . .what? Justina's first line of attack?"

"I don't know. She's never influenced the weather before, not that I know of, but she probably did inherit the ability to do it."

They sat in silence for a few minutes, listening to the howls of rising wind gusts outside, feeling the cinderblocks vibrate. The air in the room began to feel colder; the temperature outside must be dropping rapidly. They could hear the sounds of furniture being dragged around in the warehouse proper, beyond the locked door, as well as urgent voices; setting up their defensive positions, Tobias supposed.

"Tell me the honest truth," said Tobias suddenly. "Is anyone going to survive this, once Justina arrives?"

Imani paused before answering, tracing her finger through the dust on the concrete floor, which was not encouraging. "I hope so," she said at last.

He raised his eyebrows at that. "You hope so? After what they did? Shit, I wouldn't mind seeing some of these guys bite it myself, and I'm not the one they kidnapped and gave a black eye."

Imani picked up a speck of something from the floor, and flicked it away. "Emotionally, I would have. . .a hard time mourning them," she admitted, as though confessing a nasty secret. "I'm only human. But I know, objectively, that it would be much better if no one had to die at all."

"Why?"

"It's for the same reason the Order doesn't kill any person, human or not, unless it's absolutely necessary," she said.

"I always figured you just wanted to be the good guys, and good guys don't kill people. Like Batman."

Imani gave a short laugh at that. "Maybe, partly! But mostly because people are valuable to God, immeasurably valuable, so we also have to value people's lives. If we have no choice—if someone is in immediate danger, or if a powerful creature will not cooperate or stand down—then we do what we have to, but if there is a choice we always choose not to destroy a life that God values. You see what I mean?"

"I guess so," said Tobias. Just like before, hearing Imani talk about God made him feel uncomfortable and exposed.

"Essentially, if we kill a person for retribution, when we don't actually have to, we're making the judgement that they can't be redeemed, or that they shouldn't get another chance. But we don't have the ability to make that kind of call, because we can't possibly have all the information; only God can. It's way above our pay grade. If we kill someone in revenge, it's like. . .it's like we're setting ourselves up as God."

"But what does all that have to do with Justina?" Tobias was not as interested in the morality of it as he was in whether he was likely to survive.

"If she comes just to rescue me, but the situation happens so that she has no choice but to kill someone, that would be tragic. But it would be. . .not okay, but. . .at least. . .fair. But if she comes for revenge, with the intention of killing them all because she wants them dead, that could be disastrous. She would be choosing, deliberately, to follow her own way and her own will, instead of God's."

"Do you think she'll do that, though?"

Imani shivered, and hugged her knees against her chest. Tobias could tell it wasn't just because of the chill in the room. "I don't. . .think so. I don't. She will have had the entire drive here to cool down, and think through her actions. She didn't have that before, with you; you caught her off guard. But. . ."

She was silent for so long that Tobias thought she might have simply trailed off, at a loss for words. "But this is not accidental," she said finally. "I believe more and more that all of this has been orchestrated by Justina's demon-father, and he will be doing everything he can to manipulate her into making the choices he wants."

"He lost her," Imani continued after a long silence. "On the night she was born, when Sister Rebecca got her onto consecrated ground, and Brother David baptized her. He can't directly influence her any more. But he can still tempt her, manipulate her, just like he would any person. That's what he's been aiming for."

"But, shouldn't he be trying to, I don't know—" Tobias waved his hand vaguely. "Get her to, like, blow up a school bus full of kindergarteners or something?"

"That would be the end goal," she answered, and Tobias felt a chill at the simple way she said it. He tried not to imagine what it would be like, a person as powerful as Justina completely out of control and bent on mayhem like that, but he couldn't help it. It was horrifying. "But he's been tempting and deceiving people for millennia. He's good at it. He knows that just tempting Justina to do something obviously wrong wouldn't work; she'd see right through that. Instead, he's going to try to get to her through a part of herself that's good: her sense of righteous justice, and her dislike for letting people get away with doing bad things. It can be a fine line between justice and revenge, and the demon-father is trying to set her up so that she deliberately chooses to cross that line."

The two of them sat in silence for a few minutes, listening to the wind roaring outside and feeling the wall vibrate under its force.

"What happens if she does?" Tobias asked at last. "If she does. . .cross the line?"

"She won't turn into a dark nephil on the spot, if that's what you're thinking. But I think she would really. . .*enjoy* it, just cutting loose like that, and raining down wrath on people purely according to her own wishes. I think she would love it. And then afterwards she would justify why it was actually right. People are really great at doing that, and she wouldn't be any different just because she's a nephil." Tobias knew that was true; people were more than capable of any amount of mental gymnastics, if it justified them doing what they wanted to do anyway.

"He'll try to convince her she's special and superior to mere mortals, that she's an exception, that right and wrong are for creatures below her. And she'll *want* to believe it. Who wouldn't? All that power, and no one to answer to but herself." She raised her head and looked at Tobias. "Hardly anyone can really be trusted with unrestrained power like that, not subject to anyone. Not once she gets a good taste of it. If she chooses her own way today, and rains down wrath without restraint, it will start her down a really dark path, one that would not be easy for her to come back from. And even harder for her to *want* to come back from."

***

"The wrath of saints can be a far more dreadful thing than the wrath of sinners."

Leslie Charteris, *The Last Hero*, 1930.

Twenty-Four

As Imani's kidnapper had observed, there was a cold front blowing in. First it smudged the horizon to a dusty khaki color, and then the dust was overtaken by a rolling bank of heavy clouds as dark as pewter. Winter-dry prairie grass flattened itself to the ground in waves; last autumn's dead leaves rose in sudden whirls and scattered; every flag in every small town snapped and whipped, and near oil refineries, the flares of orange flame atop their spindly masts streaked out horizontally. By midafternoon, the deep overcast had hidden the sun in gray twilight, and low shudders of distant thunder boomed from the horizon.

Abrupt squalls of rain drove against doors and windows, and as the temperature plunged, the rain became driving sleet, and then snow as sharp as ice. It did not blanket the ground, but settled on the windward side of every object, and whirled and skittered in eddies across roads and sidewalks. Even the snow looked dull and pale in the slaty light.

People felt their cars shaken by the fierce gusts, and found themselves continually glancing in their rearview mirrors, every guttural, animal instinct driving them to get under cover inside sheltering walls. An ancient, wordless urgency insisted that something was wrong, something was uncanny, something was *coming*.

Inside the warehouse in Odessa, all of the freelancers but two (those two had gone into the locked office where Tobias and the girl were being kept, as a last line of defense) had turned desks and tables on their sides near the entrance, and crouched behind them, waiting. Every gun was loaded, and every person had a pile of spare magazines near to hand. They stared at each other, wide-eyed and pale, listening to the wind rise and feeling the temperature drop, against all the predictions of the local weather report that morning, their guns grasped in white-knuckled, shaking hands.

"Is the nephil causing this?" asked someone. No one knew.

As the storm peaked, all of them began to be afraid; not rationally afraid, as they should have been just before meeting a dangerous creature in battle, but afraid with an irrational, faceless, wordless fear, a child's fear of shadows and silence and shapeless lurking phantoms, an animal's fear of the hungry thing that gave chase, and gained.

A couple of the waiting monster-hunters were on the point of panic and blind flight, when without warning, something crashed against the metal door, not like a strong person trying to break in, but like a battering ram. Another blow, and the metal bowed and wrenched inward, admitting whipping swirls of snow and sleet through the gap. A third blow and, with a screech of ripping metal, the bolt and hinges all gave way at once, and the door crashed open. It fell to the floor, bent and twisted, and when the snow fell on its outer surface it hissed abruptly into steam.

The nephil stood in the doorway, framed by the storm, the wind at her back and blinding incandescence in her eyes: a creature of power, a creature of fire.

*

Imani and Tobias, locked in the old office, heard Justina arrive. So did the two hunters in the room with them; they both trained their guns on the door, eyes wide and round, teeth bared, hands shaking. Tobias had the wild impulse to ask Imani to take his confession then, after all, but he couldn't stomach the thought of being That Person who turned to God in a panic only when he was boxed into a corner. Maybe when this was all over. Imani herself, meanwhile, repeated the Our Father to herself under her breath, over and over, alternating Latin and English.

Three blows on the front door, and then a crash as the door was either violently flung open, or actually ripped off its hinges. They could all hear the sudden howl of the wind and the storm through the opening, and then, immediately, a cacophony of gunfire. Imani could pick out the crash of shotguns, the single reports of handguns and rifles, and the solid, toneless hammering of assault rifles —M-16s or something—on full automatic (what Sister Magdalena always called "full rock 'n roll"). There were shouts and yells, confused, overlapping, panicky, and then the sound of furniture being thrown violently against walls. The shouts became screams. The solid barrage of gunfire slowed to intermittence, then stuttered away to nothing.

Only then could Imani hear Justina singing. Her voice rang with the force of battle cries and blasting trumpets, and the power of it pressed against the four of them in the room like a tidal wave. She was singing a Psalm in Latin:

"*Iudica, Domine, nocentes me, expunge expugnantes me!*

"*Adprehende arms et scutum et exsurge in adiutorium mihi!*

"*Effunde frameam et conclude adversus eos qui persequuntur!*

"*Me dic animate, 'Meae salus tua ego sum!'*

"*Confundantur et revereantur quaerentes animam meam avertantur retrorsum et confundantur cogitantes mihi mala!*

"*Fiant tamquam pulvis ante faciem venti, et angelus Domini coartans eos!*

"*Fiat via illorum tenebrae et lubricum, et angelus Domini persequens eos!*"

"That may be a good sign," Imani whispered to Tobias. He jumped like a startled cat, as if he had almost forgotten she was there.

"What? What's a good sign?"

"It *may* be a good sign. I think it is. I hope it is. It's a Psalm, what Justina is singing, about calling on God to avenge and bring justice. She's trying to keep herself under control."

Rapid, heavy footsteps approached the locked office door, and for a split second there was complete silence. Tobias seemed to be holding his breath. Imani tried to continue saying the Our Father, but couldn't focus on it, and realized belatedly that she had just been repeating the same half dozen words over and over and over again.

This door was not as solid as the last one. With a crunching, rending sound, Justina simply tore and twisted the entire latch and locking mechanism loose, as if they had been made of aluminum foil, and threw the door open.

She had to dip her head under the door's lintel to enter the room, and the instant she did, all the light bulbs overhead exploded at once, in sharp flashes of light and showers of glass. The electrical outlets along the floor spat sparks and licks of flame, and the plastic wall plates began to warp and darken and melt, sending up wisps of acrid smoke. The walls, even the cinderblock wall, quivered, and Imani could feel the floor vibrating under her. The temperature in the room jumped, as if the door opened on an oven, but they could all still hear the scream of the icy storm outside.

There were no windows, and without the light bulbs the room should have been as dark as a cave. But it was not. Justina's skin actually gave off a steady hot glow, like brass heated to incandescence for soldering, and her eyes were so scorchingly, blindingly bright that everyone had to look away quickly, as though they had looked too long at the sun.

Justina had put on her body armor over her habit, as well as her full gun harness, and her odachi was sheathed across her back, but she seemed to have drawn none of her weapons. Apparently she had not needed them. Every inch of loose fabric in her clothes pulled and snapped around her, as if in the blast of heat from the opening of a pottery kiln, and her hair, its white streaks glaring, whipped and crackled around her head. Even the air around her rippled visibly, like the ripples of heat over an asphalt highway at midafternoon on a cloudless, blazing day in the dead of summer.

The two hunters opened fire, wildly. Imani, and especially Tobias, both knew that Justina could dodge bullets, but this time she didn't even bother. She didn't move a muscle, but caught the bullets with her eyes and her mind and her will, stopped them dead, and let them fall to the floor, glowing dully and melted out of shape. They lay there, blackening the concrete under them.

"Enough," breathed Justina, almost in a whisper. Tobias shivered, remembering what that one word had done to him. Sure enough, the two men both staggered to their knees, and the guns fell from their hands. With a minute flick of her chin, Justina sent the the two weapons flying through the air faster than the eye could follow, and they crunched against the back wall with enough force to bend out of shape, and gouge two divots out of the cinderblocks. Meanwhile, the two men slumped to the floor, out cold.

"Come with me, now," said Justina, in the same soft voice. Imani felt the pull and compulsion to obey, but not, she sensed, because Justina was trying to compel her; at the moment, with so much raw power pulsing through her, she simply couldn't help it. Imani scrambled to her feet and followed Justina as she turned to go, trotting to keep up with her sister's long strides. Tobias, after a moment's hesitation, followed as well.

Imani walked as close to Justina as she could. Her tendency would have been to cling like a limpet, but the heat around Justina's body was too intense to allow her closer than two or three feet; she knew that if she actually touched her sister's skin, she would be seriously burned. She kept as close as she dared.

Justina walked swiftly, her back straight, her eyes resolutely forward, her fists clenched hard with self-control. Imani guessed, rightly, that she refused to look at the men and women in this room who had injured and abducted her sister, and then tried to kill her; if she looked at them, she might change her mind and kill them after all.

Because she had not killed them. At first, Imani had not been able to bring herself to look; but she needed to know, so she took a deep breath, half-closed her eyes in case she might see blood and gore, and peeked a quick look.

For a moment she saw no one, only smashed furniture (not just overturned or pushed back, but actually thrown through the air end-over-end, as if by a tornado). Her stomach dropped, sickeningly, as she wondered if Justina might have simply *erased* everyone, reduced them to ash and dust, as *A Brief Treatise on the Nephilim* described.

But then she looked closer, and almost staggered with relief: people were hiding behind crunched and crumpled filing cabinets, desks, bookshelves, and tables, not dead, not even injured for the most part. They were just keeping their heads down, hoping that Justina would be content with her victory and leave them alone.

And she was. She was leaving the warehouse with no blood spilled, and Imani could hardly believe that the whole mess was finally over. There was no way the freelancers would keep hunting the two of them now, not after this, not after seeing firsthand both

Justina's power and Justina's restraint. They could go home! Well, Imani amended, not *home*; St. Margaret's was still being rebuilt. But back to the Order and to the sisters. And soon St. Margaret's would be repaired, and things could be normal again.

Imani was so distracted by these thoughts that when Justina stopped short, Imani nearly walked right into her. She stopped in time, but the scorching heat left her gasping, and the skin of her face and hands felt as if she had acquired an instant stinging sunburn.

No, they couldn't stop! They needed to get *out* of here, before anyone, either Justina or the freelancers, did anything that could turn this place into a slaughterhouse. Imani leaned around Justina to look at the door, desperately afraid someone was standing there, trying to block their exit.

Someone was. But it was none of the freelancers. It was not even a human, or any other kind of creature Imani knew. Just looking at it made her head hurt; not because it was blindingly bright, though it was, but because her brain seemed unable to properly accept it, as if none of her senses were up to the task, as if looking at it was the equivalent of trying to stare through darkness, or listen to a sound so low that it could only be felt as a dull throb in her bones.

It was like a tornado of fire, stretching up to the steel-girdered ceiling far overhead, throwing out waves of flame to right and left. It was like a whirling torrent of glaring eyes, of howling faces, of burning wings, merging in and out of each other. It was like rings and coils of metal, red-hot, fresh from Sister Alana's forge, twisting, interlocking, intersecting, whipping around and into and through each other. It remained in the same place, filling the doorway, but at the same time it seemed to be in headlong motion, unbearably fast, in some direction, or directions, that the ordinary three dimensions had no name for at all.

Imani squeezed her eyes closed, but then had to lift her hands to her face to make sure that she really had, because it made no difference; the thing in the door remained, as if burned into the insides of her eyelids. Colors she had no name for, colors that made her brain squirm, slid past her closed eyes (*So that's what Justina sees,* she thought dimly), and she felt herself beginning to fall. She had just enough consciousness left to reach the floor without cracking her head against it, and then the dizzy disorientation and the nameless colors closed in, and she knew no more.

*

Justina did not see what the humans saw. Or, more correctly, she was the only one actually capable of seeing it, and so instead of the maelstrom of incomprehensibility, from which human senses could only flee in shock, she saw what she had seen in her dream the night before. She saw her father, fierce and glorious and proud, wings (fire and ember, bronze and gold) stretching and reaching, skin enclosing a blinding infinity, eyes blazing with galaxies, a creature that had once sung with the morning stars.

"No," said Justina.

Nameless colors shifted, frustrated. The eyes of the fallen angel flashed, far above hers, as far her own eyes usually were above humans'. "I am not trying to hurt you, child! I am trying to set you free! I am trying to help you to throw off the chains that the Order of the Holy Lance has been piling on you all your life."

"It isn't always best to throw off chains," Justina said. "If you convinced rock climbers to do that, they would take off their safety harnesses and fall to their deaths."

The fallen angel did the last thing then that Justina had ever expected: he laughed. It was not an evil cackle, or a condescending chuckle, but a real, honest laugh, and for a moment all the world was a dance.

"You may not care about this now," he said, "but I am so happy I made you. You are truly a unique and wonderful creature. Don't think of it as throwing off chains then. Think of it as freedom. Is it not true that your Lord came into the world to set you free? To ensure that you would never be enslaved?"

Justina drew herself up, indignant. "Is that the game you want to play? Fine. Scripture also warns against using our freedom as a license for sin."

"Sin!" cried her father, and his his indignation made hers seem a small, feeble thing. "Is your desire for justice sin? Is it a sin to pursue your own soul's purpose, your own path? Is it a sin to understand the objective truth, that no mere human will ever be your equal? Would it be better for you to lie to everyone, and to yourself?"

No, Justina wanted to say. There's nothing wrong with any of those thing in themselves. But. . . She shook her head, trying to focus.

"You believe that you, a nephil with the gift of Sight, are not able to fairly judge these humans? If you can't do it, then who can?" He indicated the freelancers, lying crumpled and huddled here and there, out cold, behind their upturned tables, with a sweep of one arm, and streamers of fire followed the movement, casting a wave of ruddy shadow across the concrete floor. And he was not wrong: she could indeed see the stains, the sickness, the nastiness, the un-scrupulousness, the sneakiness and mercilessness and cowardice, all over them, like crusted mold on an unwashed casserole dish. Just the sight both sickened and infuriated her. She forced herself to look away, so she wouldn't see it.

"I don't have the right to make that judgement," Justina said, but not with any great conviction. "I can't. Only God—"

"You don't have the right!" thundered the fallen angel. "Of course you have the right! Should such things be left up to other humans, who are weak and blind and corruptible? No. You are the higher organism, and you are infallible. You have more right than anyone to judge."

His voice softened. "You must see what the Order has done to you. They have tried to force you to see yourself as the servant of humans, when you should be their ruler. No creature such as you should ever submit to humans, or serve humans, in any way. The very idea is absurd, repulsive. You are fire and lightning, and humans are mud. Even their own Scriptures admit this is true."

Justina could think of nothing to say. She tried hard to tell herself that he was lying to her, deceiving her, trying to manipulate her and get her on his side. But she couldn't help but listen. She couldn't help but see that he must be objectively right: there was no denying that she was a different kind of creature than the humans, with far more power, far more knowledge. Maybe it was right for her to rule over humans. Maybe it was her duty, even. She was not blind to the mess that human authorities often made of things. She could set that right. If people refused to act as they should, she had the power to compel them. Wouldn't that be better?

"Look at them," said her father, making another fiery sweep of his arm. "Look. Just look. These are the creatures that the Order dares to try to force you to *serve?* Look at them."

Justina looked, saw the nastiness, saw the stains.

"If you can imagine a stupid, petty cruelty, it's in this room. That one," said the fallen angel, and she knew which one he meant. "When she was nine, that one pulled her little sister's goldfish out of its bowl, and held it up over her head, just out of her reach, until it died. That one, when he was thirteen, learned what girl his friend had a secret, embarrassing crush on, then told everyone in school.

He laughed with everyone else as his friend ran, and then mocked him as he cried."

Justina closed her eyes, breathing fast, shaking, trying to control herself. Closing her eyes did not help; flickers of images (a frantic small girl, jumping up for something she could not reach, a skinny thirteen-year-old's pimple-covered face flaming with shame and shining with tears) played mockingly across the insides of her eyelids.

"Or other cruelties, maybe a bit less petty. That one." Justina tried not to look, but failed. "That one can hardly endure a day without his collection of pornography, and his requirements of it are so very specific. . .it doesn't do the job for him unless the woman is sobbing." Justina clenched her hands, tightly enough almost to break her own bones, and did not realize until later that her fingernails had cut in deep enough to let trickles of pure white blood ooze out between her fingers. "But I shouldn't say 'woman'," added the fallen angel, his voice low. "It fails to meet his exacting, discerning tastes if the little thing has even the tiniest trace of hair anywhere on her body."

Justina stood panting, and with every breath the air in the entire room seemed to heave back and forth like a tide.

"Or that one. Look at him, child of mine. Look at him well." And Justina had to. She saw a beefy man, his shoulder bandaged, his face bruised and cut. "He gave poor little Imani her black eye. But oh, if you only knew the things he's planned to do to her in the last twelve hours. How much she will bleed. How much she will scream. How much he will enjoy it. And as an added bonus, he knows that when he's through, she won't even qualify as a Sister of the Holy Lance any more. That pesky virginity rule, you see."

"Stop," said Justina, sounding as if she was being choked. Then she repeated it, her voice building to a flayed scream: "*Stop!*" The walls shook. Crumbs of mortar began to shake loose from between the cinderblocks and scatter to the floor. Curls of smoke rose from her clothes and from between her clenched fingers, and the scorching smell of burning cotton drifted into the room. Overturned desks and bookshelves slid and grated over the floor, and outside, the snow whipped in slashing spirals like a nascent tornado. The man with the broken nose did not move, but his shirt began to darken and smoke in spots, and Justina caught the meaty smell of roasting skin.

The fallen angel raised his voice as well. "These creatures are the ones the Order would have you save? Have you *serve*? Even the one you came to like, to trust, he lied to you. Not only about his name, but about his parents. Would you be interested to know that he intended to murder them both? He planned it very carefully, and with great pleasure, I might add. He stalked them. Loitered outside their house. The only reason they're still alive today is that your friend Tobias is very slightly more cowardly than he is murderous."

Justina's father drew closer, until he was almost nose-to-nose with her, his voice soft and venomous. "These creatures are beneath contempt. They are disgusting, these repulsive mixtures of spirit and mud. They are made of slime and spit and blood and meat, and everything about them stinks. They were all begotten by two squirming, sweaty, grunting animals in a bed, worse than animals because they imagined they were better, that they were different, that their rutting was somehow *meaningful*. They are stupid, slinking, deceitful, distractible creatures that will *always* fail you."

Justina fought against the simple knowledge that he was right. She fought against the relief of having someone understand, someone give voice and validation to the frustration and annoyance and distaste she had never been able to help feeling for humans. But she was losing the fight, and as she did, the chipboard and vinyl of the furniture began slowly to darken and smoke. Soon the entire warehouse would be in flames, along with the unconscious people piled inside it.

"Even your precious Imani," whispered the fallen angel, close enough to her now that his flames began to lick around her, "will always fail you. She has *already* failed you, with her fear and her timidity. She will be a weakness to you, an anchor holding you back, always."

With those words, the demon-father made his tactical error. He still wasn't wrong, not exactly—Justina knew that Imani was often afraid, and did sometimes need to be protected—but she also knew that Imani was all the braver for her fear, because she did her duty anyway.

Contemptible? Beneath contempt? Justina remembered the feel of Imani's small body clinging against her as they grieved for Sister Ella. Remembered Imani, shivering and pale, but determined, insisting that she, Justina, pursue the boo hag alone. Remembered all the times they had shared quiet meals, quiet talks, remembered burying themselves in books in the commandery library side-by side, remembered sparring and training together, and how Imani's trust in her was so complete that it seemed as obvious and unquestionable as gravity.

And even Jake—or rather, Tobias. Apparently that was his real name; at least, Justina could see no reason for the demon to lie about that. Even Tobias. He had attacked her without provocation, yes, and tried to use the rite of exorcism inappropriately, even sacrilegiously. For all Justina knew, it was true that he had planned to murder his parents. But he had also been willing to listen to reason. He had been willing to stand beside herself and Imani, and trust them enough to face a werepack by their side. He may have thought better of killing his parents (which was a little difficult, really, to call cowardice), but in the face of eight werewolves he had not bolted. Justina had seen, when she entered that room where Imani was kept, that Tobias was there too, not as a guard, but as a prisoner, so he had not turned on them. And when she threw the door open, for a split second, he had started to shift his body in front of Imani, as if to protect her.

Beneath contempt? No.

Without knowing it, Justina had let her shoulders droop and sag, as her demon-father worked his spell on her. Now she straightened, and looked her father straight in the eye. "Who took me in? Who raised me? Who loved me, even though I was strange and often a little scary and the *daughter of a demon*? Not you. You wanted me because I was useful, and now that I'm starting to come into my powers you want me for the same reason. It was the Order, made up of those humans you despise so much. And you want to enrage me with the idea of rape? It would be a lot more convincing if I didn't exist in the first place because *you* raped my mother. I don't deny anything you've said; I can see the evil on these people. But who gloried in it? Who tempted and twisted them into it? *You* did, or one like you."

She took a step forward, and didn't even notice that he drew back before her. "You're not wrong! Humans are weak, and broken, and often stupid, and sometimes evil. Objectively, they are absolutely not worth a moment of my time to defend. You're absolutely right.

"But even with all that, God sees humans as worth defending. To God, humans are infinitely, incalculably precious; in fact, God sees humans as worth actually *dying* to save. You tell me I should never lower myself to serve humans, but *God* did. God washed the feet of a bunch of men who were conceited and stupid and cowardly and even treacherous, and he knew that when he did it. If you want to call something worthless that God values as much as that, you'll do it alone."

Justina raised her voice, and the sound of trumpets rang in it again. "I was dedicated to God the night I was born. I was dedicated again when I was old enough to choose it. And I choose to be on God's side again now."

She advanced, and this time she noticed that the demon drew back. Her voice was a battle cry, and the walls rocked, as she shouted against the storm: "*Now get thee behind me!*"

***

Interlude Eleven

The Odessa American

December 2

Page B6

Cold Front Brings Sleet, Snow

Severe weather battered the Permian Basin yesterday afternoon and evening, as an unexpected cold front blew through the region. The National Weather Service reports that a fluke low-pressure system, originating in the Texas Panhandle, swept south off the Caprock and into the Permian Basin, bringing wind gusts of up to 75 miles per hour, accompanied by sleet and snow. Emergency services responded to four crashes at major intersections, and the City of Odessa has received numerous reports of downed power lines and tree branches in the wake of the storm. The city experienced scattered blackouts overnight, but spokespeople report that power has now been restored.

CBS7 News meteorologist John Wilson states, "It looks as if atmospheric conditions were just right to create a powerful cold front we didn't anticipate. It was a bit of a fluke, but the sun is out again today, and by this weekend high temperatures should be back in the mid-fifties. This is just the kind of weather Texas sometimes throws at us, folks!"

Ector County ISD announced a two-hour delay of the start of school today.

The Odessa American

December 2

Empty Warehouse Burns

During last night's snowstorm, a vacant south Odessa warehouse previously owned by Pilot Oilfield Services caught fire and burned down. The blaze began in the middle of the afternoon, and because of the high winds, was not fully controlled until 10:00 last night, according to Odessa Fire Chief Henry Garcia.

"There is no suggestion of arson at this time," stated Fire Marshall Constance Brunelle. "The Fire Marshall's Office has so far found no traces of accelerants at the scene. Instead, we believe a faulty gas line may have blown loose in the storm, allowing gas into the building, and the resulting fire was therefore accidental. However, the investigation is ongoing."

According to a Pilot Oilfield Services spokesman, the contents of the warehouse had been cleared out by November 22 in preparation for a move to a new location, but gas and electric utilities had not yet been shut off.

Four people were treated for mild carbon monoxide exposure at Odessa Regional Medical Center, and five people were treated for burns. All have been released in satisfactory condition, according to Odessa Regional.

The Odessa Fire Marshall's Office urges caution around vacant buildings, especially during severe weather, and reminds all citizens to ensure that utilities are disconnected before vacating a building.

***

Interlude Twelve

Police Report

Case No: 5764

Date: December 2

Reporting Officer: Kenny Lorenzo

Prepared By: Kenny Lorenzo

Incident: Fire at former Pilot Oilfield Services warehouse.

Detail of Event:

A fire was reported at the old Pilot Oilfield Services warehouse (1628 S. Grandview Ave.) at 4:37pm December 2. Officer Katie Wellington and I responded. There were already some people at the scene. They identified themselves as Sister Rebecca and Sister Magdalena of the Order of the Holy Lance, said that they had called us, and said that Sheriff John Whitlock of Derrick County could verify their identities and credentials. I called the Derrick County Sheriff's Office, and it checked out.

The two women informed me that they were in Odessa to meet with two other women in their order, and they saw the fire and called it in. All four of them can be reached at St. Ursula's in Lubbock (N. University Ave. and Abilene St.).

Shortly after we arrived, Odessa Fire Rescue also arrived to start to fight the fire.

There were seven other witnesses present, but no one was inside the building. According to the two sisters, they had helped get everyone out. According to the other witnesses (see attached names and contact information for the full list), they were a group of friends who were staying in the motel across the street (Yucca

Park Motel, 1627 S. Grandview Ave.) and decided to meet up in the warehouse where there was more space. They admitted to trespassing in the building, but all of them denied that anyone in their group set the fire, but claimed it began accidentally and they didn't know how. They seemed slightly confused or dazed, possibly from carbon monoxide in the building. Also, several had varying degrees of burns, but no sign of human-inflicted injuries.

We found debris just inside the building (having entered with permission from Odessa Fire Rescue) consistent with a large number of bullets, shell casings, and similar which had been exposed to high heat. However, there were no guns found, and no one had injuries related to gunshots, so the debris are probably unrelated to the fire. Additionally, the door was broken off its hinges and lying inside, suggesting that it had been breached from the outside, possibly when the witnesses entered the premises illegally. The witnesses deny doing this, but give no explanation for how it happened.

Action Taken:

We took statements from Sister Rebecca and Sister Magdalena of the Order of the Holy Lance (see attached). We also took statements from several of the other witnesses (see attached), and instructed them not to leave town for the time being. Odessa Fire Rescue EMS administered first aid on the scene, and the carbon monoxide and burn victims were taken to Odessa Regional. Samples of the bullet debris were taken as evidence just in case they turn out to be relevant. The Fire Marshall arrived, and will investigate for signs of arson or other foul play.

Summary:

So far, it appears that the only crime committed was trespassing, and possibly vandalism (if it turns out they broke down the door). No one was seriously injured, according to the Odessa Fire Rescue EMS. It appears the fire was an accident, pending further investigation by the Fire Marshall.

***

Interlude Thirteen

Excerpt from the Mission Reports: Archive at Saint Margaret's
Mission Report.

Date: December 2.

Sisters Present: Magdalena, Rebecca. Squire-novices Justina and Imani.

Location: Odessa, TX.

Creature/Spirit: N/A.

Time and specific location: Vacant warehouse, S. Grandview Ave. and Rush St. About 4:00pm.

Actions of concern: Imani was kidnapped by freelancers, with the intention of using her as bait to draw out Justina. Justina went to the rescue, and the freelancers got quite a bit more than they bargained for.

Actions taken: We arrived in the aftermath. By the time we got there, the girls were outside, and the building was already on fire. Most of the freelancers (a total of eighteen of them, by far the biggest group I've ever heard of them assembling) were also out by then, either under their own power or helped by the girls; they were all sort of staggering around, shocked and dazed and out of it, as if they'd just survived a bomb going off. I guess in a way they had. We called in the police and firefighters, though the building was honestly a goner by then, and the EMS people assumed the freelancers were suffering from carbon monoxide exposure. We didn't correct them. It wasn't carbon monoxide, though. It was Justina's demon-father, or Justina herself, or both.

Before the police arrived, we allowed most of the freelancers to leave, and take their guns with them. It felt weird to do that, but all four of us agreed that the whole thing was, in a sense, an internal matter, between monster hunters. Besides, I think they've learned their lesson, and shouldn't be messing with Justina again. That's enough.

The injured were whisked off to the hospital. Then, finally, we were able to bring Imani and Justina home.

Conclusions: It appears that over the last several weeks, Justina's nephilic powers have been increasing exponentially, along with her understanding of those powers, and her ability to control them. Especially this afternoon. Based on the records we have, she hasn't come into her full powers even yet, but today she really stretched her muscles for the first time. She isn't as powerful as she will be, but at least she's getting an idea of what she will be capable of.

Just as Imani had suspected, Justina's demon-father was behind all of this, all the way back to the boo hag and everything else back in October. He wanted to get Justina back; to maneuver her into doing very much the wrong thing for apparently excellent and justifiable reasons. For the moment, she held him off. He's bound to try again, but for now, we win.

Imani tried to describe what the fallen angel looked like. She could do no better than the prophet Ezekiel did when he tried to describe faithful angels: an effort to describe the completely indescribable, the incomprehensible, by talking about wings and eyes and flames and wheels within wheels. It seems that the mere unmasked presence of an angel (fallen or otherwise) is overwhelming enough to render humans unconscious.

The fire, as well as the snowstorm that tore through town, were apparently both Justina's doing, though she didn't mean to cause either one. Imani said that she was giving off a blistering heat, too. It seems that her heightened emotions had that kind of powerful effect on her physical surroundings. Now that she's experienced it, though, Justina believes she understands the abilities, and can keep them under conscious control (if not completely yet, at least a lot more).

Recommendations: Our littles are coming home, finally. What more do we need out of this? However, Justina also suggests that we learn the freelancers' suite of glyphs and symbols. One of them, named Tobias, offered to draw a chart for us.

Injuries: None to the sisters. Four freelancers treated for mild-moderate burns, and one treated for a serious burn.

Expenses: See attached receipts.

**

Afterward

On a bright, windy day in April, the sisters moved back into a rebuilt Commandery of St. Margaret of Antioch, and Imani and Justina went with them.

The wildflowers were in bloom: clusters of sunset-colored desert globemallow, delicate spikes of creamy-pink beeblossom and purple foxglove, tangles of white thistle poppies as lovely as roses. Fields of yellow huisache daisies drenched the air with a fragrance as warm and golden as summer.

Imani and Justina visited the commandery's cemetery, where Sister Ella's headstone stood still clean and new and unweathered on the consecrated ground. The two girls both wept there: Imani with wrenching sobs, and Justina with slow tears, and where the pearly nephil tears fell, a strong young acacia sapling grew. By the next day its feathery leaves were already pushing above the ground, and by the end of a week it had produced a few bright, cream-colored blossoms.

The night they arrived, Justina held vigil in the chapter room. The next morning she rose, and went into the new chapel, on the same ground she had once shaken as a child by singing the "Hallelujah Chorus" on Christmas Eve. All the sisters were assembled there, and Brother David stood by in his full vestments, and Justina knelt on the new and freshly-polished tiles to take her first vows.

"Lady," she said, in the old words spoken by sisters of the Order for nearly a thousand years, "I come before God and before you and before the sisters, and ask and request you for love of God and the saints to welcome me into your company and into the favor of the house, as one who wishes to be a servant of the house all the days of my vow."

Sister Deborah, her eyes only just higher than Justina's own, answered, "Have you considered well, good sister, that you wish to be a servant of the Order and leave behind your own will to do another's? And do you wish to suffer all the hardships which are established in the house and carry out all the orders you will be given?"

"Lady, yes, if it please God."

Sister Deborah stretched out her hands to all the sisters. "Good ladies, rise and pray to Our Lord that she does it well."

All the sisters stood, and recited the Lord's Prayer together; then Brother David said a prayer on behalf of Justina.

Sister Rebecca half expected a storm to rise outside: crashes of thunder, raging wind, slashing sleet, as had happened twenty years ago when Brother David had marked the cross on Justina's forehead on the night of her birth. But the morning remained calm. Justina's demon-father would make another attempt, no one had any illusions about that, but for now he had been defeated, just as he had been then.

"Now, good sister, said Deborah, addressing Justina again, "do you promise to God that henceforth all the days of your vow you will be obedient to the Chatelaine Holy Lance and whatever commander will be over you?

"Yes, lady, if it please God."

"Do you also promise to God that henceforth all the days of your vow you will live chastely in your body?"

"Yes, lady, if it please God."

"Do you also promise to God that you, all the remaining days of your vow, will live without property?"

"Yes, lady, if it please God."

"Do you also promise to God that you, all the remaining days of your vow, will labor to conquer, defeat, vanquish, and subdue, with the strength and power that God has given you, all those creatures, both seen and unseen, whether of earth or hell, which seek to harm those made in the image and likeness of God?"

Justina drew in a deep breath. Her eyes blazed white-hot for an instant, and the hair and clothes of everyone in the room whipped abruptly in a powerful, but instantaneous, gale. Flames licked out between her clasped fingers for a moment, then died away. All the candles blew out; a glance from Justina, and they sprang back to life.

"With the strength and power that God has given me, yes, lady, if it please God."

"Do you also promise to God," continued Sister Deborah, her voice shaking slightly now, "that you will not leave the Order for stronger or weaker, nor for worse or better, unless you do so with the permission of the Chatelaine and of the commandery who have the authority, before the ending of your vow?"

"Yes, lady, if it please God."

Again, Sister Deborah stretched out her hands to the sisters. "And we," she proclaimed, "on behalf of God, and on behalf of all saints, and all the sisters of the Holy Lance, we welcome you to all the blessings of the house, which have been done since the beginning and which will be done up to the end. And you also welcome to us all the blessings which you have done and will do. And so we promise you the bread and water and clothing of the house, and much pain and suffering."

Brother David stepped forward, and signed her forehead with the cross, as he had done when she was a baby. "Welcome, Justina, knight-sister of the Order of the Holy Lance. God bless you to do well."

"Amen," said Justina, and stood.

*****

ABOUT THE AUTHOR

Jenny Paxton was born in San Antonio, raised in Lubbock, and attended both Abilene Christian University and Texas Tech. After receiving her PhD in history, Jenny now teaches history at the University of Texas - Permian Basin. She loves to read, and when the story she wants doesn't exist, sometimes she simply must write it herself! Her work is strongly influenced by a love of fantastical elements blended with reality, scrupulous historical research, and her own Christian faith. Jenny currently lives in Odessa, Texas, with her four cats.

Printed in the USA
CPSIA information can be obtained
at www.ICGtesting.com
JSHW011204030923
47751JS00010B/101